UNDERSTANDING OUR BEING

John W. Carlson

UNDERSTANDING OUR BEING

INTRODUCTION TO SPECULATIVE PHILOSOPHY

IN THE PERENNIAL TRADITION

The Catholic University of America Press
Washington, D.C.

The paper used in this publication meets the minimum requirements
of American National Standards for Information Science—
Permanence of Paper for Printed Library Materials, ANSI z39.48-1984.
∞

LIBRARY OF CONGRESS CATALOGING-IN-PUBLICATION DATA
Carlson, John W.
Understanding our being : introduction to speculative
philosophy in the perennial tradition / John W. Carlson.
p. cm.
Includes bibliographical references and index.
ISBN 978-0-8132-1518-1 (pbk. : alk. paper)   1. Philosophy—
Introductions.   2. Ontology.   I. Title.
BD21.C364 2008
149'.91—dc22   2007030355

To my students across the years—

companions in the search for understanding

"It should never be forgotten that the neglect of being inevitably leads to losing touch with objective truth and therefore with the very ground of human dignity. This in turn makes it possible to erase from the countenance of man and woman the marks of their likeness to God, and thus to lead them little by little either to a destructive will to power or to a solitude without hope."

"In the present circumstances, therefore, it is most significant that some philosophers are promoting a recovery of the determining role of this [perennial] tradition for a right approach to knowledge."

"I appeal to all *philosophers*, and to all *teachers of philosophy*, asking them to have the courage to recover, in the flow of an enduringly valid philosophical tradition, the range of authentic wisdom and truth—metaphysical truth included—which is proper to philosophical enquiry."

—John Paul II, *Fides et ratio* (1998)

CONTENTS

ACKNOWLEDGMENTS

The author wishes to thank those at the Catholic University of America Press (David McGonagle, James Kruggel, Greg LaNave, Theresa Walker, and Beth Benevides) who encouraged and assisted this project through its various stages. Acknowledgment also is due to four readers for the Press (Raymond Dennehy, Steven C. Snyder, Michael W. Tkacz, and one anonymous reader), who made a number of helpful suggestions. The contributions of Steven Snyder deserve special mention. I of course am responsible for errors and infelicities that remain.

I wish to thank as well Andy Jaspers, S.J., who assisted in the preparation of figures and tables, and Ellen Coughlin, who expertly copy-edited the manuscript.

My students across the years—to whom this book is dedicated—have been a source of steady encouragement; and they have helped in many ways to make a challenging text more reader-friendly.

Finally, I thank my family, and especially my dear wife, Chris, whose unflagging support now at last is rewarded.

Omaha, Nebraska
June 2007

PREFACE

This book introduces the reader to speculative philosophy, especially as pursued in what Pope John Paul II called the "great tradition"—a historical and continuing intellectual movement inspired, in part, by resources and requirements of Christian faith. Covering a range of topics about being—what can be known of being as such; the special character of our human, personal being; and God as Source and End of being—this book is intended primarily for use in college and university courses. The author anticipates that such courses are most likely to be taught in institutions that, like his own, maintain a Catholic identity. Some historical background regarding this matter is in order.

In earlier generations, through the middle decades of the twentieth century, Catholic colleges and universities typically taught—and required students to take—separate courses on each of the above (and other) philosophical topics. Most of these courses were "Scholastic" in content and style. That is, they followed the teachings of "schools" of philosophy—in particular that of St. Thomas Aquinas—traceable to the Medieval period. Textbooks for these courses (many published in the 1950s and 1960s) tended to be highly didactic; often they contained lengthy quotations from Aquinas and his principal philosophical mentor, Aristotle, as well as from more recent Scholastics.

During the period that began shortly before the Second Vatican Council (1962–65) and now extends into a new century, there has been in Catholic circles much intellectual ferment, as well as interest in newer forms of thought—phenomenology, existentialism, personalism, etc. In the United States and other English-speaking countries, the influence of analytic philosophy also has been significant. The result has been a salutary enlivening of philosophical discourse, but also, for many, a sense of intellectual disarray when the current situation is compared to pre–Vatican II times.

Other changes have affected philosophy programs at Catholic institutions in this country. For one thing, there has been an increase in student diversity on the campuses—not only in terms of students from other than Catholic religious backgrounds, or students who represent the American racial composition, but also in terms of students from other cultures and nations: from Asia, Africa, India, and traditionally Islamic nations (or the sons and daughters of immigrants from these various nations).

Moreover, in American education generally there has been a movement toward less didactic approaches, and toward more involvement of students in their own learning. And, among Catholic institutions, a pre-professional turn in many college curricula, together with requirements of accrediting agencies in various fields and legitimate claims of other disciplines to a share of the "core," have reduced the number of class hours typically devoted to philosophy.

As suggested above, genuine good has come from these changes. However, they have made it increasingly difficult to transmit elements of the "great tradition," or, more specifically, what the late pope also called the "enduringly valid philosophical tradition." This tradition often has been referred to by Scholastic thinkers as the "perennial philosophy," and so shall we refer to it in this book. Proponents of the perennial philosophy (including the present author) believe that, properly expressed, its themes can appeal to open and reflective minds in every age and culture.

The difficulty of handing on this tradition in our day is exacerbated by the fact that the older textbooks described above, long out of print, have not been replaced in kind. Books now available for undergraduate courses tend to be anthologies and surveys, with the topics dictated by forces generally prevailing in American academic philosophy. It is extremely rare to find works suitable for the general undergraduate student that present a single, continuous thread of speculative thought, let alone one that seeks to redevelop and present the type of philosophy most associated with Catholic tradition.

This book attempts to fill the gap in question, but at the same time to accommodate irreversibly changed circumstances. While introducing students to elements of traditional "Thomist" philosophy (that is, philosophy in the tradition of St. Thomas), it at the same time incorporates genuine insights of modern and contemporary thought. It also tries to represent fairly, and outline responses to, opposed points of view.

Our book also recognizes (as good instruction always has) that in the end students must think for themselves. It endeavors to help them do this by presenting, at the end of each part, questions for reflection that might be used for classroom discussion and debate, as well as for essay assignments; and also by offering, at the end of the volume, a comprehensive bibliography. Finally, in light of the diversity of today's students—as well as questions arising from the book itself—we conclude with an Epilogue relating the philosophical tradition that has been introduced to ways of "understanding our being" that have arisen in other cultural and religious contexts.

The loss, by comparison with earlier works of Scholastic philosophy, obviously comes in the depth and level of detail to which topics can be pursued. It is hoped that this loss (which can partially be made up through instructor and student initiative, making use of sources in the Bibliography) will be compensated for in terms of usefulness in the present-day class setting.

INTRODUCTION

Philosophy

This is a book of speculative *philosophy*;[1] but what, the reader may ask, is that? From its Greek etymology (*philia,* for "love," plus *sophia,* for "wisdom"), the word "philosophy" means "love of wisdom." "Wisdom," in turn, suggests an understanding of ultimate matters—in particular, concerning the nature of our being, as well as concerning the choices proper for us, as individuals and as communities. But just how we are to achieve such ultimate understandings has been the subject of a variety of proposals.

Throughout history, and across cultures, there have been expressions of the search for wisdom. We might note, for example, the Vedas of ancient India, the sacred Scriptures of the Jewish people, the teachings of Confucius and Lao-Tzu in China, as well as of the Buddha and his followers in India and East Asia. More recently, of course, there have appeared the Gospels of Christianity and the Koran of Muslim peoples. We also should note, within the heritage of the West, the discourses of the Greek philosophers (especially Plato and Aristotle), as well as those of later thinkers. Each of the above, we might say, has offered a path to understanding—a more or less formal and rigorous means by which persons concerned with ultimate matters might pursue their objective.

Catholic tradition distinguishes three types of wisdom: infused (or mystical) wisdom, theological wisdom, and philosophical wisdom.[2] The first must be received as a direct gift from God; the second can be acquired through a study of God's revelation in light of human experience and reflection; and the third, philosophical wisdom (with which we shall be concerned), is a work of human reason itself. As Ar-

---

1. As an aid to the student, terms introduced in *italics,* along with brief accounts of their meanings, are gathered together in the book's Glossary.

2. On this matter, see Jacques Maritain, *Science and Wisdom,* trans. Bernard Wall (London: Geoffrey Bles, 1940), 22–25.

istotle pointed out (*Metaphysics,* book I, chap. 2), a search for the last-mentioned type of wisdom has its origin in *wonder*—a deep concern about how things are, and about the types of persons and communities we should strive to become. Moreover, philosophical wisdom is achieved, to the extent possible in this life, through rational analysis, reflection, and theory related to the above-noted questions. For present purposes, therefore, *wisdom* (i.e., philosophical wisdom) can be defined as a comprehensive understanding—arrived at via rational analysis, reflection, and theory—concerning the way things ultimately are and the way we humans ultimately should act. And philosophy itself can be said to be a love of or a search for wisdom, understood in precisely this way.

In this book we develop and explore one approach to philosophical wisdom—an approach rooted, as noted in the Preface, in what the late Pope John Paul II termed the "great tradition."[3] Our focus will be the dimension of that tradition represented by the school of St. Thomas Aquinas. But before undertaking this task, we should note a number of other preliminary points.

First, although there are wide differences in people's ways of reasoning about how things are, there also are certain remarkable affinities. Writers sometimes speak, therefore, of a "common sense" understanding that lies at the base of philosophy. In this vein, John Paul himself spoke of an "implicit philosophy" that is shared in some measure by all and that thus "should serve as a kind of reference point for the different philosophical schools." Indeed, he went so far as to refer to "a core of philosophical insight" that includes, for example, "the principles of non-contradiction, finality and causality, as well as the concept of the person as a free and intelligent subject, with the capacity to know God, truth and goodness" (*Fides et ratio,* sec. 4). Some may wonder whether all people can be said to share, even implicitly, all of the ideas just noted. However, the success of such ventures as the United Nations' "Universal Declaration of Human Rights" (1948)

---

3. See John Paul II, *Fides et ratio* [On the Relationship between Faith and Reason], Vatican translation (Boston: Pauline Books and Media, 1998), sec. 85. [Hereafter, references to this document often will be made in the text, with the title followed by the section number.]

suggests that a common fund of human wisdom indeed is in some way possessed by all peoples. Moreover, regarding basic judgments and distinctions about reality, philosophical notions that are truly implicit in the common sense of all humankind (insofar as such notions can be discerned) are surely to be trusted, unless compelling evidence requires their rejection or revision.[4]

Another point to be noted is that, from the Middle Ages on, but especially in recent times, philosophy formally speaking has been held by most scholars to relate to a body of thought that in principle is available to all—irrespective, in particular, of their religious commitments or lack of such commitments. This is a key to what sometimes is referred to as philosophy's "autonomy." Thus, for a position or argument to be properly philosophical, it must be expressed in terms that represent (or allegedly represent) what is available to common human experience and rational reflection. Theories or understandings that require special insight or special data may well occupy theologians or, in their own ways, natural scientists and other specialists; but philosophical reflection is a work of human reason as such. Of course, to speak here of "common" experience is not to imply that the articulation and assessment of such experience is easy. On the contrary, as we shall see, it sometimes is quite difficult. Moreover, due to various cultural factors, as well as the difficulty of the topics pursued, the various philosophical traditions and schools display considerable diversity: in their inspiration, their language and methodologies, and their specific results. Even within a single tradition or school, philosophers are liable to disagree on a number of finer points. And, while it may seem that nearly everyone can hope to increase to some extent his or her grasp of ultimate matters, it also seems that a "complete" understanding of subjects so broad and so deep is an ideal that can only progressively be approached, never finally achieved.

---

4. We would emphasize that we are here speaking of common sense understandings about basic and general philosophical matters. The present statement does not hold regarding the more particular beliefs and hypotheses investigated by the natural sciences; nor does it hold of certain pictures or images associated with common sense. (As we shall see, these distinctions become important in several philosophical subject areas.)

Lastly, we should mention that philosophers since the time of Aristotle have distinguished between *speculative* (or theoretical) wisdom and *practical* (especially moral) wisdom—and accordingly between the types of philosophy that pursue them. The first pursues an understanding about, as we have put it, how "things ultimately are"; the second pursues an understanding about how "we humans ultimately should act." As suggested by the subtitle of our book, the present text will be concerned primarily with matters of the speculative sort.

"Christian Philosophy" and the Perennial Tradition

Philosophy has interacted with Christian faith since the original preaching of the Gospel, when St. Paul encountered the philosophers of Athens at the Areopagus (see Acts of the Apostles, chap. 17). Some early Church thinkers regarded "pagan" philosophies as simply false, and they held that Christian faith presented the "true philosophy." Others found in the writings of the philosophers arguments which, at least if suitably adapted, might contribute to the promotion of faith—either by preparing minds and hearts to hear the Gospel, or by assisting in theological reflection upon it. Still others sought in the Christian message themes that might inspire properly human or rational lines of reflection that could be shared with all interested parties.

These various issues, trends, and emphases have been represented throughout Western history. During the twentieth century, in particular, there was considerable discussion as to whether there was, or could be, such a thing as "Christian philosophy"—especially in view of the prevailing understanding, noted above, of philosophy's autonomy vis-à-vis religious faith. Pope John Paul II's *Fides et ratio*, written in the wake of these discussions, offered several helpful clarifications and proposals. (It may be noted that, during the early years of his career, the late pope, under his given name Karol Wojtyła, was himself a professor of philosophy at the Catholic University of Lublin in Poland.) Let us discuss a number of John Paul's central points about *Christian philosophy*—which may be characterized most simply as philosophy pursued in the context of Christian faith, or philosophy occurring in a Christian condition or state.

First of all, like other instances of the discipline, Christian philosophy is truly philosophy; in particular, it is to be distinguished from theology, both as to its content or object, and as to its sources and methods.[5] Philosophy treats those ultimate matters that can be understood, at least in principle, by human intellect or reason. Thus, when it speaks of God, philosophy does so only in terms of what can be known of God from the nature of the world, including the nature of our human selves. *Theology*, on the other hand, articulates and inquires into specific religious mysteries—for example (for Christians), God as Trinity or the Incarnation. Regarding sources and methods, philosophy proceeds in terms of common human experience and "unaided" human reason; that is, it does not formally rely on religiously revealed propositions in its speculations or arguments. Theology, by contrast, while it may incorporate elements of philosophy, makes full use of what the believing community accepts as matters of faith.

The above points safeguard and indeed emphasize philosophy's autonomy. But religious faith nonetheless can play a role in the philosopher's work; and it can do so, according to John Paul, in two ways—"subjectively" and "objectively" (*Fides et ratio*, sec. 76). Regarding the former, one's Christian commitments can have a salutary effect on one's attitude toward the philosophical task and toward oneself as a person undertaking it. It might be suggested that it is an "occupational hazard" of philosophy that its practitioners may become prideful people: those who regularly pursue an understanding of how "things ultimately are" are very apt to have an elevated sense of self! Christian faith induces—or should induce—the virtue of humility, and with this an appropriately modest set of goals for one's rational understanding. Of course, as will be discussed below, the goals of Christian philosophy cannot be unduly modest; and a religious form of life will include, in addition to humility, the virtues of courage and hope—virtues that are important in facing the rigors of intellectual thought, to say noth-

5. See *Fides et ratio*, sec. 9. This understanding of the distinction between philosophy and theology has been common in Catholic thought since the time of St. Thomas Aquinas (1225–74); it was formally recognized by the First Vatican Council in the document *Dei Filius*, IV.

ing of the disappointments that often attend philosophers' efforts to reach agreement about their ideas and theories.

On the "objective" side, Christian faith can help to identify philosophical topics that otherwise might be left untreated. It is important to understand this point clearly. It does not take back the idea of philosophy's autonomy; it does not suggest, for example, that the philosopher formally presupposes any statements of faith, or uses them in his or her reasoning. But it stresses the fact that—as the history of philosophy itself confirms—humankind's appreciation for, e.g., the splendor of existence, the dignity of human personhood, and the transcendence and the immanence of God as Creator, are enhanced when philosophical reflection upon these themes is pursued under the inspiration of faith.

Moreover, at least as it seemed to John Paul II, "the word of God"—that is, divine revelation—sets certain "requirements" for philosophies that aspire to be adequate to the vision it expresses. Three requirements in particular are mentioned in *Fides et ratio,* secs. 80–85.

The first is that philosophies, and the persons pursuing them, should be mindful that they are called to a sapiential undertaking. The word "sapiential" comes from the Latin *sapientia,* which means "wisdom." Thus here we find a reinforcement of the original and etymological understanding of "philosophy," as discussed at the outset. It is important, according to John Paul, to stress this discipline's search for wisdom in view of the temptation—so prevalent in the contemporary world—to regard all studies as specialized and fragmented, or as oriented toward solving technical problems, rather than toward probing the mysteries of the universe and ourselves. To avoid this result, philosophy must seek its rightful place as providing the "ultimate framework of the unity of knowledge and action, leading them to converge toward a final goal and meaning" (sec. 81). This is not to say that philosophy, in and of itself, will succeed in producing a truly final account. Christian faith teaches that the directly revealed word of God (and thus theology) is necessary for an understanding of reality in its fullness. But philosophy should explore the naturally attainable aspects of—and thus in effect should prepare the way for—this more ultimate understanding.

The second requirement listed in *Fides et ratio* is that philosophy must recognize and authenticate the human capacity to "come to a knowledge which can reach objective truth," or to "attain to reality itself as knowable" (sec. 82). According to this requirement, the philosopher operating in the context of Christian faith must seek to vindicate the mind's ability to grasp intelligible features of reality (rather than, e.g., merely apprehend and respond to sensory data) as well as the mind's ability, at least to some degree, to articulate reality's intelligible features.

A third requirement is said to follow from the preceding two—that philosophy should be "of genuinely metaphysical range"; that is, it should seek to go beyond "the factual and the empirical" and come to know the "transcendent and metaphysical dimension in a way that is true and certain, albeit imperfect and analogical" (sec. 83). The term "metaphysical" comes from the Greek *meta* (meaning "beyond" or "coming after") plus *phusika* (meaning "the physical" in the very general sense of what happens within or according to nature). Now, the philosopher must recognize limits regarding both the quality and the type of knowledge that can be developed in a metaphysical way (notice that John Paul II called such knowledge "imperfect and analogical"); but the philosopher also must—if his or her work is to cohere with "the word of God"—push on toward a result that is truly fundamental.

Summarizing these points, we may say that John Paul called on philosophy 1) to return to its original task, which arises out of human wonder, of seeking wisdom; 2) to pursue this task by way of developing and authenticating a genuine knowledge of reality; and 3) to understand that philosophical knowledge must transcend the phenomena of nature and aspire to be metaphysical or foundational. Of course, one need not accept these three requirements in order to be called a philosopher. And many, as we shall see, do not. But a Christian philosopher, as here understood, will accept these requirements—at least in principle and insofar as they bear on the subjects of his or her inquiries.

A little later in *Fides et ratio,* the late pope acknowledged that accepting the above tasks can appear daunting—especially in the present intellectual climate, which includes a good deal of skepticism about the very possibility of the approach to philosophy being advocated. But he suggested that philosophers who respond to this call can look to the "great tradition" that precedes them. More fully, and more specifically, he wrote as follows: "I believe that those philosophers who wish to respond today to the demands which the word of God makes on human thinking should develop their thought . . . in organic continuity with the great tradition which, beginning with the ancients, passes through the Fathers of the Church and the masters of Scholasticism and includes the fundamental achievements of modern and contemporary thought" (sec. 85). As models of Christian philosophers who have engaged contemporary intellectual culture, John Paul listed such twentieth-century figures as Jacques Maritain, Etienne Gilson, and St. Edith Stein (sec. 74).

One aspect of this "great tradition" consists in what has been called the *perennial philosophy* (in Latin, *philosophia perennis*).[6] This term suggests both a wisdom that is available to all historical periods and cultures, and a wisdom that is in need of regular renewal. Indeed, one of the thinkers just mentioned, Jacques Maritain, called the perennial philosophy a tradition that "is eternally young and always inventive, and involves a fundamental need, inherent in its very being, to grow and renew itself" in every age.[7]

This tradition, as John Paul II noted, began with the ancient philosophers, Plato and especially Aristotle. It continued, informed by Christian faith, in certain early writers of the Church—in particu-

6. This term in its present usage appears to derive from the historian of philosophy Maurice de Wolf; for a recent account, see the article *"philosophia perennis"* by Ralph McInerny ("R.M.") in *The Cambridge Dictionary of Philosophy,* ed. Robert Audi (New York: Cambridge University Press, 1999), 580. In at least one place in his early writings, Karol Wojtyła/John Paul II himself referred to the *"philosophia perennis"* and the "Thomist school"; and he identified himself with them. See "The Human Person and Natural Law" (1970), in Karol Wojtyła, *Person and Community,* trans. Theresa Sandok, O.S.M. (New York: Peter Lang, 1993), 181. Moreover, in the official Latin text of *Fides et ratio,* the heading for the paragraphs directly focused on the thought of Aquinas (secs. 43–44) reads: *"Perennis sancti Thomae Aquinatis sententiarum novitas."* For further specification of "perennial philosophy" as the term is understood in the present text, see note 15, below.

7. Jacques Maritain, *A Preface to Metaphysics* (London: Sheed and Ward, 1945), 2.

lar St. Augustine of Hippo (354–430). And it came to maturity in the Christian Middle Ages, after Aristotle's thought was re-introduced into the West by way of Islamic and Byzantine Greek sources. For many, a high point in the development of the perennial tradition came in the thought of St. Thomas Aquinas (1225–74), a priest of the Dominican order who taught at the University of Paris, counseled popes, and wrote voluminously on both philosophical and theological topics. Significantly, John Paul devoted two full sections of his 1998 document to Aquinas's achievements.

At the heart of the perennial philosophy is a *realism* (recall the second "requirement" for Christian philosophy noted above); this may be characterized as holding that the human mind can and typically does make contact with the real, and that its judgments can and typically do have a reliability and a truth-value that go beyond the mere expression of sensations and ideas. In developing this position, the tradition, at its best, has avoided realisms that are "naïve" or "one-dimensional." It has recognized, that is, a need to critique human judgments, as well as to attend to diversity in the modes of being and, correspondingly, the modes of human knowing and articulating being.

In the later Middle Ages, and throughout most of the Modern period, the perennial philosophy somewhat languished. Except for the work of a few key figures, this tradition was kept alive primarily by repetition and codification, rather than—as Maritain would have urged—by growing and renewing itself in keeping with the age. Following the call of Pope Leo XIII in the encyclical *Aeterni patris* (1879), attention once again was paid to the authentic thought of the Medieval masters, in particular Aquinas, as well as to ways their thought might interact with that of modern philosophers. Here one might mention, for example, the historical studies of Gilson[8] and the creative philosophical explorations of Maritain.[9]

---

8. See, for example, Etienne Gilson, *The Christian Philosophy of St. Thomas Aquinas* (New York: Random House, 1956).

9. In addition to the works mentioned in notes 2 and 7 above, see, for example, Jacques Maritain, *The Degrees of Knowledge,* translated under the supervision of Gerald B. Phelan,

Up to and including the decade of Vatican Council II (1962–65), such perennial philosophy held pride of place in Catholic colleges and universities in this country. With the "opening of windows" initiated by Pope John XXIII, there occurred in succeeding years (indeed, it had already begun) much ferment in Catholic thought, philosophical as well as theological. The result has been a good deal of diversity and uncertainty (some would say chaos) in Catholic intellectual circles. John Paul II's 1998 encyclical clearly called for another renewal of the perennial philosophy (as well as a parallel revitalization of fundamental theology) at the outset of the twenty-first century—a renewal that would produce, as we might put it, "new blossoms" on the stem of the great tradition.

We ourselves hope to contribute to such a renewal, and especially to help make it available to students. But before doing so we should note the presence of a variety of contrary trends in contemporary intellectual culture. These trends in effect challenge the very possibility of the philosophical enterprise that John Paul so strongly recommended. At this point, we shall merely identify and sketch general features of these movements of thought; they will receive greater attention—as well as critical discussion and response—in the final sections of each of the three main parts of the book..

Twenty-first-century Challenges and Opportunities

Toward the end of *Fides et ratio*, John Paul himself specifically mentioned a number of challenges to the perennial tradition. For purposes of our discussion, such challenges may be gathered into three general groups. The following are the most significant in each, with brief characterizations provided by the present writer.[10]

In the first group are to be found *scientism* and associated posi-

---

and with a new Introduction by Ralph McInerny (Notre Dame, Ind.: University of Notre Dame Press, 1995); and *Integral Humanism*, trans. Joseph W. Evans (New York: Charles Scribner's Sons, 1968).

10. It should be noted that the various "isms" here discussed are to be understood as general types; it is not implied that every thinker who might be categorized in a certain way holds exactly the position described.

tions. "Scien*tism*," it should be noted, is to be distinguished from "sci-en*ce*." The latter term can be used of any organized body of knowledge and theory; today, of course, it is applied especially to studies that are rooted in precise observations of the physical world. Scientism, on the other hand, is a philosophical view. It makes a claim about the na-ture and limits of knowledge—specifically, the claim that all genuine knowledge is to be achieved through the methods of the natural sci-ences, i.e., methods that are "empirical" or, as they are also called, "positive." Now, genuine science—at least when properly employed—is not a threat to any person or any sound form of thought; indeed, it has proven to be a great boon to humankind. But scientism would ren-der impossible or ineffectual any other approaches to the knowledge of reality—e.g., ones that are philosophical or theological. In particular, it would reject, as John Paul put it, "the [philosophical] notion of being in order to clear the way for pure and simple facticity" (*Fides et ratio*, sec. 88). And a restriction to pure and simple "facticity" would elimi-nate metaphysical aspirations such as those discussed above.

A scientist, it should be made clear, need not accept the philoso-phy of scientism. (Likewise, a person need not be a scientist in order to be a proponent of scientism.) But some scientists in fact do accept and promote this general view—for example, the evolutionary biolo-gist Richard Dawkins and the physical chemist Peter Atkins. The lat-ter gives a particularly clear expression of the "scientistic" position (by contrast with a properly "scientific" one) when he states that his orientation toward the knowledge of reality springs from a "belief that science is all-competent."[11]

As noted just above, the natural sciences are sometimes also re-ferred to as "positive" sciences. Here we should mention a related challenge to the perennial philosophy called *positivism*. One form of this challenge, inspired by the nineteenth-century French thinker Auguste Comte, emphasizes a supposed lack of practical value in any

---

11. Peter Atkins, "Purposeless People," in *Persons and Personality*, ed. Arthur Pea-cocke and Grant Gillett (New York: Basil Blackwell, 1987), 13.

speculations beyond matters "posited" (or "set down") by the sciences. Another form of positivism, even more extreme in its theoretical views, is logical positivism. First developed by the "Vienna Circle," a group of scientists and philosophers in Austria in the 1930s, logical positivism holds that the very meaningfulness of a word or statement is to be called into question if it cannot be expressed in terms that admit of empirical verification.

Scientism is also associated with *reductionism*, which holds that all the elements of one order of thought can be reduced to, and explained within, another order—for example, and in particular, that the whole of what we refer to as the "mental" or "psychical" can be reduced to the material or physical. (For obvious reasons, this form of reductionism is also characterized as a type of *materialism* or *physicalism*.)

Clearly, scientism and associated views, as we have briefly described them, are serious threats to the perennial philosophy—a philosophy that holds, as *Fides et ratio* put it, that the human mind can and should orient itself toward "the transcendent . . . dimension" of reality, not simply toward the empirical dimension.

A second group of contemporary challenges includes what are known as *historicism* and *progressivism*. Such views hold that ideas and practices that develop later in human history are probably or even necessarily better; or, alternatively, that at least in the long run humankind inevitably makes progress. Now, as regards a detailed knowledge of the physical world, historicism makes good sense. However, if the question is one of philosophical wisdom as earlier described, the matter is—to say the least—not so clear. Moreover, an embracing of historicism would be incompatible with the honoring of an intellectual tradition that began with ancient thinkers. Regarding progressivist views about the human project—e.g., those of Marxists and certain positivists, those who hold, in John Paul II's words, that "thanks to scientific and technical progress, man and woman may live as a demiurge, single-handedly and completely taking charge of their destiny" (sec. 91)—it can readily be seen that such views would be incompatible with Christian faith. After all, this faith emphasizes the vicissitudes and uncertainties of the human project, while at the same time offering a supernatural hope (by contrast with a purely natural one) for humanity's fulfillment.

Although not explicitly mentioned by John Paul II in the document from which we have been quoting, a further trend can be associated with the ones just mentioned. This is the trend called *secularism*. So far from embracing any type of supernatural hope, secularists regard the very idea of a realm beyond the natural as a mere vestige of past modes of thought. For secularism (from the Latin *saecula*, meaning "the ages"), temporal reality is all there is—or at any rate it is all that should concern us as human beings. It should be noted that an acceptance, as in Western democracies, of the idea of a "secular order"—including, in particular, a this-world and human-centered form of government—does not in itself entail secularism; for one can recognize the proper autonomy of the present realm and at the same time hold that it depends upon and answers to a realm that is "higher." The latter view, in fact, was the one expressed by the American founders in the Declaration of Independence. Secularism, by contrast, rules the idea of a higher realm out of play. Thus it is, like historicism and progressivism, a trend that challenges a renewal of the perennial philosophy, especially if this renewal is in any way associated with religious faith.

A third cluster of challenges includes *relativism* or, as John Paul II also called it, "undifferentiated pluralism." Any educated person today recognizes that people—individuals and groups, as well as whole cultures and civilizations—are divided by beliefs and attitudes. Sometimes the divisions seem quite fundamental. However, the relativist holds that this is the case not only in fact, but also in principle. That is, the relativist argues that there is no way of showing that any one fundamental view is correct and others incorrect or false; indeed, such a thinker holds that there is no rational basis even for preferring one fundamental belief to another. Relativism also is incompatible with the philosophy of the "great tradition," which maintains that there is, in fact, objective truth about ultimate matters—even if such truth is very difficult to formulate and establish in a manner persuasive to all. (Significantly, John Paul's successor—Pope Benedict XVI, the former Cardinal Joseph Ratzinger—also has consistently expressed this point. In a speech just before the conclave at which he was elected pope, he warned of the dangers to the contemporary world of what he termed a "dictatorship of relativism.")

Beyond the sociological data alluded to above, another source of today's relativism is the school of philosophy called "atheistic existentialism." Writers of this school, such as Jean-Paul Sartre, hold that there is no essential reality to human persons or other types of being, because there is no God to conceive such essential realities. Rather, each human individual determines—and cannot avoid determining—what his or her "essence" will be. At this rate, clearly, there can be no objective justification of any philosophical framework. Supposed "wisdoms" or "understandings of our being" will be irreducibly plural because they are simply and freely chosen.

John Paul II also referred to *postmodernism*. As the name suggests, this cultural trend—especially popular in Western Europe but also represented in the United States—springs from a rejection of the supposed certainties propounded by certain modern philosophers, especially those called "rationalists." The latter sought to establish systems of truth deductively from sets of a priori principles.[12] According to postmodernism, all such efforts belong to a prior age of thought. As expressed by the French thinkers Jacques Derrida and Michel Foucault, as well as by the American Richard Rorty, the postmodern philosophy claims that all forms of knowledge and speech are embedded in particular viewpoints. Thus it is impossible to ground, or even to

12. We shall explore modern "rationalism" in section 1.1 of this book. For good, brief accounts of postmodernism (and ones that are helpful for our purposes), see Rosalind Smith Edman, "Feminism, Postmodernism, and Thomism Confront Questions of Gender," in *Postmodernism and Christian Philosophy*, ed. Roman T. Ciapalo (Washington, D.C.: American Maritain Association/The Catholic University of America Press, 1997); and Warren Murray, "Science, Postmodernism, and the Challenge of Philosophy in the New Century," in *Faith, Scholarship, and Culture in the 21st Century*, ed. Alice Ramos and Marie I. George (Washington, D.C.: American Maritain Association/The Catholic University of America Press, 2002).

claim rational priority for, one's preferred understanding of reality. It is interesting to note John Paul's reaction to these ideas. He wrote that, while in their fullness they obviously conflict with both Christianity and traditional speculative philosophy, "the currents of thought which claim to be postmodern merit appropriate attention" (*Fides et ratio*, sec. 91). That is (at least as this writer interprets the pope's remarks), there is something correct in rejecting an overemphasis upon reason. However, the thinkers who call themselves "postmodern" tend to carry this theme too far. Indeed, they tend to fall into the position called "nihilism."

It is *nihilism*, according to *Fides et ratio*, that is the ultimate challenge to perennial philosophy—as indeed to contemporary religious faith. The term in question derives from the Latin word *nihil*, meaning "nothing"; as John Paul understood it, it expresses "a denial of the humanity and the very identity of the human being" (sec. 90). To put the matter in a slightly different way, a nihilist holds that human life and indeed the whole universe are purposeless or totally without meaning. As indicated in a passage quoted on the epigraph page of this book (taken from section 90 of the document), the late pope attributed the rise of the nihilist philosophy to a "neglect of being." Such neglect, he said, has had the effect of erasing from people's awareness "the marks of their likeness to God." This in turn has led individuals and whole cultures "either to a destructive will to power or to a solitude without hope."

The German philosopher Friedrich Nietzsche—who wrote just over a hundred years ago and who coined the phrase "will to power"[13]—often is said to be the founder of nihilism. This may or may not be historically accurate. It is clear, however, that events of the twenty-first century are again shaking civilization to its core; and that a renew-

---

13. See *The Will to Power*, ed. and trans. Walter Kauffman (New York: Knopf Publishing Group, 1968). It should be noted that this book was not prepared for publication by Nietzsche himself. (He had intended to do so, but he abandoned the project.) Thus the texts gathered under this title are selected by editors from Nietzsche's notebooks, and in some places are amended for the sake of continuity. (For another discussion of "will to power" by Nietzsche, see his *Beyond Good and Evil*, trans. Helen Zimmern [New York: Dover Publications, 1997], esp. nos. 43–44.)

al of perennial philosophy will need to articulate the basis of human meaning in the world.

From the side of religion itself come other challenges to the perennial tradition. One such challenge John Paul II called *biblicism* (see *Fides et ratio*, sec. 55); in this country it is better known as (biblical) *fundamentalism*. According to this view, all relevant knowledge about our being already has been expressed in the Bible, which (for fundamentalists) is to be interpreted literally in all its parts. Thus rational analyses and reflections based on common human experience—such as those called for by philosophy—are held to be quite unnecessary, and even, perhaps, dangerous to the religious faith of those who participate in such modes of thought.

Another challenge—closely related to biblicism or fundamentalism—is *fideism*. This last term, which comes from the Latin *fides*, meaning "faith," refers to the position that religious questions, and more generally all questions about transcendent matters, are to be settled by sheer faith, unsupported by human reasoning. It may be noted that Christianity always has had adherents who have adopted such a position.[14] Moreover, the Christian life obviously is rooted in an entrusting of oneself to God as revealed in Jesus Christ: his words, his deeds, and the traditions of his Church. This, however, does not entail that reason has no important role to play in the life of faith. And fideism, taken as a general position, is incompatible with the traditional search for a "harmony" between faith and reason, and especially with the idea that philosophy—a work of reason—can make substantive contributions to this harmony.

At the opposite end of the spectrum are those who hold to a purely metaphorical, or figurative, or symbolic interpretation of Biblical and similar texts. This line of interpretation—sometimes called *noncognitivism*, since it takes religious terms to be rooted in the exercise of emotion or poetic creativity, rather than acts of knowledge—poses a

---

14. See, for example, the passages from the ancient Christian writer Tertullian, and from the nineteenth-century Danish writer Søren Kierkegaard, in *Faith and Reason*, ed. Paul Helm (New York: Oxford University Press, 1999).

challenge that is equally obvious. For there can be, on its view, no literal or designative language, i.e., no language that expresses its object
by way of a genuine concept, either about God or about the world's
relations with God. Of course, much religious language, in its original and continuing use, clearly is figurative and symbolic in character.
And such language does involve both a strong emotional dimension
and the resources of the poet. But on the severe restrictions proposed
by non-cognitivism (which we also will call "symbolism"), no realist interpretation of ultimate language would be possible; its meaning, that is to say, would forever be shrouded in the mists of image and
metaphor.

It is perhaps needless to say—but it is worth pointing out—that
analogues to these various challenges arise for philosophers, or students of philosophy, from other religious traditions. Thus, for example, there is to be noted within Islam a kind of fundamentalism
and a kind of fideism related to the Koran. And a Hindu devotee may
well consider just how literally or how symbolically the stories of the
many gods of his or her ancient and multilayered religion are to be understood. Moreover, all religious traditions—including the primarily
oral traditions of Native American and other indigenous peoples—are
challenged by contemporary movements such as scientism, secularism, and nihilism.

We see, then, that thinkers interested in redeveloping the perennial philosophy (as well as thinkers from other cultural contexts with
whom they might engage in positive dialogue) face many significant
challenges. But it is important to note that there are, in these early
years of the twenty-first century, genuine opportunities as well. A
number of recently developed types of philosophy have shown promise of making contributions to the ongoing tradition. Prominent examples would be phenomenology, personalism, and some strands of
linguistic or analytic philosophy. *Phenomenology*, according to its
practitioners, seeks to record and to reflect upon the realities of experience as immediately apprehended, apart from intervening conceptual apparatus. Philosophers called *personalists* stress the unique fea-

tures and possibilities of human personal and interpersonal life—e.g., encounter in dialogue, communion with others, and the higher forms of love. For their part, *analytic* philosophers emphasize careful attention to the analysis of language as the key to progress in philosophy—an emphasis in part shared, as we shall see, by Aristotle, Aquinas, and others in the Scholastic tradition.

In his own early philosophical work, John Paul II himself was influenced by phenomenology and personalism. He regularly made use of themes from these philosophical schools—as well as from that of Aquinas—in his various writings. Other phenomenologists and personalists associated with Catholic thought are St. Edith Stein, Dietrich von Hildebrand, Gabriel Marcel, and, in this country, Robert Sokolowski and John Crosby. The insights of analytic philosophy have been made available to the great tradition through the work of English-speaking philosophers such as Elizabeth Anscombe, Peter Geach, John Haldane, and, in this country, Norman Kretzmann and Eleonore Stump. None of these newer philosophies is particularly strong in what John Paul termed the "metaphysical dimension." However, insofar as their insights might be grafted onto the perennial philosophy the prospects for the latter's enrichment seem bright. In the present book, we shall incorporate points from the newer movements when they illuminate the topics in question.

Equally important, in the judgment of the present author, is a noticeable renewal among students and young adults of a desire for such human wisdom as may be available. (This comes after a period marked by much random intellectual experimentation, or, alternatively, ennui.) It is especially to such readers, who seek a philosophical approach to "understanding our being," that this book is addressed. Our aim is to develop in some detail one such approach—not the only such approach, to be sure, but one that the author hopes is well articulated and accessible to the reader, as well as one that is in continuity with the perennial tradition. Our effort in effect responds to *Fides et ratio*'s concluding call: "I appeal . . . to philosophers, and to all teachers of philosophy, asking them to have the courage to recover, in the flow of an enduringly valid philosophical tradition, the range of authentic wisdom and truth—metaphysical truth included—which is proper to philosophical enquiry" (sec. 106).

In articulating this philosophical approach, we shall make use of the works of recent writers of other types or schools insofar as they supplement, or correct in matters of detail, or facilitate a helpful contemporary expression of, basic ideas of St. Thomas Aquinas. That is—with due respect for those who adopt other paths to wisdom—our presentation, on essential matters, will be "Thomist."[15]

We would re-emphasize at the outset of this book that, while the tradition of philosophy to which we seek to contribute has flourished under the inspiration of Christianity, precisely as philosophy there is nothing essentially or formally Christian about it. Supposing it to be viable, it in principle is available to all, regardless of religious tradition or lack thereof. In a very few sections we shall explicitly pursue certain religious and theological concerns. For the rest, our proposals will be strictly philosophical. Indeed, it will be a relevant criticism of them as philosophical if they seem formally to depend, in whole or in part, on a revelation accepted in faith.

15. John Paul II was careful to point out that, while certain philosophies are incompatible with Christian faith, the Church does not require adherence to a "specific school" of thought (*Fides et ratio*, sec. 83). Moreover, regarding Aquinas's philosophy itself, it is not always a simple matter to determine what counts as "essential." However, insofar as other philosophies do reject Aquinas's thought, or alter it in essential ways, they would not, strictly speaking, fall under our concept of "perennial" philosophy—although they might be part of what John Paul II called the "great tradition" more broadly conceived.

Our touchstone for the interpretation and development of Aquinas's speculative thought will be the work of the twentieth-century Thomist Jacques Maritain, as well as his students Yves R. Simon and Pierre-Marie Emonet, O.P. (As it happens, all three of these writers were Frenchmen by birth, although both Maritain and Simon spent many years in the United States and Simon became a naturalized citizen.) We also will refer to other recent Thomist philosophers—e.g., Etienne Gilson, William Wallace, O.P., and W. Norris Clarke, S.J. The work of these various figures is continued in meetings and publications of the American Catholic Philosophical Association, as well as those of more specialized groups such as the American Maritain Association. Also of relevance to the perennial philosophy are a number of recent books (many of them mentioned in the main parts of this volume and listed in the Bibliography), as well as articles in the journals *The Thomist*, *American Catholic Philosophical Quarterly* (formerly *The New Scholasticism*), *The Modern Schoolman*, and the recently inaugurated English-language edition of *Nova et Vetera*. (For further information, see the introductory note in the Bibliography.)

As suggested above, the present book also will attend to other positions—including ones opposed to our own—that have become prominent in recent times. In this way the student can experience the interplay of philosophical arguments and themes, and at the same time judge, at least in a preliminary way, whether our brief responses to competing views are cogent. Thus, it is hoped, the student himself or herself will be drawn into the life of philosophy.

In keeping with John Paul II's call for a philosophy "of genuinely metaphysical range," part 1 of this book is devoted to the philosophy of being. Here we shall consider the ways we can know being, the constitutive principles of being itself, and other very general themes of perennial philosophy. In part 2 we apply a number of these themes in developing an account of our personal being. We shall especially be concerned to note the features—and the apparent implications of the features—discovered in our human powers of knowing and willing, as well as in our distinctive modes of sociality. In part 3 we turn to philosophical reflection about God, understood as being's Source and End. Here we shall pursue the topics of reasoning to God's existence, the nature of statements about God, difficulties regarding God's providence and creative activity in light of evil in the world, and, finally, the idea of a divine revelation that would respond to our continuing quest for self-understanding.

Our final section is an Epilogue concerning prospects for dialogue among world cultures and religions, and concerning the role of philosophy in such dialogue. This theme is suggested by topics in part 3, as well as by the increasingly communal nature of our world, together with the consequent need for intercultural understanding. In the document from which we have been quoting, John Paul II pointed out that "philosophical thought is often the only ground for understanding and dialogue" with those who do not share one's faith; and that such thought might provide a basis for "clear and honest collaboration between Christians and the followers of other religions and all those who, while not sharing a religious belief, have at heart the renewal of humanity" (*Fides et ratio*, sec. 104). The present writer shares the hope thus expressed. Since readers of this book are likely to represent a range of cultural and religious backgrounds, they will be in a position to discuss the value of suggestions we make about these matters—and to make suggestions of their own.

After this rather lengthy Introduction, we now are ready to begin exploring the perennial philosophy and its approach to "understanding our being."

SUMMARY

• Philosophy is a search for wisdom that formally relies on common human experience and modes of reasoning. Speculative philosophy seeks an understanding of being or of the way things ultimately are.

• Christian philosophy is to be distinguished from theology, although it takes inspiration from, and pursues its topics in light of, religious faith.

• The "perennial" tradition of philosophy draws upon earlier expressions of wisdom (in particular, those of Aristotle and St. Thomas Aquinas), while seeking to renew itself in the context of contemporary intellectual culture.

• A number of challenges to perennial philosophy arise today—e.g., scientism, historicism, and nihilism; trends among certain religious believers themselves (fideism, fundamentalism, and non-cognitivism) also call this philosophical approach into question.

• In a highly pluralistic world, philosophy perhaps offers the best hope for mutual understanding and dialogue.

QUESTIONS FOR REFLECTION

1. Given the understanding of philosophical wisdom articulated in this Introduction, how close do you think a person might come to actually achieving it? Are people of certain backgrounds or temperaments more likely to make progress in philosophy than others? Explain.

2. Suppose a critic of the idea of Christian philosophy says, "You let religion influence your thinking, but I go by reason alone and thus am able to produce a purer form of philosophy." How might a Christian philoso-

pher (or a philosopher from some other religious tradition) respond to this; and how cogent would the response be?

3. Of the various challenges to the "great tradition" identified by John Paul II and discussed in this Introduction, which do you regard as the most significant or the most threatening? Why?

4. Might the position identified as "fideism" be appropriate in relation to certain types of transcendent matters, but not others? Alternatively, should reason play a role even in the acceptance or rejection of teachings that are proposed in a specifically religious way? Explain.

5. At this early point in our study, what do you think of the possibilities of intercultural and interreligious dialogue? Do you see any concrete ways in which philosophy might be helpful in this undertaking?

PART I

BEING

1.1 KNOWLEDGE OF BEING: A REALIST APPROACH

Identifying the Object of Wonder

Philosophy, as we noted in the Introduction, has its origin in wonder. For the speculative philosopher such wonder, or awe, is directed primarily at the very being of things. In the Introduction, we mentioned wonder at "the splendor of existence" in noting how Christian faith can inspire and enhance one's philosophical thinking. But a person need not be a Christian, or formally religious at all, to share a sense of wonder. Aristotle clearly did so. And, just before his death, the American philosopher and professed atheist Sidney Hook (1902–89) confided that "there were many times in his life . . . that he often felt well up within him the desire to say thanks that things, which might have gone badly, worked out in existence as they had."[1] A large number of people, it seems reasonable to suggest, have had some such experience during their lives. Whether or not it is accompanied by gratitude, the capacity to be struck by and filled with awe at the very existence of things is shared by very nearly everyone.

But while philosophy begins in wonder, it must proceed to think about its object—that is, being—in a disciplined and systematic way. Let us undertake some preliminary reflections about how this might be done.

What is it to think, or to philosophize, about being? One recent proponent of the perennial tradition, Pierre-Marie Emonet, introduces the topic as follows: "(I)n sounding the depths of the primary data of the intelligence common to us all . . . the philosophers of ancient Greece were able to tap the source of philosophical wisdom. They demonstrat-

---

1. This episode is recounted in Michael Novak, *On Cultivating Liberty*, ed. Brian C. Anderson (Lanham, Md.: Rowman and Littlefield, 1999), 190.

ed that the evidences of intellectual awareness are pregnant with the most profound truths."[2] Emonet's point is that to philosophize about being (in the manner of, e.g., Aristotle) involves approaching the world in the deepest possible way—through the "primary data of the intelligence," or the "evidences of intellectual awareness." The speculative philosopher, that is to say, seeks out basic intellectual data (i.e., data that can ground fundamental concepts and principles), rather than the more obvious and more prevalent, but at the same time more superficial, data of sensory awareness. Again, the judgments formulated by the philosopher are most universal; some of them apply to all that is or can be. By contrast, judgments formulated by specialists in other disciplines (e.g., biochemistry or history) are—from the standpoint of intellectual understanding—more particular and, in a way, derivative. That is, while these latter types of judgments have their own proper significance and are to be assessed in terms of criteria specific to their respective disciplines, they also reflect, or presuppose, the more basic judgments of the philosopher—e.g., the judgment (to be discussed in the next section) that physical reality fundamentally consists of "substances," along with their various features or attributes (traditionally called "accidents").

Moreover, the types of evidence used in philosophy are, in Emonet's words, "common to us all." That is, as we put it in the Introduction, they in principle are available to everyone, without regard to special training or prior systems of belief.

But how do we search for these primary data or evidences? How do we know when we have found them? And how is it that these put us on a path to "understanding our being"?

In responding to such questions, philosophers in the tradition of St. Thomas Aquinas point to certain very general facts about reality— facts which, if we reflect upon them properly, enable us to formulate basic philosophical concepts and principles. In this first of our book's three main parts, we shall discuss a number of such general facts, as

2. Pierre-Marie Emonet, O.P., *The Dearest Freshness Deep Down Things: An Introduction to the Philosophy of Being,* trans. Robert R. Barr (New York: Crossroad, 1999), 3.

well as concepts and principles to which they can lead. It is the latter that equip us to think about being; it is through reflection incorporating such concepts and principles that there emerge, in Emonet's words, the "most profound truths."

Before proceeding with this line of inquiry, however, we must be sure that we have properly identified the being that is the object of wonder. In particular, we must beware of a common confusion: mistaking real being for what might be called the being of logic. To approach this matter, let us note that logicians often distinguish two aspects of a term's or concept's meaning. The first is the range of individuals the term picks out; this is called its "extension," or "denotation," or range of "reference." The second is the term's intelligible content, or what it says about the individuals it picks out; this is called its "intension," or "connotation," or "sense."

In light of this distinction, consider the following series of terms: "college student," "human being," "living being," "natural being," "being." Here, it may seem, we have progressively wider sets of things picked out (and thus wider extensions or denotations or ranges of reference), but at the same time progressively less intelligible content (and thus less intension or connotation or sense). The last term of the series, "being," clearly applies without restriction; for of everything we can say that he or she or it "is," or that they "are." However, while this concept's denotation is thus all-inclusive, it may seem that its connotation—what it expresses about things—must be regarded as utterly empty.

Now, the danger for the beginning student is to assume that the being said to engage philosophical interest just is this being—or what might rather be termed "pseudo-being"—consisting in membership in the widest class of objects of thought. And, in fact, when we hear the word "being" (as well as its cognates "is" and "are," etc.), it is easy to think that they express no more than such membership. But if we do think of these terms in this way, they will seem to lack any specific meaning (for they express nothing that differentiates the terms' intensions, or restricts their extensions in any way); moreover, they will seem to connote something static (namely, class membership), rather than something full of actuality. Such words, accordingly, may come to be regarded as banal, indeed "the most banal . . . of all."[3]

In light of all this, the student may be inclined to ask: How could reflection on being be thought to have philosophical significance? How could it be said to lead to "the most profound truths"? And, in fact, many professional philosophers—under just the impression described above—have doubted the possibility of a metaphysical study of reality as envisioned by John Paul II and the perennial tradition. Thus, for example, R. G. Collingwood spoke for many English-speaking thinkers of the twentieth century when he said that there could be no science or discipline of "pure being" because such a study "would have a subject matter entirely devoid of peculiarities; a subject matter, therefore, containing nothing to differentiate it from anything else, or from nothing at all."[4]

To the philosopher who has learned from Aristotle and St. Thomas Aquinas, Collingwood's remark involves a deep misunderstanding; for "being" taken simply as the term with the widest range of reference does not express real being at all. However, the very prevalence of this misunderstanding shows that we must take special care to see that the object of our study is, in fact, real being. We must focus on the intelligible features of reality or actuality itself, insofar as we can come to know them.

Here the question arises: Can we in fact come to know such features? At this point the philosophy of being needs to be supplemented by a philosophy of knowledge (or, as it also is called, an *epistemology*)—that is, a very general account of knowledge's nature, its types, and their interrelations. Thus we need to articulate, as we put it in the Introduction, a critical and ordered "realism"—one in which the knowledge of being, just as being, is assigned its proper place, along with various types of knowledge of being as qualified in such-and-such respects (biochemical, historical, etc.).

3. Emonet, *Dearest Freshness*, 5.
4. R. G. Collingwood, *An Essay on Metaphysics* (Oxford: Clarendon Press, 1957), 14. As we shall see, a study of "pure being," as Collingwood seemed to understand it, is not what the perennial philosophy has had in mind.

The Theory of Critical Realism

Jacques Maritain said of being that it is, paradoxically, a mystery hidden "in plain sight."[5] That is, being is so present to us in all our conscious moments that we tend not to notice that, first of all, beings simply are. But this indeed is the case. Moreover, things first make themselves known to us just as beings: when we were infants, even before we developed a specific recognition of, say, our mothers, we already had a vague awareness of reality.

The human mind—at least when it begins to philosophize—craves an account of the mystery called "being," as well as our access to it. Before outlining the account given by perennial philosophers, let us consider epistemologies of two other types. Both were developed during the period called "Modern Philosophy," which historians commonly take to begin with the French thinker René Descartes (1596–1650). These approaches to knowledge are called "rationalism" and "empiricism," respectively.

Rationalism in its modern form originates with Descartes himself. As a student he had been taught a version of Scholasticism—which, as we noted in the Introduction, at that time often involved mere repetition of the ideas of Medieval thinkers. Disenchanted with his formal education, the young Descartes decided that he would begin the quest for knowledge anew. As he expressed the matter in his *Discourse on Method* (1637), in order to preserve himself from error he developed four rules that he tried to follow with "firm and unwavering resolution." The first was "never to accept anything for true which I did not clearly know to be such . . . and to comprise nothing more in my judgment than what was presented to my mind so clearly and distinctly as to exclude all ground of doubt." From such starting points— from what he termed "objects the simplest and easiest to know"— Descartes sought to proceed, "step by step, to the knowledge of the more complex."[6]

5. See Jacques Maritain, *A Preface to Metaphysics*, 87.
6. René Descartes, *A Discourse on Method*, trans. John Veritch (La Salle, Ill.: Open Court, 1901); reprinted in *Discourse on Method and Meditations on First Philosophy* (New Haven, Conn.: Yale University Press, 1996).

The perfect model of rational knowledge, as understood by Descartes, was mathematics, and in particular, perhaps, geometry. Succeeding rationalist philosophers looked to this model as well. Thus they all began by grounding their work in what they took to be direct insights into natures and relations (insights expressible via what Descartes had called "clear" and "distinct" ideas); they then moved by deduction to conclusions about reality that would follow from these insights. For example, and most famously, Baruch Spinoza (1632–77) developed an entire system of the mind and the world (including implications for ethics) following what he termed "the manner of geometry" (in Latin, *more geometrico*).[7]

Although the rationalists thought they were developing knowledge of reality, they are considered by philosophers of the realist tradition (as well as others) to have fallen into *idealism*. That is, they took as their intellectual foundation things that can be sharply defined only in the realm of concepts; accordingly, their systems relate primarily to ideas, rather than to reality as such.

During this same Early Modern period the natural sciences were burgeoning forth. These studies of course depended upon observation and experiment, rather than abstract concepts and thought. It is not surprising, therefore, that a very different account of knowledge also developed among Modern philosophers, namely, empiricism.

Empiricism derives its name from the Greek verb for "to experience" *(emperein)*; as an epistemological theory it involves an account that has seemed—to some thinkers—to cohere best with the actual approaches to knowledge that characterize modern scientific investigations. One originator (or, perhaps better, precursor) of empiricism was Francis Bacon (1561–1626), a near contemporary of Descartes who lived and studied in England. But it was succeeding thinkers from the British Isles—specifically, John Locke (1632–1704), George Berkeley (1685–1753), and David Hume (1711–76)—who produced full-fledged articulations of empiricist views about knowledge and reality. Hume, in particular, declared that "all the perceptions [i.e., objects of experi-

---

7. Baruch (Benedict) Spinoza, *Ethics*, in *A Spinoza Reader: The Ethics and Other Works*, ed. and trans. E. Curley (Princeton, N.J.: Princeton University Press, 1994).

ence] of the human mind resolve themselves into two distinct kinds, which I shall call Impressions and Ideas." The former category comprises immediate "sensations, passions and emotions, as they make their first appearance in the soul"; the latter category comprises the generally much fainter "images of these in thinking and reasoning."[8] According to Hume, even our loftiest and most general concepts ultimately are reducible to original "impressions" of sense or feeling; indeed, this is the case regarding everything we call knowledge, whatever its type or complexity.

In connection with the empiricist theory of knowledge, we should mention a related theory about what is real. This is called *phenomenalism* (from the Greek word *phainesthai,* "to appear"). According to phenomenalists, reality consists simply of appearances or the data of sense. An early articulator of this theory was the aforementioned George Berkeley, a fierce opponent of what he understood to be "materialist" philosophies of reality. According to Berkeley, "to be is to be perceived" (in Latin, *esse est percipi*)—or, alternatively, "to perceive" (in Latin, *percipere*).[9] More recent English-speaking proponents of this tradition, e.g., the twentieth-century British philosopher A. J. Ayer, have sought to combine its theories of knowledge and reality with modern developments in logic. The resulting theory often is referred to as "logical empiricism" or, as we expressed it in the Introduction, "logical positivism." Perhaps the most ambitious project along this line came in the work of the American philosopher Nelson Goodman, whose 1951 book *The Structure of Appearance* sought to develop a logical program for building up out of "basic individuals" (i.e., sense-data or phenomena) the entire world of our everyday experience.[10]

Empiricism and related views have not been limited to English-speaking countries. For example, the French existentialist Jean-Paul Sartre offered a view similar to phenomenalism in his best-known

8. David Hume, *Treatise of Human Nature,* sec. 1; reprint ed. D. F. and M. Norton (New York: Oxford University Press, 2000).

9. George Berkeley, *Treatise Concerning the Principles of Human Knowledge,* ed. Jonathan Dancy (Oxford: Oxford University Press, 1998), secs. 3 and 7.

10. Nelson Goodman, *The Structure of Appearance* (reprint, Dordrecht, Netherlands: Kluwer, 1977).

philosophical work, *Being and Nothingness*. There he wrote, "Being is nothing more than the closely joined series of its manifestations."[11] That is, there is no integrating reality that provides the basis for a thing's acting, or for its being experienced, precisely as a being. For Sartre, as for British and American phenomenalists, there simply is no being beyond appearances or sensory data (including, for Sartre, internal or subjective data).

In empiricism, and especially in phenomenalism, we find another approach that is contrary to traditional realism. Unlike the rationalists, who focus on abstract ideas, empiricist philosophers take immediate objects of sensation or emotion, precisely as experienced, as the only realities to be recognized—or, at any rate, the only realities to which the human mind has genuine access.[12]

Having reviewed two competing approaches, let us now introduce the theory of knowledge articulated by twentieth-century proponents of the perennial tradition, in particular, Thomists such as Jacques Maritain and Yves Simon. As Frenchmen, these philosophers were very familiar with the rationalism of Descartes. Moreover, as thinkers who had studied the modern sciences, they were well aware of empirical methods and their achievements. However, first and foremost they saw themselves as heirs of the realist philosophical tradition, as originally developed by Aristotle and then redeveloped by Medieval Scholastics. That is, they were committed to articulating anew an account that confirmed, in John Paul's words, the human capacity to "come to a knowledge which can reach objective truth," or to "attain to reality itself as knowable."

Now, some modern "philosophers of common sense," especially in England and Scotland, also had sought a return to realism. Their efforts,

---

11. Jean-Paul Sartre, *Being and Nothingness*, trans. Hazel Barnes (New York: Washington Square Press, 1966), lxvii. The present English rendition follows the translation of Sartre's statement in Pierre-Marie Emonet, *The Greatest Marvel of Nature*, trans. Robert R. Barr (New York: Crossroad, 2000), 86.

12. At this point there also might be mentioned the philosophy of "skepticism," which has attracted few modern adherents as a general philosophy of knowledge (although the aforementioned David Hume seemed, at some places in his writings, very close to embracing it). We shall consider skepticism in relation to a specific knowledge of human, personal being in section 2.1.

however, were rejected by many as "uncritical" or "naïve," as well as "one-dimensional." That is, these philosophers were thought to have ignored the ways in which experience can mislead us in our judgments, as well as the range of complementary approaches available to our effort to understand being. By contrast, the perennial philosophy (especially as developed by Thomists) has sought to develop a realism that is both critical and ordered.[13] As critical, it is aware that everyday experience and common sense beliefs (e.g., that the sun "passes over" the earth, or that the earth is "flat") often need to be supplemented and corrected by more refined forms of experience, as well as by sound scientific theory. As ordered, it is sensitive to the diverse modes (and to interrelations among these modes) of being, knowledge, and the verbal expression of knowledge. Regarding the last point, Thomist writers have articulated an account that marks different "orders" and "degrees" of human knowledge—an account that we shall begin to explore in the immediately succeeding pages, then take up more fully in section 1.3.

Empirical and Philosophical Approaches

Whatever may come to be said about "orders" or "degrees" of human knowledge, it seems clear that we first formally encounter being in our experience of and attempts to understand the world of nature. At this point, the student may be inclined to ask: Is not the world of nature precisely the province of the modern natural sciences? What substantive contributions can philosophy make to our understanding of it? And, supposing it can make contributions, how is the discipline of philosophy to be distinguished from and related to those of the natural sciences? These are very important questions; let us consider them at some length.

As we have noted, the rapid expansion of the natural or empiri-

13. See, for example, Maritain's seminal book, *The Degrees of Knowledge,* as well as refinements in Maritain's account introduced by Simon in, e.g., *Foresight and Knowledge,* ed. Ralph Nelson and Anthony O. Simon (New York: Fordham University Press, 1996); and *The Great Dialogue of Nature and Space,* ed. Gerald Dalcourt (South Bend, Ind.: St. Augustine's Press, 2001). Another good, general presentation of the realist approach to knowledge is that by the Jesuit scholar R. J. Henle. See his *Theory of Knowledge* (Chicago: Loyola University Press, 1983).

cal or positive sciences during recent centuries has largely been due to an increase and improvement in methods of observation, and, with these, in controlled experimentation and therefore verification. It is the careful attention to features of things that are available to the senses—i.e., the gathering, describing, measuring, comparing, hypothesizing and testing, and, where possible, mathematical systematizing of such features—that has led to our detailed acquaintance with and ever-increasing mastery over the physical world.

But now let us consider how modern scientific knowledge, precisely as a type of knowledge, should be characterized. Empirical studies, in every case, are related to matters of observation, i.e., to the ways things manifest themselves via features available to our powers of sense perception. Such studies, without doubt, can lead to one genuine kind—or, perhaps better, one set of kinds—of knowledge: namely, an increasingly precise and systematic understanding of things in terms of their observable features. As indicated above, this knowledge is sometimes called "positive" knowledge, since it is directly rooted in things "posited"—i.e., the relevant phenomena. (It should be clear, incidentally, that these points do not necessarily entail the philosophy—discussed earlier in this section—of empiricism or phenomenalism. That is, one can recognize the significance for our knowledge of access to the observable features of things without holding that reality consists only in such features, or that our knowledge is restricted to them.)

Connected to all of this is the following point: the types of concepts developed in the natural sciences themselves always relate to matters of observation. As perennial philosophers have put it, matters of observation figure essentially in these concepts' "degree" of abstraction within the general "order" of our knowledge of nature. By way of example, let us borrow from a discussion by Simon, and consider the way in which a study of the element silver is approached in the positive science of chemistry.[14] Taken as an empirical nature or species, silver initially is distinguished from other elements by such features

14. Yves R. Simon, "Maritain's Philosophy of the Sciences," in Jacques Maritain, *Philosophy of Nature* (New York: Philosophical Library, 1951); reprinted in *Philosopher at Work*, ed. Anthony O. Simon (Lanham, Md.: Rowman and Littlefield, 1999), 30–31.

as color, texture, hardness, etc. Over the centuries, as the science of chemistry has progressed, these features have been subject to increasingly fine measurement, as well as mathematical analysis and organization. In addition, other experientially based but mathematically organized facts about silver have come to be recognized: the element's melting point; its ability to combine with other elements (e.g., in the case of silver, the ability to combine with chlorine to form the salt silver chloride); its atomic weight and number; etc. It may be noted that as chemistry merges with physics at one edge of the discipline, a reliance on mathematical modeling tends to increase; as it merges with biology at the other edge, this is progressively less the case. However, throughout the natural sciences, the role of phenomena—i.e., the empirical or sensible features of things—are recognized as foundational in the development and application of concepts.

In light of all this, when we consider the natural sciences, or their principal characteristics, as "pure types," and seek to characterize them from the standpoint of their general approach to knowledge, we may come to say, with Maritain, that they are *empiriological* (from the Greek *emperein* once again, plus *logos* for "account").[15] That is, they seek to give an account of natural beings by reference to their observable features. Maritain marked a contrast between such empiriological approaches and ones he called *ontological* (from the Greek *on* for "being," plus *logos*). The latter seek to understand natural beings in terms of their type of being or reality, rather than in terms of their empirical manifestations.

Developing another pair of contrasting notions, Maritain further characterized the positive sciences as *perinoetic* (from the Greek *peri* for "about," plus *noein* for "to know").[16] This term suggests that the modes of study in question enable us to have, via empirical observation, knowledge about their objects, although not direct knowledge of the objects' natures as they are in themselves. The latter type of knowledge would be, on Maritain's account, *dianoetic* (from the Greek *dia*,

15. Maritain, *The Degrees of Knowledge*, 156–58.
16. Ibid., 215–24.

for "through," plus *noein*)—as if to say that such knowledge would "cut through" observable features to things' very centers or essences.

Whether the above terminology provides an adequate or completely accurate account of the natural sciences has been a matter of some controversy, including among followers of Aristotle and Aquinas. It has been suggested, for example, that Maritain's account makes natures into mysterious "x's" that are forever impenetrable by the human mind, whereas in fact we can achieve genuine definitions of, e.g., silver and the other elements, and we can do so precisely by way of noting such things as their atomic structures, degrees of hardness, and melting points.[17] In light of this, Maritain's student, Simon, doubtless was correct to emphasize that the terms "empiriological" and "ontological" are to be applied in different gradations to the diverse actual studies of nature, and that terms like "knowledge" and "definition" are (as we shall come to say) "analogous," rather than "univocal" or precisely the same, in the various instances of their use.[18] The author of the present text would suggest as well that, insofar as accounts of an empirical and metrical sort do give a kind of knowledge of natures, this is due to the fact that at the level of reality comprised by elements and compounds there is less actual being to be known than there is in the case of, say, advanced living species. Thus sensible features more immediately and clearly point to the actual natures of things at the chemical level than they do at higher levels of reality. Here, accordingly, philosophy can more directly make use of the results of the positive sciences than is possible in certain other areas of inquiry (e.g., concerning the nature of our human, personal being).

It also may be remarked that not all distinctions that are appropriate and useful from an empiriological point of view necessarily correspond to real or ontological distinctions. Some are simply convenient tools in the development of scientific descriptions. Conversely, certain real or ontological distinctions may be glossed over by an exclusive

17. See, e.g., the review of Maritain's *Philosophy of Nature,* including Simon's article, by William H. Kane, O.P., in *The Thomist* 16 (1953): 127–31.

18. Simon, "Maritain's Philosophy of the Sciences," 38–39. On analogous vs. univocal terms and their meanings, see section 1.4 below.

attention to observable features. An important instance of the latter sort, to be discussed in part 2, involves our own nature. Biologists and anthropologists typically "define" *homo sapiens* in terms of observable similarities to and differences from associated biological species. But the perennial philosopher will ask: Is it things such as these—e.g., having a brain of a certain size, or walking on two legs—that most deeply characterize our distinctive reality as a type of natural being?

Whatever the possibilities of ontological or dianoetic knowledge, it seems clear that we humans have an innate desire for it. As Aristotle expressed the point (*Metaphysics*, book I, chap. 1), "All people by nature desire to know." That is, we want to apprehend the real natures of things, and to explain by reference to those natures the things' behavior and other phenomena. Moreover, if it perhaps has come to seem that such knowledge is largely an ideal rather than a genuinely prospective human achievement, it surely remains a common belief that the world we experience is made up of things that *have* natures, together with their observable features. For all their practical usefulness, "definitions" of things in terms of purely empirical and mathematical concepts seem less than complete or adequate to the natures in question. As suggested above, this perhaps is especially the case with regard to higher order beings such as ourselves.

Turning to a related point, it should be noted that the sensible features of things are impermanent and, in fact, constantly changing. In themselves, therefore, such features are unable to account for the relative stability and continuity we attribute to beings of our experience. Similarly, they are unable to account for these beings' "knowability," even if only obscurely, in terms of their general natures. Moreover, sheer phenomena, or the material and measurable as such, are without "centers"—they consist, in a phrase used by Aristotle, of "parts outside of parts." Thus they provide no explanation of why things "hold together." In light of all this, we are led to ask: How is it that the things that make up natural being—individual elements and compounds, plants, animals, and human persons—are, and are understood to be, unified and integral wholes, i.e., entities that remain somehow the same things as long as they are in existence?

In this way, the perennial philosophy comes to propose that a fully intellectually satisfactory account of natural being requires that the empirical sciences be supplemented by, and their principles or starting points be examined in light of, a more fundamental type of study. Such a study would treat natural being just as natural—that is, as comprising being that emerges, develops over time, is altered by way of internal factors as well as by contact with other things, etc. Central concepts in such a study (traditionally called *philosophy of nature* or *natural philosophy*, but perhaps more accurately called "philosophy of natural being") would be "nature" itself, plus several others we shall come to consider such as "substance," "form," and "change." This discipline will complement the empiriological sciences by trying to articulate, even if only very generally, natural being "as it is in itself"—that is, as it can be understood as a type of real being, not as it is apprehended by sensory perception or further treated via mathematical forms (which, precisely as mathematical, are not directly concerned with things' reality or actuality). Of course, to propose a study of nature or substance as such is likely to strike the practicing biologist or chemist as far too general and abstract. No "requests for proposals" ("RFPs") for the funding of such studies are to be anticipated from the National Science Foundation! And indeed, this is quite understandable, given the precise aims and methods of the empiriological sciences. But that does not mean that philosophical inquiries of the sort here indicated do not lead to genuine knowledge of natural being. As we shall now try to indicate, they do. Moreover, they set the stage for the even deeper knowledge of being—metaphysics—that will occupy us in later sections of part 1.

SUMMARY

• Speculative philosophy seeks to understand features of real being, by contrast with being in the logical sense—which consists simply in belonging to the widest class of objects of thought.

• The perennial tradition espouses a critical and ordered realism; according to this account, the human mind can gain genuine knowledge of reality that is differentiated according to types ("orders" and "degrees").

• While recognizing the significance of the modern empirical sciences, perennial philosophers point to the need for a more general approach to natural being that accounts for the stability amid change of such being, as well as our knowledge of it.

1.2 PHILOSOPHY OF NATURAL BEING

A Philosophy Rooted in "Facts"

Let us turn, then, to natural philosophy, which is said by the perennial tradition to share with pure natural science the first "order" of abstraction, i.e., the physical, while being abstract or general to a higher "degree." It is often remarked that the natural sciences are rooted in or based on facts. By a *fact* here is meant an individual reality, or conjunction of realities, judged to be such by experience. (In an extended sense, the term "fact" also applies to things judged to be realities by the equivalent, or near-equivalent, of experience—such as a well-founded theory of what experience would deliver if it were possible in the case in question, e.g., an event that is so distant or so small as to preclude observation even by way of instruments.)

For followers of Aristotle and St. Thomas (unlike the thinkers mentioned earlier who are properly termed "rationalists"), speculative philosophy also is rooted in facts. The difference among the types of facts comes in terms of their degree of generality, and, in the case of "philosophical facts" (as they might be called), their relevance to and adequate formulation by the philosopher. Reflection on such facts leads to the development of philosophical concepts and principles.

Let us consider a set of facts relevant to the philosophy of natural being, facts that are completely general within our experience of nature, by contrast with the particular and detailed facts utilized by the empiriological sciences. Here is a miscellany of such facts:

There is natural being—that is, things emerge into being, persist for a while according to their specific types, and then go out of being.

The beings we experience consist of individual wholes (e.g., oak trees or human persons), along with characteristics attributable to them. Such wholes are real, not mere constructs of the mind out of their parts or characteristics. Beings of nature are irreducibly diverse in number and kind. A single individual cannot have two contrary physical characteristics (e.g., being spherical and being cube-shaped) at the same time. Natural beings are subject to change. Some changes (e.g., in color or size) are compatible with the being in question remaining the same individual whole; other changes (e.g., the death of an organism) are not. Natural beings have various relations of real dependency in their being and coming to be. Natural beings display tendencies, according to their specific types, toward definite states of completion (e.g., acorns grow to be oak trees, tadpoles grow to be frogs), as well as definite types of interaction (e.g., mixing an acid with a base yields a salt plus water). In living beings, some acts (e.g., cutting and building) result in changes in an object or objects other than the agent; other acts (e.g., breathing or maintaining an internal flow of fluids) terminate in the agent itself.

Notice that while the philosophical facts here assembled are completely general, this does not mean that our statements of them are vague; indeed, contrary to what is often supposed about philosophical statements, they can be seen to be quite precise. Of course, this set of facts does not pretend to be exhaustive, for as noted above the status of such facts as philosophical in part is determined by their usefulness in philosophical reflection—which can follow various modes and the course of which is not predictable. Still, all of the above statements reflect common experience and common sense; thus they are, in the words of John Paul II, proper "reference points" for philosophy.

This is not to say that the facts in question have never been challenged. The pre-Socratic philosopher Parmenides believed that all reality must be one and undivided (for, he reasoned, what could there be beyond being but sheer non-being?). Thus he in effect challenged all of the above statements. Another early Greek philosopher, Heraclitus, believed to the contrary that there are no permanent realities—no beings or relatively stable wholes that are the subjects of changing characteristics. Rather, he held, what is real is only the flow of characteristics or phenomenal features themselves (for, he noted, this is all that our senses can reveal to us). Accordingly, he also in effect challenged at least some of the above judgments of fact. The school of St. Thomas holds that Aristotle's philosophy, to be spelled out below, adequately resolved such problems about "the one and the many" (as they came to be called) posed by the speculations of Parmenides and Heraclitus. Much later, in the eighteenth century, the Scottish empiricist David Hume (mentioned in section 1.1) questioned whether we can have genuine knowledge of personal identity, or of causal relations. As with the musings of the pre-Socratics, such thinking seems—from the standpoint of common sense—to be aberrant. But how can it be shown to be such? Since the positions challenged are so general and so basic, it falls to philosophy rather than to other, more particular disciplines to give them such "defenses" as they need or are capable of having. These defenses often are termed *dialectical*—which in this context means that they proceed by pointing out the unacceptable consequences of holding a contrary position, rather than by seeking directly to prove what is most basic and thus not strictly "provable" itself.

Substance and Accidents; Form and Matter; Change

In reflecting on the above facts, and in considering how to respond to challenges to their genuineness, perennial philosophers—following the lead of Aristotle[19]—have developed concepts and principles relat-

---

19. Emonet stresses, and offers accounts of, the large number of terms that Aristotle either originated or adapted in speaking of natural being. See *Dearest Freshness*, esp. 31–33. Among these terms were *phusis* ("nature," with the image of "thrusting" or "unfolding toward the light of day"); *eidos* ("idea," or "organizing power," whereby a thing becomes an autonomous whole); *morphe* ("form," the organizing idea insofar as it works on *hule* or "matter"); *entelecheia* ("having its end or perfection *[telos]* from within itself") and *ousia* (the primary type of "being"—"that which is capable of standing fast" or "enduring"). As we shall see, many of these terms—or ones derived from them—continue to be used by philosophers in the present day. (It should be noted that some scholarly controversy surrounds the precise meanings Aristotle himself gave to terms such as *phusis* and *eidos*. In this book we present these meanings as they, and their Latin and English equivalents, have come to be understood in the perennial tradition.)

ed to natural being just as such. As with the facts on which they are based, these concepts and principles are very general; but again this does not mean they are vague. (Here, incidentally, there is to be noted an important contrast with our "everyday" or "pre-reflective" understandings of nature—which indeed often are vague.) As we shall now try to indicate, the basic elements of natural philosophy are, in their respective ways, as precise as those of any other discipline.

The initial, and most fundamental, concepts within this branch of speculative philosophy can be articulated as follows.

Substance and Accidents. We begin with the primary *category,* or the first among the most general types of being. *Substance* (from the Latin *sub* plus *stare,* "to stand under") represents the individual, integral whole—that which exists and in principle is knowable in itself rather than as a modification of another; that which exercises characteristic powers and acts; and that which persists through various changes in individual features. Examples of substance would be the chemical solution in this beaker, the tree in the front yard, the dog down the street, etc.—not primarily insofar as they are observable, but insofar as they are centers of act and intelligibility. Parts of substance are recognized (e.g., organs and limbs—the tree's branches, the dog's hind legs, etc.); however, it is substance itself that represents the unity and stability of the natural being. Moreover, substantial activity is attributed to the whole being. For example, it is not, strictly speaking, the eye that sees (although it is the eye that is affected by the external object and that transmits data to the brain via the optic nerve); rather, seeing is an activity of the whole animal that possesses this power— an activity that it carries out by means of the organs in question.

Contrasted with substance, including parts of substance, are *accidents* (from the Latin *accidit,* meaning "it happens to"). These are instances of natural being that cannot exist on their own, but rather are attributes or characteristics or modifications of substances. Aristotle distinguished what have come to be recognized as nine categories of accident, of which the most important for speculative philosophy are *quantity, quality, relation, action,* and *passion* (in the sense of "passivity," i.e., undergoing a process or being acted upon). Examples of accident would be the weight of a newborn baby (quantity), the color of a rose (quality), a basketball player's being shorter than the person he or she is guarding (relation), the running of a horse (action), and the contraction of a gas due to an increase in pressure (passion). All of these are real instances of natural being, but they depend for their being on the substances that manifest the respective characteristics.

Form and Matter. These are sometimes called *principles* (from the Latin *principium,* meaning "starting point") of natural being; that is, they are "starting points" of a thing's being precisely insofar as it is physical. *Form* and *matter* are philosophically distinguishable yet mutually conditioning factors in such a being's constitution. Things of our world thus are said to be "composites" of these two principles: matter is "that out of which" a being comes to be; form is "that which determines" a being to be what it is—e.g., an individual with the nature of oak (a case of "substantial" form), or the color green, or the height seventy-five feet (cases of "accidental" form). In light of the Greek equivalents of "matter" *(hule)* and "form" *(morphe),* the present analysis of natural being is sometimes referred to as *hylemorphism.*

In the case of substance, the material principle is called "primary" or "first" matter (Latin *materia prima*). Matter in this special, philosophical sense actually exists only as formed or determined; and substantial form, at least as treated in natural philosophy, is always a determiner of matter—e.g., that by which an individual thing is, and can be known as, an instance of oak (whether it be in an acorn state, sapling state, fully developed state, or diseased or otherwise physically threatened state). Neither matter nor form, precisely as a principle of substance, is equipped to exist on its own.

The present account of natural substance, form, and matter can be represented by the following model, adapted from the writings of William A. Wallace, O.P.[20]

20. See, e.g., *The Modeling of Nature* (Washington, D.C.: The Catholic University of America Press, 1995). In speaking of matter as a principle of natural substance, Wallace prefers the term "proto-matter," so as not to confuse it with matter as ordinarily understood

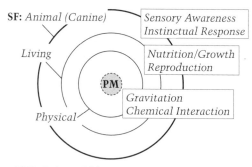

Note: "SF"= "substantial form;" "PM" = "primary matter"

Figure 1. Model of Natural Substance

The center of the model is designated "PM." This stands for "primary matter" (or, as Wallace also calls it, "proto-matter"). It is surrounded by a hashed circle—with the hashes indicating that primary matter is not, just as such, formed in any specific way, but simply is open to physical formation. The series of concentric circles represent specifying forms, with interior ones operating in conjunction with exterior ones and ultimately in conjunction with the being's substantial form ("SF"). Powers associated with the various levels and types of being in question are represented by rectangular boxes on the respective circles. The ultimate specifying form, substantial form, is represented by the outermost circle; it is marked by a **bold** line. (One might view the diagram as a tapered cylinder, as seen from the top; each successive circle would represent a higher specifying form, along with associated powers.)

Let the above diagram represent the natural being of an animal, e.g., a dog, with the innermost (unbroken) circle signifying physical

in everyday life and the natural sciences. In a somewhat similar way, W. Norris Clarke, S.J., speaks of "the raw energy of the material (space-time extended) universe": *Explorations in Metaphysics* (Notre Dame, Ind.: University of Notre Dame Press, 1994), 22–23; and Pierre-Marie Emonet speaks of "the matter-matrix": *Dearest Freshness*, 50, 53. (For the actual construction of the present model, as well as the complementary one in section 2.5 representing the substance of the human person, I am indebted to Andy Jaspers, S.J.)

form and its powers (e.g., toward gravitational and chemical interactions), the next circle signifying living form and its powers (e.g., toward nutrition/growth and reproduction), and the third circle signifying specifically animal (in this case, canine) form and its powers (i.e., the dog's specific ways, involving sensory awareness and responsiveness, of interacting with other things in the world).

Although, as noted above, the terms "matter" and "form" are applied most fundamentally to constitutive principles of a substance—e.g., a molecule of water, a tree, or a dog—they also can be applied to accidents. In the latter case, the substance itself is said to be "matter," in relation to "forms" that consist of particular quantities, qualities, relations, etc. For example, a particular dog may, as a matter of fact, share in the characteristic of having a smooth coat. Other good examples of natural substance receiving additional forms are products of art. Consider the famous statue *The Thinker*, by the French sculptor Auguste Rodin. The matter in this case is the bronze out of which the statue is made (the bronze already being a natural substance—or, strictly, an alloy of substances); the form is the configuration that represents a man sitting and pondering.

Change. In the philosophy of natural being, this term is used in a most general sense. That is, *change* consists in any type of coming to be (or "becoming") of formed matter. Scholastic philosophers have used the word "motion" (from the Latin *motus*, meaning "change") in the same, very general sense. (Sometimes the Latin term *mutatio* has been used in this most general sense, with *motus* reserved for instances of continuous and successive change, e.g., the digestion of food.) Motion is taken as a defining feature of our current subject matter, namely, natural being; accordingly, natural philosophy is sometimes said to study "mobile being" (Latin *ens mobile*) just as such.

Change or motion in the most general, philosophical sense consists in going from not having a particular form (or having it to one degree) to having that form (or having it to another degree). The initial state is said to be that of *privation*—i.e., a lack of the form that is to result from the change. In the process itself the subject is said to go from "potentially" to "actually" possessing the form (or the degree of the form) in question; or from possessing it "in potency" (or "in potentiality") to possessing it "in act" (or "in actuality"). Aristotle accordingly offered the following definition of change: "the actualization of what exists in potency insofar as it remains in potency"—for the process of change itself will cease when the actualization in question is completed (*Physics*, book III, chap. 1). Sometimes processes of change fall within the category of action (as in the case of the horse's running); sometimes they fall within the category of passion (as in the case of the gas's being contracted).

As suggested by these examples, changes typically occur in accidents—that is, in quantities, qualities, relations, etc. But change also occurs in substances, in which case it is sometimes called "absolute" change. Here an individual, integral whole goes from not-being to being, or vice versa. Among living beings, substantial change obviously occurs at death, as well as at the first emergence of an organism. Among non-living beings, the notion of substantial change can be rather obscure in its application; and the actual occurrence of such change can be difficult to discern with certitude. (For example, when water is demineralized through ion exchange, does this constitute a substantial change, or only a change in accidents? A case might be made for either type of philosophical analysis.)

Several additional, related concepts are needed in the philosophical discussion of natural being. The most important among these are the following:

Causality. For perennial philosophers, *causality* consists in relations of real dependency in a thing's being or coming to be, whether as a substance or as an accident. Every change in a thing, and indeed every present state, involves causes or explanatory factors (in Aristotle's Greek, *aitiae*) that in some real way bring about, or affect, the thing or characteristic in question. We shall offer a much fuller analysis of causality in the subsection immediately following, but one thing should be noted at once: a cause is always a principle (i.e., once again, a starting point); but a principle is not always a cause. In particular, something can be a starting point in the analysis of a being or a becoming without constituting a real factor that explains some aspect of the thing in question. (This applies, for example, to the notion of "privation" discussed above.)

Time and Space. These notions, for the philosopher, represent two measures of mobile being. *Time* is a measure related to the fact that natural beings' mode of being involves successive stages (sometimes this mode is called "successive duration"); and to the fact that we experience this mode of being as involving such succession. A system of time is an organized way of measuring or numbering successive changes in terms of "before" and "after" along a continuum. Different systems of time—the Gregorian and lunar calendars; seconds, minutes, and hours; light-years; etc.—depend on different changes or motions, as well as on diverse systems of measurement (which in turn reflect the cultural or scientific interests of people using these systems).

A somewhat similar account can be given of *space.* In natural philosophy this notion has to do with the condition of physical bodies whereby each has its own dimensional characteristics and occupies a particular place; in this way each physical body can be located and configured in relation to others. Interestingly, the whole universe, on this account, will not be said to occupy a place; indeed, Aristotelian philosophical concepts of both space and time include a note of "relativity." Thus they complement well—while serving a different function—the notions of space and time as these have developed over the past century in the positive science of physics. In fact, the philosophy of nature articulated in these pages shows that the ideas of "absolute" space and time, as used in the earlier Newtonian physics, suffer serious conceptual flaws—or at least they do if they are understood literally, rather than as features deriving from mathematized modes of presentation. All concrete characteristics pertaining to time and space depend on concrete conditions and acts of physical, changing beings.

Transitive and Immanent Acts. These terms distinguish types of operations of living beings insofar as they bring about diverse products or effects. An act or operation is said to be *transitive* (or, sometimes, "transient") insofar as it causes a state of affairs to occur in an object or objects other than the agent (in the example noted earlier, the act of building—e.g., a house). An *immanent* act also brings about a state, but one that remains in the agent (in the examples noted earlier, the acts of breathing or maintaining internal fluid flow). Other examples of transitive acts would be cooking and writing; other examples of immanent acts would be growing (i.e., maturing) and thinking. It might be noted that a single activity can have effects of both a transitive and an immanent sort: e.g., lumber mill work, in addition to producing, say, redwood boards, also typically develops strong muscles in the worker.

Causal Explanation in the Philosophy of Nature

As is the case with disciplines generally, a philosophy of nature has structure and organization. Specifically, as developed in the perennial tradition, it begins with an articulation of general principles, which then are linked to more particular statements and accounts of natural phenomena.

It should be noted that, in the present context, the notion of *principle* is used differently than it was when we spoke of matter and form as "principles," or starting points, of substance. In speaking of "principles" of a discipline, we mean starting points in the articulation of knowledge, i.e., basic statements within the discipline. Principles of natural philosophy in this second (and, in fact, more ordinary) sense will incorporate the general concepts outlined in the preceding subsection—substance, accident, change, causality, etc. Indeed, such principles will be formulated in terms of these very concepts. Because of this, the principles in question—by contrast with those of mathematics and of rationalist philosophy—will be grounded in experience. Three such starting points of our knowledge regarding natural being would be the following:

"All natural being is either substantial being or accidental being."

"Natural being is subject to change—either the alteration of features or states within a substance, or the coming into being or going out of being of a substance itself."

"Change always involves causality, i.e., the real dependency of one physical being on another or others, or on another aspect of the being in question." (This principle is commonly referred to as the "Principle of Causality.")

Such principles of course are very general—as indeed they must be if they are to underlie all of our thinking about nature. More significantly, insofar as they are well formulated, the general principles of natural philosophy can be seen to hold across historical eras, even though the positive sciences of nature undergo regular and sometimes profound changes.

To gain a fuller sense of the organization of natural philosophy— and to appreciate a set of subprinciples that cluster under the Principle of Causality—let us consider what are recognized as four different types of cause, i.e., four different types of real factor involved in the explanation of a thing's being or coming to be. These four types are traditionally designated as follows:

1) *formal*—factors that determine the being to be what it is, including the species or type of thing that it is;

2) *material*—the stuff or "that out of which" the being is or becomes;

3) *efficient* or *agent*—that which produces the change or coming to be, or is responsible for a thing's continuing in being; and

4) *final*—the end (Latin *finis*), or the state of completion or fulfillment, toward which a being or an activity or change is ordered.

As with certain concepts discussed earlier, helpful examples here can be drawn from the realm of art. Recalling the statue *The Thinker*, we may attribute formal causality to its shape and configuration; material causality to the bronze; efficient or agent causality to the sculptor, Rodin; and final causality to the idea of the completed statue that guided and motivated the sculptor in his work.

It should be noted that this fourfold analysis can be carried out at different levels; and that causal factors can operate in different degrees, as well as different modes, in a thing's being or coming to be. Thus, for example, an account of the matter of *The Thinker* might be taken to the level of the particular atoms and molecules making up the bronze. The specific positioning of the subject's right hand and chin is a formal feature of the statue, while at the same time contributing to the overall form. Further, beyond the efficient or agent causality exercised by Rodin himself, a secondary and instrumental causality can be attributed to the equipment he used—as well as to the people who assisted him in the project. Lastly, it might be suggested that a more remote, or less immediate, type of final causality was exercised by Rodin's desire to earn fame as a sculptor. In their respective ways and degrees, all of these were real factors contributing to the coming to be of the statue.

Let us return to the general term "nature," for which we now are in position to construct an account. This term obviously can refer in a diffuse way to the whole of physical reality; it has this use in both everyday language and the empirical sciences. However, in the philosophy of natural being "nature" also refers, and refers primarily, to a type of formal factor—namely, the characteristic dynamism or energy (in Aristotle's Greek, *energeia*) that acts as an internal principle of a thing's being what it is (e.g., this molecule of water, that oak tree, or the person over there), as well as having certain powers that orient the thing toward specific activities, each with its proper end (e.g., freezing at thirty-two degrees Fahrenheit, developing broad branches, or thinking and choosing in light of recognized goals). At the same time, nature or natural form can be said to be the basis of efficient causality, insofar as substantial form is responsible for a being's range of natural activities. (These latter activities, of course, can be studied in their specifically material or mechanical dimensions in the various disciplines of positive science.) Natural form can be associated with final causality as well, insofar as—via the prospect of its being expressed in a completed state—such form serves as the end or goal of the particular being's processes of growth and development.

Whether in art or in nature, if a thing is to exercise causality along any of the four lines, it must enjoy actuality of the relevant level and type. Rodin's tools in and of themselves could not serve as efficient causes of a statue; rather, they participated in such causality insofar as they were used by him. Nor could the bronze, in and of itself, make itself into a statue. The sculptor alone has the actual art that enables him or her to impart form, and thus to exercise such causality in the primary sense. Similarly, the natural process of forming acorns can be traced, at one level, to a type of formal causality exercised by DNA in the cells of the oak. However, such causality does not occur simply on its own; rather, the protein chains that make up the DNA have their specific configuration and roles in conjunction with ontologically more primary factors, i.e., the nature and end of oak. Of course, the nature in question could not be propagated to a new generation of trees if the requisite proteins were not themselves present—just as a statue of *The Thinker* could not come to be unless bronze (or other suitable material) were available to the sculptor. Thus in both types of case we find a complex, mutually conditioning set of factors.

With the above references to atoms and molecules in the bronze of a statue, and DNA in the cells of an oak, we see that natural philosophy—insofar as it seeks to account for particular phenomena—depends in part on data from the empiriological sciences. It also should be acknowledged that a concept long in use by philosophers may need to be reconsidered and reformulated as human experience grows and as the positive sciences progress. For example, with modern theories of thermodynamics, reformulations have been necessary regarding the understanding of formal and efficient causality in the propagation of heat. The ancients believed that things that are hot are so because of their sharing in the "element" (among the ancient four) that is hottest—i.e., fire. This, of course, is a view that no educated person holds today, when heat and other physical properties are explained in quite different ways. Moreover, whereas Aquinas rejected what was, at the time, a rather crude version of the theory of the propagation of smells, a contemporary understanding of particulate matter, as carried along by wind currents and as affecting an animal's olfactory system, today is rightly incorporated within natural philosophy.

In spite of the philosophy of nature's progressive character, it should be re-emphasized that the most general concepts and themes of this approach—e.g., the analysis of physical reality in terms of substance and accidents, form and matter, change and the four types of cause—have remained constant, even while dramatic developments have taken place in the empirical sciences. Thus, for example, the discovery of microorganisms and their role in certain disease processes was an important event in the history of science and medicine; Aristotle and his Medieval followers knew nothing about them. Nonetheless, philosophically speaking, microorganisms are to be understood as types of substance, ones that—unfortunately for us—have natural orientations and activities involving specific types of agent causality (which medical science and practice seek to counteract).

By way of concluding this section, we may say that, at the level of the particular case, causal analyses in natural philosophy are varied and complex—perhaps as varied and complex as ones in the empiriological sciences, although in ways that are quite different from the latter. Given the specific types of understanding it seeks, natural philosophy attends to levels and modalities of four types of causality, as well as to the types of substantial and accidental being these bring about or modify. Given the rather different aims of the positive sciences, the latter bring to bear a variety of empirical (including experimental) and mathematical methods, along with the development and testing of hypotheses and theories, in an effort to explain (and sometimes to predict) the occurrence of particular phenomena. In the next section we shall explore further the relations between these two approaches, as well as the types of "abstraction" that characterize each.

SUMMARY

- The philosophy of nature has its origins in certain very general and universally recognized facts of experience—e.g., that natural beings undergo changes while remaining the same beings; that such beings have real relations of dependency on one another; etc.
- By reflecting on such general facts, philosophers are able to develop concepts and principles (regarding substance, accidents, change, causality, etc.) related to natural being as such.
- The differentiation of four types of real factors in a thing's being and

becoming (i.e., material, formal, efficient or agent, and final) enables the
perennial tradition to develop a philosophy of nature that illuminates and
contextualizes—but also is enriched by and sometimes corrected by—the
empiriological sciences.

1.3 IMPLICATIONS OF NATURAL PHILOSOPHY

Abstraction's Orders and Degrees

We noted in section 1.1 that the perennial philosophy proposes a
type of realism that is critical and ordered. This means, in part, a realism that is sensitive to diverse modes (and to interrelations among
the modes) of knowing. According to the Thomist account, we come
to know and express the being of things by way of processes of abstraction. These processes and their results (i.e., universal concepts) can be
distinguished into three general "orders."[21]

As understood in philosophy, *abstraction* is the process by which
the mind forms concepts, through picking out or apprehending ("ab-
stracting") intelligible features. A thorough discussion of this intellectual process must wait until the next part of our book, where we treat
the cognitive dimension of our human, personal being. Here we wish
simply to mark relevant distinctions—and the logical bases of the distinctions—regarding the results of processes of concept formation.

Our experience is always of individuals—particular rocks, plants,
animals, human persons, etc. Individual objects and their characteristics can be very familiar to us; and individual persons and their qualities can be intimately known by us. But no individual as such is the
subject of a formal body of knowledge. Such knowledge always has
an element of universality, because it is achieved through the appli-

---

21. Many Thomists seem to prefer the term "degrees" here. However, we follow Yves
Simon in speaking of three general "orders" of abstraction—thus making room for a distinction among "degrees" within the first order. See "Maritain's Philosophy of the Sciences,"
23–25.

cation of concepts (which in principle are always general). As indicated above, concepts distinguish or pick out intelligible features. These features are shared among different individuals of the type in question. Thus, at a minimum, a thing's individual sensible characteristics—i.e., its particular color, size, spatial relationships with other objects, etc.—are "abstracted from," or ignored, in the formation and use of concepts applying to that thing as well as others.

The "first order" of abstraction, in terms of which we study physical and changing being as such (by contrast with its condition as subject to quantification and measurement) involves concepts of precisely the above sort. Scholastics sometimes have said that such concepts abstract from "individual matter." For example, the concept "squirrel" ignores particular colorations of individual squirrels; and the concept "salt" ignores particular elements (e.g., sodium) that can combine to make up a salt.

Especially in light of developments in the natural sciences, it is important to distinguish different "degrees" within this first order of abstraction, or, to put it another way, different levels in the study and definition of natural reality.[22] Thus we have spoken of certain concepts as being more or less "empiriological"—i.e., as dealing primarily with things' sensible features or manifestations and with descriptions and accounts of these manifestations (not as individual instances, but as grouped into classes and types). The concepts of the modern sciences generally are of this sort. (See, however, the discussion two paragraphs below on "mixed sciences.") By contrast, we have spoken of other concepts as being more or less "ontological"—i.e., as dealing with things primarily insofar as they are instances of natural being (e.g., as subject to coming into being, to processes of change of various sorts, and, finally, to going out of being). The concepts used in the philosophy of nature—"substance," "form," "matter," and the rest—share this more ontological character. Maritain and Simon offer an account of the way

---

22. For a recent discussion of modes of definition within studies of nature, see Matthew S. Pugh, "Maritain and Postmodern Science," in Ciapalo, ed., *Postmodernism and Christian Philosophy*.

concepts of the two sorts may be distinguished. They ask us to consider whether the concepts are "resolvable" by analysis into terms referring to sensible features or, alternatively, into terms expressing more general and more basic ontological concepts. They also note that sometimes the same word—e.g., "living"—is used both in empiriological and ontological types of analysis. In the former case, the word "living" will be understood in terms of typical observable features of living things (e.g., respiration and the internal flow of fluids), by contrast with features of things that are non-living. In the latter or ontological case, "living" will be understood as referring to a type of natural being—one that has an internal principle of self-movement or development. The latter concept, "having an internal principle of self-movement or development," in turn is resolvable into a more fully ontological concept—one in which the mind moves beyond the first order of abstraction—namely, "self-actuating being."[23] Here we have an example of what we shall come to call a "metaphysical" concept, i.e., one that does not in and of itself involve reference to any observable or material features.

The "second order" of abstraction characterizes mathematics; in this type of case the mind abstracts from what Scholastics have called "common matter," as well as from individual matter. Here, that is to say, the intelligible features are simply quantitative, and they are represented through constructed or idealized "objects." In the case of mathematical abstraction, what remains is sometimes called "intelligible matter," in order to contrast it with the common sensible matter referred to in direct studies of natural being. In its various concepts and demonstrations, a discipline of the second order of abstraction—e.g., geometry or the calculus—uses constructs with ideal features (point, line, class, number, function, curve, etc.), rather than actual physical realities such as substances, various types of change, and real causal factors.

Since antiquity it has been recognized that there are *scientiae me-*

---

23. See, e.g., Jacques Maritain, *Philosophy of Nature,* 74; and Simon, "Maritain's Philosophy of the Sciences," 26–27.

diae or "mixed sciences"—that is, ones in which the proper object, or "matter," is physical, but the mode of treatment, or "form," is mathematical. Classical examples of such sciences are mechanics, which treats forces and weights in moving bodies and, more generally, the quantitative aspects of motion; and optics, which treats visible objects via the study of light rays. (Astronomy, which makes use of light rays coming from heavenly bodies, also can be included in this classification.) Today it is recognized that much of "natural science" turns out to be of this mixed sort. That is, the principles of explanation and proof in most regions of physics and chemistry, and even in some regions of the life sciences, tend to be mathematical rather than, strictly speaking, natural or physical.

As noted above, mathematical concepts, symbols, and models are ideals; although they can be based on reality, they are intellectual constructions. Thus they do not, in and of themselves, represent natural being. To use the language of the Scholastics, the objects of such concepts are *entia rationis* ("beings of reason"), rather than forms of real being as they might exist in nature and be grasped by the human mind. Thus, with all due respect for their enormous practical value, "mixed sciences" must be carefully analyzed and reflected upon if we are accurately to gauge the extent to which the knowledge they offer is knowledge of reality "as it is"—rather than as reality's observable features may be quantitatively ordered and systematized.

Additional points should be made regarding the positive sciences' relations with natural philosophy. First, as already suggested, a closer examination of relevant empirical evidence may indicate the need for revisions in philosophical concepts and judgments—especially insofar as the latter undertake to characterize the world in detail, as with accounts of the propagation of heat. Similarly, Aristotle's Medieval followers, including Aquinas, fell into error on a number of points regarding the types of causality involved in sensation.[24] Such error in part was due to these thinkers' not always distinguishing philosophi-

---

24. For a discussion of inadequacies in Aquinas's treatment of sensation, see Simon, "An Essay on Sensation," in *Philosopher at Work*, 63, 84–88.

cal from empirical studies (the latter, of course, were in a rather primitive state in their day). To take still another type of example, the now overwhelming evidence for certain types of evolution in living species has entailed the recognition—not present in the perennial philosophy of earlier periods—that natures, as well as concrete individual beings, have a history.

Approaching the relationships among the disciplines from the other side, we may note that certain insights of natural philosophy can suggest fruitful paths for empirical research—for example, regarding the processes involved in human and animal recognition of types of physical being. Moreover, we shall see in the next subsection, it can happen that the natural philosopher will conclude that a particular philosophical interpretation of a scientific theory (e.g., a purely physicalist interpretation of the theory of evolution) cannot survive the test of philosophical reflection.

Secondly, it should be pointed out that certain terms in natural philosophy have analogues in the natural sciences that are similar but not the same in their specific meanings. For example, the term "cause" as elaborated above—a relationship of real dependency along one of four lines—is crucial in the philosophical understanding of natural being. However, when employed in empiriological sciences, terms like "cause" and "explanation" do not necessarily signify real dependency at all. Sometimes they refer simply to antecedent conditions in a statistically established relationship, or to the subsuming of an empirical regularity under a higher, more general empirical regularity. Inattention to such points can lead to misunderstandings between philosophers and natural scientists, as well as to confusion about the proper relationships among the diverse disciplines that study physical nature.

Thirdly, let us consider the application of natural philosophy's concepts to the realm of what physicists call the "very small." Chemical elements and compounds can be said to have natures or forms. But what of subatomic particles such as protons, neutrons, and electrons—or, at still more basic levels, baryons, mesons, and quarks? Do these

too have "natures"? Clearly this question tests the limits of philosophical analysis. It has been suggested by William A. Wallace that
subatomic particles should be regarded as "transient entities"; for they
cannot be said to have natures in the strict sense, although they enter into elements and compounds—which latter, as just noted, and as
elaborated in our earlier discussion of silver, do have natures.[25] Here, it
might be said, philosophy reaches the end of the line in its investigation of natural form.

Another complex issue stems from the fact that the term "matter" has had a long history of meanings in both philosophy and the
empiriological sciences. For some scientific purposes this term has
given way to the more mathematically precise and manipulable notion of "mass."[26] In the philosophy of nature, two specialized meanings of "matter" are to be noted. First, as was mentioned in our introduction of terminology in section 1.2, when perennial philosophers
have wished to speak of matter as a co-principle of form in the constitution of natural substance, they have used the phrase "primary" or
"first matter" (Latin *materia prima*). Such a concept is necessary in
the philosophical explanation of absolute or substantial change—e.g.,
the death of an organism—where no single, general organizing form
continues through the change. Accordingly, "primary matter" expresses a sheer principle, a sheer potentiality for natural form—any form
that it is possible for natural reality to take. Secondly, when Scholastic philosophers have wished to characterize physical reality just insofar as it manifests quantity, and thus as it is subject to being measured,
counted, etc., they have used the phrase *materia signata* ("signed" or
"signate matter" or, perhaps better, "marked-off matter"). Matter as
generally understood in the sciences and everyday discourse is, in this
sense, "marked-off."

Finally, let us consider whether natural philosophy and the pos-

---

25. See William A. Wallace, "Is Nature Accessible to the Mathematical Physicist?" in
Science, Philosophy, and Theology, ed. John O'Callaghan (South Bend, Ind.: St. Augustine's
Press, 2006).

26. See Ernan McMullin, ed., *The Concept of Matter* (Notre Dame, Ind.: University of
Notre Dame Press, 1963), especially 18–27 of his editor's Introduction.

itive sciences may be subject to unification or synthesis. This idea was proposed throughout the latter half of the twentieth century by Thomist thinkers who were dissatisfied with what they took to be Maritain's strict distinction between "empiriological" and "ontological" studies. A philosopher mentioned above, William A. Wallace, developed a rather full account of the "unification" theme in his book *The Modeling of Nature*, to which he gave the subtitle *Philosophy of Science and Philosophy of Nature in Synthesis*. As he remarked in the book's preface, its "explicit aim [was] to present an understanding of modern science that is explicitly based on the concept of nature."[27] According to this understanding, the positive sciences in effect are extensions of the philosophy of nature; that is, they trace out and specify more concretely—and, to the extent possible, with greater mathematical precision and systematization—concepts and principles articulated in philosophy.

Not surprisingly, Maritain and his closest followers—even those who emphasize that the distinction between empiriological and ontological is one of degree—have been skeptical about the possibilities of an actual synthesis between the two approaches. According to their way of thinking, philosophical and positive studies of nature are to be seen as "complementary," but not "continuous."[28]

In general, the present writer accepts the "complementarity" view. As we have noted, the concepts and principles of natural philosophy may need to be revised in light of developments in the empiriological sciences. Moreover, different kinds of complexity have been seen to attend studies of the two sorts. And, while methods in the positive sciences are generally inductive, working from instances to generalizations, the order in natural philosophy is the reverse. That is, beginning with general principles (which themselves, as we shall see, are supported by the still more general and abstract principles of metaphysics), the philosopher proceeds deductively, and by way of application, to more particular judgments about nature.

27. See William A. Wallace, *The Modeling of Nature*, xiii.
28. See Maritain, *Philosophy of Nature*, especially 93ff.

However, the efforts of thinkers such as Wallace reveal one important point: the principles of the positive sciences can, in a sense, be analytically "reduced" to those of philosophy. The former types of discipline focus primarily on the categories of quantity and quality, in both their questions and their accounts and theories. But quantity and quality, as we have seen, are modes of natural being that depend upon substance. In light of this, there indeed is reason to take the "synthesis" model as a kind of ideal goal. And, if it seems that this model represents only an ideal, and that it is more realistic to speak of natural philosophy and the natural sciences as mutually complementary, it nonetheless is true that philosophical studies, in one important way, are foundational to their empirical counterparts. For philosophical concepts and principles ultimately ground and explain the ontological significance of those of the positive disciplines.

Questions Arising from Our Philosophical Account of Nature

Reflection on our philosophical approach to natural being leads the attentive reader to a number of additional questions—questions about implications of key aspects of such being as it has been characterized in the preceding pages.

A first such question relates to the nature of change or motion. We have seen that, as articulated by Aristotle and his followers, change consists in going from not possessing a form to possessing it—or, more strictly, from possessing it only in potency to possessing it in act. (Change also can consist in going from sharing a form to one degree to sharing it to another, which itself is a kind of movement from potency to act.) Moreover, we saw that in order for change or activity to occur among beings of nature, the ones undergoing change must be really affected by others, i.e., their causes. These causes in turn must be in act, and indeed in relevant types and degrees of act.

Now, while a cause, precisely as causing, must be in a state of act, a natural cause, considered strictly in terms of its specific type of being, is in a state of potency to such act. That is, in itself such a being has only the power to act in the relevant way. Here Emonet asks: "Could it [i.e., a being of nature that exercises real causality] find *in itself alone* the cause of its 'going into action'? . . . However deep one may delve into a power to act, one shall not be able to find there the power to pass over to action."[29] The natural being's state of potency is precisely a limit to its state of actuality, a limit that must be overcome through the agency of another natural being in the relevant state of act. And, in this regard, what is the case for each individual natural being would seem to be the case for all of them together. That is, the whole realm of corporeal being is one of act that is limited by potency, of being that needs to be brought to act.

But now we must ask: In light of the present account, is activity and development within corporeal being really intelligible by itself? Could it be the case that everything in act, without qualification, also is limited by potency? In that case, how would there be anything in act at all? It appears from this line of reasoning that natural philosophy points beyond our realm of being to what exists and acts of itself, i.e., exists and acts without potency or the need for causal stimulus by another.

A second set of questions arises in relation to final causality: How is it that beings of nature are oriented in their activities toward specific ends or modes of fulfillment, ones related in each case to their natures or the types of beings they are? Of course, in the case of human agents, there is (at least with regard to our consciously chosen acts) an answer ready to hand. For we explicitly formulate ends or goals for ourselves, and then select means to pursue them. But apart from our own case—and we shall suggest in part 2 that even here something very important falls outside the range of choice—it seems that beings of nature display no intelligence whereby they might consciously formulate ends. And, even granting that there might turn out to be intelligent life elsewhere in the universe, it surely is the case that the vast majority of natural beings do not share this quality or characteristic.

29. Emonet, *Dearest Freshness*, 40.

Moreover, we are aware—often painfully so—that we humans do not determine how things of nature are oriented to act. At best, we can anticipate, e.g., the force of a hurricane, and then react to and try to accommodate its internally based tendencies and its effects.

But to be oriented toward ends is a real feature of natural beings; that is to say, we are speaking here of real relationships. And real relationships of the present sort—being positively oriented in such-and-such ways—are a sign of intelligence at work. For positive orientations require directedness, not merely factual (e.g., spatial) relationships. Thus philosophers from the time of Aristotle (and even before Aristotle)[30] as well as proponents of the perennial tradition today have held that we must postulate some primary intelligence that lies beyond the realm of nature. Such intelligence would be that by which things have natures and thus are oriented toward ends. It would be "primary" not in a temporal sense, but rather in the sense of enjoying a higher order of actuality than all that lies within the natural realm.

At this point, it may be objected that the positive sciences, including biology, have little if any use for the concept of natural ends. Instead of appealing to final causality, contemporary biologists study, in ever greater detail, the workings of genetic programs and other material and mechanical factors in the activity of living beings. However, this fact about the science of biology should come as no surprise; neither does it have the philosophical implications the objector thinks it does. For, as a primarily empiriological science, biology is limited by its own aims and methods to factors resolvable into sensory data, and, in some instances, to the mathematical analysis of such factors. Thus final causality does not come directly under its purview. However, as we noted in considering the organization of natural philosophy, different levels of causality can operate within the same order (material, formal, efficient, or final). Moreover, a single phenomenon can reflect causality of more than one order or type. Thus the concrete expression of a genetic program in the context of environmental factors—e.g., the

30. See the discussion of Aristotle and the pre-Socratic philosopher Anaxagoras in Emonet, ibid., 37.

actual height attained by a particular tree—will reflect, in addition to the genetic program's proper agency as impinged upon by a variety of material factors, that program's status as an instrument operating in accord with, and for the sake of, the tree's natural form and end.

In short, from the standpoint of philosophy (although not necessarily or even ordinarily from the standpoint of the positive sciences), we do need to speak of ends in nature. And, recognizing such ends, we also realize that we are unable to give an adequate account of their presence in terms of natural being itself. For, once again, to be really related to an end bespeaks the operation of intelligence, which is not generally present within the material realm. Thus our reflection on such factors seems to point to a mode of being beyond this realm.

Finally, let us note the implications of recognizing degrees within natural being. During the past century and a half, the positive sciences of biology, paleontology, and geology have brought to light in a compelling way another pervasive feature of our world. Not only do individuals display a history of development—species do as well. This leads to a new question for philosophy: How is such "trans-form-ation," or such evolution in natural species, to be understood and explained from the standpoint of being?

We now know that there is much greater variety in natural forms (at least as this can be judged empirically) than was supposed by the ancient writers; and we also know that, contrary to the general belief up to the time of the biologist Lamark (1744–1829), the number and kinds of natural species are not fixed, let alone (as was thought to be the case by some) "eternal." Indeed, very many species that once existed no longer do, and there can be discerned evolutionary relationships by which one species has prepared the way for another. By the same token, however—and this indeed was clearly understood by Aristotle and his Medieval followers, although it sometimes is obscured in the empiriological approaches of today—the natural world reveals, via things' characteristic operations and activities, a diversity in levels of actuality. In particular, as will be discussed more fully in part 2, we must distinguish among living beings those that have merely vegetative functions, those that operate by way of sensation and sensory response, and those that know and act in an intellectual way. Thus there has been an (ontological) "ascent," as well as what Charles Darwin called a (temporal) "descent," of natural kinds or species. Philosophically, we must ask how there can have been this increase in levels of actuality within natural being; and, in attempting to answer this question, we need to apply natural philosophy's fourfold scheme of explanation.

Material and efficient causes—e.g., the processes of "random variation," "adaptation," and "natural selection" studied by evolutionary biologists—clearly are involved in the ascending levels of actuality. However, just as in our effort to understand orientations toward ends among individual beings, so also in connection with species, we must inquire as well into the other types of explanatory factor, i.e., formal and final causes. For these, and especially the formal, are the factors that directly specify the diverse levels and types of actuality.

Emonet quotes a contemporary French biologist who says, "Life is born of matter—indeed non-living matter." He then puts the question about such being "born": Can the more come from the less? While the issue is of no concern to empirical scientists, "philosophers," he says, "cannot escape this question."[31] At one level, of course—that of temporal sequence—the answer obviously is Yes. That is, later species sometimes manifest greater actuality than earlier species. But can the earlier species, or indeed any set of natural, physical, or corporeal factors, provide an adequate explanation of an increase in actuality? Can what has less of being literally, in and of itself, be the cause of what has more of being? As Emonet says, philosophers "must neither deny the facts [i.e., the facts of species evolution], nor try to explain them with absurdities."[32] And, in the judgment of the perennial philosopher,

---

31. Ibid., 49. The biologist is Yves Coppin. As we have noted, Emonet's philosophical mentor was Jacques Maritain. But another Thomist scholar cited by John Paul II, Etienne Gilson, produced in his later years an important and sadly neglected book on philosophy and evolution. See *From Aristotle to Darwin and Back Again*, trans. John Lyon (Notre Dame, Ind.: University of Notre Dame Press, 1984). For an excellent recent account of these matters, see W. Norris Clarke, S.J., *The One and the Many* (Notre Dame, Ind.: University of Notre Dame Press, 2001), 245–60.

32. Emonet, *Dearest Freshness*, 49.

it would be absurd to answer the above question—once it is articulated and understood in its full ontological significance—in the affirmative. What has less of being simply cannot be the cause of what has more of being, except in the sense of providing material and efficient factors that operate in conjunction with a more primary form of being. Thus, understood philosophically, being of a genuinely new, higher level of actuality can be produced—or, perhaps better, "educed"—only by being of a still higher level of actuality. And if, as will be argued in part 2, our personal reality includes types of act that go beyond the limits of matter, the higher actuality involved will need to be seen as transcendent to the physical world.

Toward a More Profound Study of the Real

As we have indicated, certain key points in the above reflections—e.g., the level of actuality manifested by human persons—require support through discussions still to come. However, as they stand these reflections suggest that natural studies by themselves cannot give us a fully satisfactory account of being. Indeed, philosophical questions arising from a consideration of scientific data point beyond the natural realm. If we are to develop a full and adequate account of the being of experience, we shall need, so it seems, to refer to being that is strictly unlimited, that is possessed of originating intelligence, and that constitutes transcendent actuality.

But can a phrase such as "transcendent actuality" designate the object of a rational study? So far, staying within the confines of natural philosophy, we seem able merely to gesture toward such being, as that which would explain what is not explainable within the philosophy—or the empirical sciences—of nature. If there is to be a disciplined approach to transcendent actuality it must be rooted in a more profound study of the real. Such a study, in fact, would need to be of another order—a "third order" of abstraction. Let us consider what such a study would involve.

The positive sciences can be said to investigate being as changing and sensible, with an emphasis on change and sensation. Natural philosophy also can be said to investigate being as changing and sensible, but with an emphasis on being. The discipline now envisioned would study being just as being. That is, it would study being as shared by diverse individual beings in their respective ways; and it would study the intelligible structure and properties of being without regard to whether these are found in physical nature alone, or beyond such nature as well. Now, the Greek word for "beyond" is *meta*; this word can mean "coming after" as well. Accordingly, since the most profound study of being would go beyond or come after physical studies, it is given the name *metaphysics*.

But important and difficult questions arise about this type of study: How is it possible to develop concepts of being, or other metaphysical "objects," that are not limited to the realm of the sensible? Is there, in fact, any genuine intelligibility that lies deeper than that which characterizes things as natural beings? Finally, is it possible to answer the preceding questions without first knowing with certainty whether there actually are any beings beyond physical nature?

As we noted in our general discussion of abstraction, any discipline's concepts must be rooted in an apprehension of intelligible features. The question of how this is possible in the case of metaphysics has produced disagreement even among perennial philosophers.[33] It is not difficult to see why this is the case. For if, as some have held, the discipline of metaphysics cannot begin until it has been proven that there exists some immaterial being, it would appear that this discipline must wait upon the full and successful articulation of natural philosophy. Indeed, in light of the preceding section, it should be said that even this would not strictly be adequate. For natural philosophy, just by itself, involves concepts which are restricted to the "first order" of abstraction—and thus concepts which, by definition, cannot be applied in a direct way beyond the natural or corporeal realm. But if,

---

33. This controversy has been surveyed, and given a resolution similar to our own, by Matthew S. Pugh, in "Maritain, the Intuition of Being, and the Proper Starting Point for Thomistic Metaphysics," *The Thomist* 61 (1997): esp. 405–8. Also helpful on this matter is the essay by Raymond Dennehy entitled "Maritain's Realistic Defense of the Importance of the Philosophy of Nature to Metaphysics," in *Thomistic Papers VI*, ed. John F. X. Knasas (Houston, Tex.: Center for Thomistic Studies, 1994).

as others have held, metaphysics can begin as soon as it is recognized that the concept of "being" is not inherently restricted in its application to material beings, the danger is the one noted at the beginning of part 1: such a "discipline" may deal simply with a most general and in fact empty concept. In what follows, we will pursue a middle course regarding this matter.

Let us first note that the objects of metaphysical concepts indeed would be, of their very nature, immaterial in what can be called a "negative" or "neutral" sense. That is, taking as an example our earlier concept of "self-actuating being," we see that its specific intelligible features would be such that the associated concepts must ignore all sensible and material elements. Moreover, metaphysical concepts would not depend for their formal meaning on the materiality or physicality of things to which they apply.

It is important to understand this point clearly. Concepts of the third order of abstraction would treat all real beings alike whether they are material or (if there are such beings) immaterial. That is, these concepts would be "neutral" as regards their objects' being material or immaterial. Of course, the question of whether there in fact are beings that are immaterial cannot be settled in a purely conceptual manner. As a substantive philosophical issue it calls for reflection and judgment, which will continue in sections of the book to follow. But as the preceding subsection has shown, certain questions arising from reflection on natural philosophy ("Could act in all cases be limited by potency?" "How is it that things are really oriented toward ends?" "Can what has less of being literally cause what has more of being?") already argue that not all of being can be construed as material or physical. Thus we have a positive basis—in addition to that given by the "negatively" or "neutrally" immaterial character of the concept of "being"—for undertaking a more profound order of abstraction. Such an order of abstraction will enable us to inquire into being as such.

On both conceptual and substantive grounds, therefore, we are led to make what Scholastic philosophers have called a "judgment of separation" (in Latin, *separatio*). That is, we are led to the proposition: "Being is not essentially tied to materiality." And, if being is not essentially tied to materiality, then—responding to the call of John Paul II—we should undertake the discipline of metaphysics.

SUMMARY

• Our knowledge of the real is characterized by different degrees and orders of abstraction; it is important to note the distinctive characters and objects of purely physical sciences, mathematical sciences, and mixed sciences.

• A philosophical account of nature gives rise to certain questions (e.g., "Can what has more of being be fully explained by reference to what has less of being?") the answers to which point beyond the boundaries of natural being.

• Thus there can be envisaged a more profound study of the real, one that would treat being apart from the question of whether it is physical or observable, and apart from the question of whether it is subject to mathematical systematization; such a study ("metaphysics") will involve a third order of abstraction.

1.4 METAPHYSICS PROPER

Being as Being; Essence and Existence; Subsistence

In the course of his writings (e.g., the *Commentary on Aristotle's Metaphysics* [book IV, lesson 1]), St. Thomas Aquinas described the subject matter of metaphysics in a variety of ways: e.g., *ens qua ens* ("being as being"), *ens secundum quod est ens* ("being just insofar as it is being"), and *ens commune* ("being as enjoyed in common"). It is most important that we come to understand such notions clearly and correctly.

As noted in section 1.1, there is a danger of coming to think that the object of metaphysics is simply the range of reference of a term ("being") that has the widest possible extension, and thus a term that lacks any specific meaning or sense. But what, the reader may ask, is the alternative? So far, we have not answered the question of how intelligible features of being as such are to be elicited, or how concepts of the "third order" are to be developed. To this task we must now turn.

Every discipline articulates, for the purposes of organized study, concepts that express supposed intelligibilities. But "being as being" and "being as enjoyed in common" do not express intelligibilities that can be arrived at by abstraction in the ordinary sense. As Jacques Maritain elaborated the matter, such intelligibilities are grasped rather through a distinctive "intuition" or, as he also called it, "eidetic visualization." (The word "eidetic" comes from the Greek *eidos*, for "idea.") By way of such an *intuition of being*, arrived at through reflecting on our acts of judgment about existence in its various modes, our intellect attains a special type of reality—one that "can possess only in the mind the conditions of its existence [as] one and universal."[34] This reality, i.e., being, comes to be understood, accordingly, as a unity amid diversity. The present writer would express the point in the following way: The mind, via reflection on its own most basic judgments, comes to grasp that the "*ways* to be" are diverse, but at the same time that they are all "ways *to be.*"

Through the process just described, that which itself is precisely not a nature or characteristic (namely, the very existence of things) nonetheless can become the object of a concept. Indeed, for Maritain, and for those who follow him in this account, it is only through the intuition of being that metaphysics can be given a proper, experientially grounded subject matter. It is only in this way that the inevitably sense-related character of our concepts of natural being, as well as the inevitably vague character of our common or everyday notions of

---

34. Jacques Maritain, *A Preface to Metaphysics*, 58. In a footnote, Maritain adds: "It is only with a precarious grasp that the metaphysical intuition of being is 'possessed.' . . . On the one hand its object is supremely inexhaustible, and is presented to us as such; on the other hand this intuition . . . [is such that] we actualize it at will but in a fashion usually imperfect." Ibid., 60n. (Recall John Paul II's remark, quoted in the Introduction, that expressions of metaphysical knowledge are "imperfect" and "analogical.")

being, can be overcome; and it is only in this way that being as such
(with its genuine mysteriousness now displayed) can be studied in its
amplitude and inexhaustibility.

The amplitude of being requires that certain concepts developed
in the philosophy of nature come to be understood, in metaphysics, as
"analogical" (the notion of analogy will be discussed in the subsection
to follow). Indeed, in some cases, the concepts in question are seen to
need significant transformation. Thus the natural philosopher's form/
matter dyad, which cannot strictly apply beyond the corporeal realm,
is transformed by the metaphysician into the more universal dyad of
act/potency.[35] As we have seen, any physical change involves some instance of matter going from potentially to actually having a particular
form, or having it to a particular degree. Similarly, but now more generally, any being, material or immaterial, that undergoes a process of
alteration or development will be said to go from a state of potency to
a state of act in the respect in question.

Again, the concept of "nature" strictly speaking applies only within the physical realm; in metaphysics it is folded into the broader concept of "essence" or "quiddity" (i.e., the "what it is" of a thing—which
answers the Latin question *"Quid est?"* or "What is it?"). *Essence* thus
will be a system of intelligible necessities, something that must characterize any being, whether that being is material or immaterial. (For
an example of the latter, we may think of the human soul—or the
type of pure but created spirits called angels—as these are spoken of in
Christian and other religious literatures.) Moreover, materiality or cor-
poreity itself comes to be regarded as a form of limitation or finitude;
the fundamental contrast for metaphysics accordingly is that between
the whole of "finite" being and what can only be called "infinite" being—the latter term understood, at least initially, simply as a negation
of the former.

In a corresponding way, *existence* is no longer understood against
the background or matrix of "primary matter," i.e., the principle of or

35. For a full discussion of this matter see Clarke, *The One and the Many*, 109–22.

the potentiality for corporeal being. Rather, existence is understood in relation to, and by contrast with, complete "nothingness" or non-being. Moreover, so far from being a static quality, or something that merely happens to attach to beings, existence, for the perennial philosopher, is the very perfection or actuality involved in the exercise of being. Aquinas stresses this point when he characterizes existence as the "actuality of all things without exception, the actuality of all the forms of being" (*Summa Theologiae*, I, q. 4, art. 1 ad 3).

This leads to the further point that, within all finite or limited being (whether material or immaterial), there is a real distinction between a being's essence and its existence—between, as we might put it, the "what it is" and the "that it is" of the being. This real distinction is grasped through reflection on the fact that we can understand a thing's essence (at least in general terms) without knowing whether instances of it actually exist. ("Are there intelligent life-forms in other regions of the universe?") Of course, the actual beings of our experience are such that, in them, essence and existence are always found together. Nonetheless, while they are not separated in fact, they are said to be distinct as constitutive principles of being. To put the matter in another way, we are here referring not merely to two different concepts, but two different perfections or types of act. Emonet expresses the point with poetic force: "These two acts, essence and existence, call to one another in order to join in the remotest depths of things."[36] That is to say, only through such "joining" do we have, within the realm of finite reality, an actual being of a particular type—i.e., a thing with a determinate essence (or system of intelligible features) that actually exists.

One final pair of metaphysical notions needs to be introduced. These have been expressed by Scholastics as "subsistence" and the "supposit." Regarding the former, let us recall that in everyday speech it sometimes is said that a bare minimum of financial resources pro-

---

36. Pierre-Marie Emonet, O.P., *God Seen in the Mirror of the World*, trans. Robert R. Barr (New York: Crossroad, 2000), 13.

vides a family with the "means of subsistence"; that is, it enables
them simply to keep living. The metaphysical notion is related to this.
Subsistence, it may be said, enables a being to receive and exercise individualized existence. Why is such a notion needed in our account of
being? Consider that neither of the principles of being, i.e., neither essence nor existence, can be what individualizes a being as such. For
essence—to be a horse, a cow, a human person, etc.—is by definition
something "shareable" or, as is sometimes said, "communicable."
And existence, although exercised distinctively by each concrete being, is shared by all of them in the way we shall come to call "analogous." Thus a third notion, subsistence as defined above, seems to be
necessary at this point. And, it should be noted, it is the whole individual being (or what can exercise existence in an individual manner)
that is said to "subsist" or be a "subject" in the profoundest, metaphysical sense. The latter concept—that of metaphysical *subject*, i.e.,
that which is capable of exercising individualized existence—also is
sometimes expressed as *supposit* (in Latin, *suppositum*, from *sub* for
"below," plus *ponere* for "to place"). This etymology correctly suggests that subsistence, or what enables a thing to exist as *this* individual (i.e., as *this* substance, qualified by *these* accidents), lies, ontologically speaking, at the very depth of a being.[37]

In light of the above, we can see that every real thing—even one
that is manufactured by human technology—is unique in some way
and to some degree. Thus, for example, each member of a stack of a
particular edition of the daily newspaper is unique insofar as it consists of *this* concrete product of a wood-pulp processing plant, with
this concrete configuration of printer's ink marked upon it. Such,
however, is clearly a minimum level of uniqueness, since for almost
all ordinary purposes one copy of today's newspaper is "the same" as
any other. But the more fully being or actuality is enjoyed by things
of a particular type, the more unique or "incommunicable" is each

---

37. For further discussions of subsistence and the supposit, see Emonet, *Dearest Freshness*, 65–66; and *God Seen in the Mirror of the World*, 99–101. See also Maritain, *The Degrees
of Knowledge*, 245–47 and 458–64.

metaphysical subject.[38] Thus flowers of the same species have greater uniqueness than copies of the daily newspaper (a sign of this is that
each blossoms in its own peculiar way); and animals and human persons, as we shall discuss in part 2, are still more incommunicable in
their metaphysical subjectivity.

Returning to being and its principles, let us note that since there
are many "ways to be," being itself is not simply generic. Recalling the
language of section 1.1, we may say that being as spoken of in metaphysics, unlike the being or "pseudo-being" of logic, has a much fuller, as well as internally diverse, intension than that which is connected with mere membership in the widest class of objects of thought.
Moreover, within any individual being essence and existence are pro-
portioned to each other. Thus it can be said that each being, each supposit or metaphysical subject, exercises existence in proportion to the
type of essence it enjoys. As Emonet expresses the point, things that
are constitute a "symphony" of being, one that is elaborately orches-
trated. Fundamentally, however, the "music of being" is "made up of
only two notes, essence and existence."[39]

The recognition that there are various "ways to be" also leads to a
consideration of those qualities perennial philosophers call "transcendental" and "pure" perfections. In order to pursue this topic we first
need to discuss the nature of analogous language.

Analogous Language as a Tool of Metaphysics

Any disciplined study requires careful attention to language and
language's relations with the mind and with reality. Such relations are
especially important in the context of speculative philosophy.

Let us begin our consideration with general remarks about *literal*
or *designative* language. By contrast with language that is metaphorical or symbolic (whose nature and application we shall discuss further
in part 3), when we use terms in a literal way we seek to designate

38. See Dennehy, "Maritain's Realistic Defense of the Importance of the Philosophy of
Nature to Metaphysics," 119–20.
39. Emonet, *Dearest Freshness*, 89.

real features of being through the application of concepts expressive of those features. According to the perennial tradition, literal or designative language can be divided into three categories or types; these are called "univocal," "equivocal," and "analogous."

A *univocal* term (from the Latin *unum* for "one," plus *vocare* for "to call") has the same meaning in each instance of its normal use. Examples of such terms abound in everyday life, as well as in the disciplines. The science of biology, for example, depends on the use of univocal terms for species: "cat," "dog," "horse," "human being" *(homo sapiens)*, etc. So plentiful and useful are univocal terms that many people—even philosophers—sometimes think that all designative terms either are or should be of this sort. But, as we shall see, this is not the case.

A term is *equivocal* if it has two or more distinct and unrelated meanings. Although the disciplines try to avoid the use of such terms, they arise rather frequently in natural languages. Examples in English would be "bat" (for the nocturnal mammal, and for the hitter's instrument in baseball), and "bank" (for the side of a river, and for the financial institution). As far as one can tell, these diverse uses of the same word, or diverse concepts commonly named, have arisen in English by accident. No sameness or similarity seems intended; moreover, from an account of one meaning of the term we can gather nothing of the other (or others).

Analogous terms lie, in a sense, midway between the univocal and the equivocal: they are partially the same and partially different in their meanings; or they have distinct but similar or related meanings. Importantly, in analogy strictly speaking the relationships that hold among the meanings of a word are rooted in relationships among the realities named. Thus, for example, the term "healthy" is applied primarily to organisms (signifying, let us say, their being whole and functioning well); and the same term also is applied in related ways, e.g., to diet and exercise as causes of health, or to results of a blood test as a sign of health, in the organisms in question. Analogy of this sort is called by Scholastic philosophers "analogy of attribution" (because in a typical case the various meanings are related as attributes are to a substance). Another kind of analogy, called "analogy of proportionality," involves a similarity or proportion among the meanings of a term. For example, we speak of a meal as "good" and a lecture as "good" even though there is no real relationship or common feature shared by the things in question. There is, however, a "proportion"—one involving the respective natures of a meal (where to be good is to be tasteful and/or nutritious) and a lecture (where to be good is to be clear and comprehensive or insightful). This type of analogy may be expressed by way of the following formula: "To be a good x is to the nature or essence of x as to be a good y is to the nature or essence of y." Parallel accounts would be given for other instances of analogy of proportionality, e.g., the terms "large" and "small."

We may be inclined to think that analogous terms must involve some sort of sameness. This, however, would be a mistake. If a term is genuinely analogous, its uses are irreducibly plural and polyvalent, even though these uses display intelligible similarities, relations, or proportions.

In a particular case, it may be wondered whether the use of a term should be called analogous or merely metaphorical.[40] A further complication is that Scholastic philosophers sometimes have spoken of analogy as including metaphor, or of metaphor as being a type of analogy.[41] However, strictly speaking—especially in the context of metaphysics—we should mark a clear, if abstract, distinction between the two. In a case of genuine analogy, the diverse meanings and their connections have their adequate basis in reality; whereas with metaphors such bases lie in the minds of poets or creative writers. It is the latter fact that allows for the multiplication of associations in cases of human creativity, by contrast with those of disciplined inquiry. Consid-

---

40. For example, "green" is applied by some speakers of English to a new worker or team member, as well as to the color of a tender shoot of a plant. Reflecting on similarities among these cases, a person might regard this use as analogous. But one also might think that "green" has the color as its original and normal meaning, with its application to a new person in the organization constituting an instance of metaphor. (Still another—perhaps less plausible—way of analyzing the matter would be to say that the term "green" is simply equivocal.)

41. See Simon, "On Order in Analogical Sets," in *Philosopher at Work*, 137. See also Clarke, *The One and the Many*, 47, where the author expressly identifies metaphor as an "improper" or "non-literal" form of analogy.

er, for example, the following poetic mode of address to a famous Parisian landmark:

> O shepherd Eiffel Tower! How the flock of bridges bleats this morning![42]

Here, it may be said, the honking automobiles that crowd bridges around the French city during rush hour are associated with bleating sheep. As the literary critic M. C. Reverdy writes: "External reality does not live in poetry as it does outside. It is transformed there, and occasions the bursting forth of relationships."[43] It thus can be seen that, while we may be uncertain in a particular instance whether to speak of analogy or metaphor, the theoretical difference between the two is quite important.

This especially is the case when we consider the use of analogy in metaphysics. (Recall the remark from *Fides et ratio*, quoted in the Introduction, that metaphysical knowledge by its nature is "analogical.") For, in this discipline, one's attention is focused on characteristics of real being, or, as Scholastic philosophers also call them, *perfections*—that is, features through which beings enjoy their present states of actuality and completeness. (The corresponding Latin term *perfectio* comes from the roots *per*, meaning "through," and *facere*, meaning "to make." It should be noted, incidentally, that "perfection" in this general, philosophical sense does not convey the idea of being ultimate or highest; rather, a perfection is any characteristic that contributes to the real being of a thing.)

Whether they come to be named univocally or analogously, it is the real perfections of things that underlie the associated elements of designative language. Consider, for example, the redness of a dress, the goodness of a meal, and the freedom of a human person: each of these perfections in its respective way provides the ontological basis for the corresponding descriptive term—"red," "good," and "free." As we shall now see, the latter two types of example hold special interest for the speculative philosopher.

---

42. Guillame Apolinaire, *Alcools*; quoted by Emonet in *Dearest Freshness*, 101.
43. Quoted in Emonet, ibid., 92.

Transcendental and Pure Perfections

Within metaphysics, the analogy of proportionality is the primary type of analogy. This is due to its role in accounts of "transcendental" and "pure" perfections. (The analogy of attribution does play an important role in the development of rationally grounded statements about God; we shall explore this point in part 3 of our book.) Perennial philosophers approach the respective characteristics by identifying them as two among three types of perfections of real being.

The first and most obvious type of perfections consists in those that are restricted to physical realities and conditions. These are often called *mixed* perfections, because they are, in all cases, bound up with (or "mixed" with) matter. The term "red" and other color words designate such characteristics, as do innumerable other terms related to natural categories of substance and accident, as discussed in section 1.2 above. Mixed perfections have little significance for metaphysics, except insofar as they represent one mode of real being, the mode that is familiar to us from sensory experience.

The second category of perfections is comprised of the *transcendentals*. These are so named because they are represented across the categories of being; indeed, as their name suggests, they can be instantiated in ways that go beyond ("transcend") nature. That is, while such characteristics in fact are found in material conditions, they do not require such conditions for their being, or for their being known and verbally expressed. Moreover, in expressing these characteristics the philosopher relies on the type of language called "analogous"—in which, as will be recalled, the meanings of terms are essentially plural or polyvalent, while at the same time being similar or proportional.

In principle there might be discerned any number of transcendental perfections; Scholastic authors traditionally have focused upon five: being, oneness or unity, truth or intelligibility, goodness, and beauty.[44]

---

44. The following characterizations of the transcendental perfections draw especially upon Emonet, *Dearest Freshness*, 101–16.

Being (in Latin, *ens*), taken as a transcendental, is simply the perfection by which a thing has or shares in existence. It is the primary perfection in the sense that, in relation to being, all the other transcendentals are, to use St. Thomas's term, "inseparables." That is, while they may be mentally distinguished from being, they are never found apart from it; nor is being ever found apart from them: "Never," says Aquinas, "do they abandon one another" (*Commentary on the Sentences*, d. 8, q. 1 ad 3).

Oneness or *unity* is that perfection according to which each being is a consistent, integral whole, indivisible and distinct from all other beings as long as it remains itself. The oneness of an organism, for example, is such that the particular elements and compounds of which it is a synthesis have their being in and through the organism, even if, by way of a substantial change (i.e., the organism's death), they may come to exist "on their own," independently of any living form.

Truth, as a transcendental (rather than as an achievement of the mind in correct judgment, which we shall discuss in part 2), is that perfection according to which any and every being has *intelligible*, i.e., understandable, characteristics. It sometimes is called, metaphorically, the "light of being"—i.e., that by which beings can come to be objects of knowledge.

Goodness is the perfection by which all beings are desirable or suitable, in their various respects, because of their sharing in existence. As already suggested in our discussion of analogous language, the type and degree of desirability or suitability will depend on the type and degree of being. ("What about evil?" it may be asked. "Is it too a transcendental perfection?" From the metaphysical point of view, evil signifies precisely some lack of suitable being. This point will be considered in part 3, when we discuss what is termed the "problem of evil" in relation to God.)

Beauty is the perfection according to which, when a being is beheld or understood, it awakens delight. It may be called the "splendor of being"—that by which the being in question is an immediate, absorbing presence to the senses and/or the intellect.

Other transcendental perfections sometimes mentioned by writers in the perennial tradition are to be a "definite something" (in Latin, *aliquid*), and to be an agent (with the term here taken in a most general sense, as designating anything that brings about a change or engages in an activity).

As already has been suggested regarding essence and existence, an analysis of the transcendentals reveals that there are ordered hierarchies within the perfections named by "being," "unity," "truth," "goodness," and the rest. Moreover, it can be said that the less a transcendental perfection is bound up with materiality in a given case, the more purely and intensively it is held by the subject in question. Thus the unity that can be attributed to a living organism is more intensive (it enjoys a fuller measure of reality) than the unity that can be attributed to a chemical compound; and the goodness that can be attributed to a virtuous person is more intensive than the goodness that can be attributed to a well-formed plant.

Members of the third general type of perfection are called *pure* perfections. They have a special place within the hierarchy of being: they are never found in a condition that in itself is material. It may be wondered whether we can know that there actually are any such perfections and, if so, which they are. By way of response let us consider the nature of free choice. As will be discussed more fully in the next part of our book, freedom (as we know from our experience as human beings) is a real perfection whereby choices are not determined in any material way. Freedom, in fact, is an ability to exercise a higher type of causality—an ability that is present in those beings in which unity and independence of agency achieve a level characteristic of persons. Personhood itself can be regarded as a pure perfection; there are lower and higher orders of personhood (and, thus, of freedom)—with God, as understood within Christianity, occupying the highest, indeed infinite, order.

Like the names for transcendental perfections, the names for pure perfections ("rationality," "freedom," etc.) follow the analogy of proportionality. The difference here is that such perfections have a "floor" at the level of human beings.[45] Beneath our level of reality there are

---

45. See Clarke, *Explorations in Metaphysics*, 132.

to be found only perfections of the mixed and transcendental types.

Both the transcendental and the pure perfections are said to exist and to be shared by *participation.* That is, such characteristics or features, as we apprehend them in real beings, are instantiated in various degrees. (Reflection reveals, however, that they are not, within any objects of our experience, instantiated in the highest possible degree.) A clear example of such participation from an earlier section of the book would be the artistic quality shared by a sculptor's equipment. Rodin's tools indeed produced a beautiful statue; but they were artful only insofar as they participated in the sculptor's own art—the ultimate origin of which, since it consists in the orientation of a limited (i.e., human) being toward the transcendental quality beauty, itself might inspire philosophical wonder.

One must exercise caution in declaring which qualities present in natural being are of this participative sort. As noted in section 1.2, Ancient and Medieval writers—including St. Thomas Aquinas—thought that heat was such a quality. They thus said that a pot of water boiling on the stove was hot because it "participated" in the element that is hottest—i.e., fire. With the advent of modern chemistry (in particular, the kinetic molecular theory), we now have a much different and better understanding of material elements, as well as their interactions and results; in fact, to say that the water "participates" in what is hot would for us clearly be a metaphorical use of language. Genuine examples of participated perfections would be those that are properly regarded as transcendental and pure perfections—e.g., being, goodness, beauty, rationality, and freedom.

SUMMARY

• Metaphysics formally treats "being as being." Its concepts typically involve an analogical extension of ones from natural philosophy (e.g., potentiality and actuality as analogical extensions of matter and form). Other key concepts of metaphysics are existence, essence, and subsistence—all treated without regard to whether the subjects of these perfections are physical or non-physical.

• An important conceptual tool for metaphysics is analogy. In such a use of language, the meanings of a term are not the same; however, due to real relations among the things named, they are similar or related. A particularly important form of analogy is called analogy of "proportionality."

• The perfections of being can be divided into three types: those limited by matter (i.e., "mixed" perfections), those attributed by way of analogy across all that is (i.e., "transcendental" perfections), and those that can exist only in a condition that is, in itself, free of matter (i.e., "pure" perfections).

1.5 FUNDAMENTAL PRINCIPLES AND THEIR IMPLICATIONS

Central Metaphysical Principles

Having considered key metaphysical concepts (being; potency and act; essence, existence, and subsistence; and transcendental and pure perfections), let us now proceed to metaphysical principles—i.e., statements expressing the intellect's most fundamental judgments. Like the realities expressed by terms such as "being," these principles are arrived at through what Maritain called "intuition" or "eidetic visualization." That is, we become aware of them through reflection on other, more immediate types of knowledge and awareness, rather than through direct experience. Three such metaphysical principles are commonly recognized. They were alluded to in the Introduction via a remark from John Paul II, and they have been discussed by perennial philosophers throughout history. These three principles generally are known as the Principles of Identity, Sufficient Reason, and Finality.[46] Let us explore each in turn.

---

46. Maritain's discussions are to be found in *A Preface to Metaphysics*, 90–116.

The Principle of Identity

Every being is what it is.

This principle is, in one important respect, the first and most basic of all. Maritain approaches it by noting that when we reflect on an instance of knowing extra-mental reality, we find that our awareness is comprised of two objects. The first is the thing under consideration; the second is the perfection or particular determination attributed to that thing. Then, says Maritain, "the mind intuits that in these two functionally different notions [i.e., being as definite existence, and being as concrete intelligible] it is thinking of the same thing. It sees intuitively the first principle."[47] That is, the mind sees that, in the concrete, *this* instance of existence and *this* intelligible characteristic are inextricably bound up with one another, and that the same is true in relation to all other instances of real being.

There is a corollary to the Principle of Identity:

No property can be both shared and not shared by a being at the same time in the same respect.

This corollary is grasped when we see that the intelligibility of being precludes contradictory realities from being present in a single, concrete, existing thing. No actual instance of being can be, e.g., both spherical and non-spherical.

It will be recalled that John Paul II, in his discussion of metaphysical principles quoted in the Introduction, referred to the principle of "non-contradiction." This principle may be expressed as follows:

Nothing can be both affirmed and denied of a subject at the same time in the same respect.

Strictly speaking, since this formula refers to the mind's act of attributing a property rather than to the property itself, it should be regarded as a logical, rather than a metaphysical form of the Principle of Identity—or, perhaps better, of the corollary principle just mentioned.[48]

47. Ibid., 92.   48. See ibid., 94.

When we combine the above discussion with our earlier one on the transcendental character of being, we come to appreciate that the Principle of Identity applies not simply to the physical order of reality. Rather, in Maritain's words, it "expresses the extra-mental coherence and overflowing wealth of being in all its analogous degrees."[49] That is, throughout reality—from a single atom of hydrogen to the Being Christians and others worship as God—each being is what it is.

The Principle of Sufficient Reason

Everything that is, to the extent that it is, has a sufficient reason for its being.

Here again we have two objects of thought; however, in this case a different sort of relation holds between them. The intelligibility of being requires that every real thing be such that it can "explain itself" to the intellect (although not necessarily to our human intellects). That is to say, every being, everything that is, has that whereby it is.

Maritain notes that the Principle of Sufficient Reason is broader in scope, yet analogically related to, the earlier mentioned Principle of Causality.[50] The latter, as we have seen, is a principle of natural philosophy, restricted in its range to the material or corporeal world. But the Principle of Sufficient Reason, apprehended via the "third order" of abstraction, relates to our knowledge of being just as being, or *ens secundum quod est ens.* Therefore, this new principle applies without restriction. If we inquire, for example, how it is that human persons can appreciate jokes, part of the "sufficient reason" is that we are rational and thus able to see the relationships (and lack thereof) on which many jokes depend. This type of reason refers to a distinctive feature of our nature, a feature we have identified as a "pure" perfection and thus one that, strictly speaking, operates beyond the limitations of matter. Again, as we shall discuss in part 3, the being of God is simply without cause, although God's being does have sufficient reason. Therefore, the two principles—Causality and Sufficient Reason—

---

49. Ibid., 97.   50. See ibid., 99.

are not identical. In fact, the former principle can be subsumed under the latter, more general principle. (It should be noted that some philosophers use the phrase "Principle of Causality" in a wider sense, so as to be equivalent to what we are calling the "Principle of Sufficient Reason." Although this usage obscures an important difference, if no confusions are thereby caused it can be regarded as acceptable, if not completely precise.)

The Principle of Finality

This principle can best be treated in two stages; the first may be expressed as follows:

Potency essentially refers to (or is related to) act.

To approach an understanding of this formula, let us recall the meanings of the metaphysical concepts "potency" and "act." These concepts, we have seen, subsume but are analogically broader than those of "matter" and "form" in natural philosophy. The whole realm of finite being is divided into potency and act; all concrete beings are metaphysical syntheses of the two. If we take a particular being such as the current president of the United States, his or her holding of executive office involves having within his or her range of potency the ability to undertake a number of official functions; and we may say that his or her undertaking of these functions constitutes the exercise of the U.S. presidency in act. Throughout finite reality the enjoyment of a potency or tendency is due to a being's orientation toward a particular act or perfection. (This applies, we might note, even to what we earlier identified as "primary matter." As sheer potency such matter does not exist in and of itself, but it is oriented toward existing in conjunction with an indeterminate range of physical forms.) An individual, determinate being—e.g., this rose—does actually exist; it is possessed of essence, which itself (as earlier discussed) is made actual by the act of existence. With the rose's primary actuality come tendencies toward further modes of perfection—e.g., blooming forth in pink or yellow. (Scholastic philosophers accordingly distinguish between a thing's "first act," or existing as a being of a certain sort, and "second act," or carrying out activities appropriate to such a being.)

The second stage of the Principle of Finality can be formulated in this way:

Every agent acts toward an end.

The types of act or perfection toward which things tend is in part determined by the types of thing they are: physical beings in general are oriented toward change; acorns are oriented toward becoming oak trees; United States presidents, by virtue of their office, are oriented toward marshalling and deploying the nation's military resources; etc. As will be discussed in part 2, in the case of properly human acts the immediate ends (as well as the related means) are freely chosen; however, in the vast majority of cases throughout the natural world, the objects of a thing's acts are not a matter of choice. But whether a thing acts freely or simply operates by nature or animal habit, it always acts so as to fulfill some purpose or objective. Thus we arrive at the second statement of the Principle of Finality.

Additional Principles; Summary Reflections

Beyond the central metaphysical principles just considered, there are a number of others of importance.[51] These other principles do not have commonly accepted designations, but they may be introduced and discussed as follows.

Perfection is due to act; limitation is due to potency.

This principle follows closely the second formulation of the Principle of Finality. That is, some concrete perfection is the end of each act; however, that perfection is limited by the specific type of being (and thus the specific type of power) that exercises the act. For example, persons by nature will the good; such willing is present in any human being in act (i.e., any human being that exists or is alive). Never-

---

51. See the discussion of some of these principles in ibid., 151–52.

theless, since we are not directly acquainted with the good in all its comprehensiveness (this is a feature of our specific condition of potency), our concrete judgments about what in fact is good can, and sometimes do, fail to be correct.

Another important principle holds:

The operations of a thing follow its being.

This, too, clearly relates to the Principle of Finality, especially in its first formulation. It should be noted in this regard that different modes and levels of being are to be distinguished—the purely physical; the type of life shared by plants; the level of being and activity typically enjoyed by human persons; etc. In each case, the mode or level of being can be associated with certain consequent natural operations; thus a plant, but not a rock, can physically incline toward sources of light or water (phenomena that botanists call heliotropism and hydrotropism, respectively). And human persons, but not, as far as we know, other living things, can organize their understanding of reality via physical and metaphysical principles.

Next, we may take up this basic judgment:

Every change presupposes a subject of change.

Here we have a principle that subsumes, and extends by analogy, another statement of natural philosophy. In connection with the latter, the changes that occur are all physical. By contrast, the metaphysical principle applies to all finite being, whether material or immaterial. This includes the human soul and the various types of change and development it can undergo—say, passing from a state of potentially understanding to a state of actually understanding, or from a state of being non-virtuous to a state of being virtuous. (These and other relevant examples will be elaborated in the next part of our book.)

Finally, let us consider the following:

Any perfection of a being either is possessed by way of the being's essence (or some determination of its essence), or it is possessed by way of participation.

At one level, as already suggested, this principle can be applied, e.g., to Rodin's equipment as participating in his art: the sculptor has his art by virtue of what he has become and now is; the tools share in this art by virtue of being used by him. A more significant application of the principle relates to what we have called "transcendental" and "pure" perfections—which, as we have seen, are possessed in respective degrees. When we reflect on our actual experience of such perfections (being, goodness, freedom, etc.), we realize that such experience is never of the characteristics as they might be possessed in the highest possible degree. Moreover, we come to realize that the things of our direct acquaintance cannot, of themselves, provide a sufficient reason for their possession of transcendental and pure perfections. These perfections' ultimate "home," as we might put it, somehow transcends the realm of experience.

In our formulations of various metaphysical principles we in general have followed suggestions of Jacques Maritain. However, Maritain himself noted that metaphysical principles are subject to diverse formulations. (For example, some perennial philosophers have expressed the Principle of Identity as "Being is not non-being.") Although this may seem to introduce unwelcome complications, in itself such diversity is not a bad thing. Rather, variations and even disputes about these matters indicate, as Maritain noted, that what is crucial "is not a matter of formulas, but a living intuition . . . [that] transcends all the words in the dictionary."[52] Metaphysical principles indeed are difficult to express in ways that everyone can understand and accept; still, whether or not they are precisely articulated or explicitly recognized, they form the bedrock of all human reflection about reality.

It should be noted that since metaphysical principles are most general and fundamental, they cannot be "proven" in any ordinary sense. Initially, they are "intuited" or (intellectually) "seen," sometimes after a period of reflection on relevant, very general facts. However, as we suggested earlier, fundamental principles can be defend-

52. Ibid., 94.

ed dialectically, by demonstrating the unacceptable consequences of rejecting them. For example, one who rejects the Principle of Non-Contradiction is faced with the possibility of having to accept a statement that a particular being is both spherical and cube-shaped, or both finite and infinite, at the same time. It seems reasonable to suppose that no reflective person will want to be in such a position.

Let us note as well that philosophical analysis enables us to explain certain principles in terms of other, more fundamental principles. Thus the Principle of Sufficient Reason can be reduced to the Principle of Identity by noting the relationship between a being's intelligible basis (its "sufficient reason") and its ability to be what it is (to have a certain essence or "identity"). In fact, reflection reveals that, at least implicitly and indirectly, *all* other speculative philosophical principles can be understood in terms of the Principle of Identity. For example, the Principle of Finality ("Every agent acts toward an end") can be elucidated by noting that the term "end" signifies a kind of fullness of a thing's being, to which by its essence it is ordered.

It might be asked, "Would a complete and integrated set of metaphysical principles be possible? And could there be only one such set?" Interestingly, although Maritain and other perennial philosophers are "systematic" in their approach to philosophy, they have not tried to produce a complete or closed "system" of metaphysical principles. The present writer would suggest that such open-endedness is both a sign and a guarantee that the perennial philosophy is always subject to further development, in light of new insights and conceptual frameworks.

We have noted that metaphysical concepts and principles, and the facts upon which they are based, are most general and most purely ontological. This means that, unlike certain concepts and principles of natural philosophy, they are not apt to be overturned by, or to need modification in light of, new scientific data.[53] Their formulation

---

53. Philosophers of "process" (e.g., the British thinker Alfred North Whitehead and his followers such as the American Charles Hartshorne) have sometimes suggested that Aristotle's basic category of substance should be given up in favor of a more "dynamic" view sug-

and recognition are independent of the current state of investigations in the empiriological disciplines. To illustrate this point: while the causes of a particular type of cancer can be studied in ever-finer detail, and while particular biomedical hypotheses may suffer setbacks and even need to be abandoned, that there is a set of causes or a sufficient reason for this type of cancer is not itself ever called into question.

It might be asked whether the empiriological sciences—as well as natural philosophy—depend in some way on metaphysics; or again, whether it is possible to project a unified and appropriately layered system of all human knowledge about reality. This question is similar to the one discussed in section 1.3 regarding knowledge of the physical world. Ideally, one might hope for a unification or synthesis insofar as this is possible. But the situation here is even more complex than it was in connection with Wallace's projected synthesis of natural philosophy and the positive sciences. For the disciplines now under consideration—that is, all the disciplines that there are—do not even share a single "order" of abstraction. Their modes of concept formation and definition are to be differentiated into at least the three orders we have discussed—the purely physical, the mathematical, and the metaphysical.

On the other hand, it can be seen that the principles of natural philosophy are analytically reducible to those of metaphysics, somewhat as those of the empiriological sciences are reducible to those of natural philosophy. Natural philosophy, as we have seen, studies being insofar as it is sensible and physically changeable; and these aspects depend on natural things' materiality—which, as we noted, falls under the heading of "potentiality." Potentiality in turn may be characterized as a "can-be," or as a "not-being that in principle is." And, with

---

gested by the modern sciences. See, for example, Whitehead's *Process and Reality*, corrected edition by David Ray Griffin and Donald W. Sherburne (New York: Free Press, 1978). It should be noted, however, that to the extent there is a significant issue here it would have to do with the philosophy of nature, not with metaphysics properly understood. Moreover, as we have shown in section 1.3, Aristotelian philosophical categories seem well able to accommodate the latest developments in, e.g., physics and evolutionary biology. (For further discussion of the influence of process thought—especially on Christian philosophers and theologians—see the discussion of Nicholas Wolterstorff's views in section 3.3.)

these latter notions, we clearly have arrived at the realm of metaphysics. Thus, while natural philosophy can be developed independently of metaphysics, just as the positive sciences can be developed independently of natural philosophy, *all* studies of reality can be appreciated in the most ultimate and comprehensive way via the principles of metaphysics. This, we would suggest, is the key to philosophy's serving what we saw John Paul II call its "sapiental function"; this is how it can prepare the "ultimate framework of the unity of knowledge and action" (*Fides et ratio*, sec. 81). Such a function of wisdom does not involve merely stringing together disparate elements. Rather, it involves, at least in outline and in principle, a transformation of our understanding of these various elements into a single, ordered whole.

Let us conclude our elaboration of the perennial metaphysics by considering how it leads to what might be called a gateway to Absolute Being. We would suggest that such a gateway can be approached along two related paths.

To appreciate the first, let us reflect a little further on the fact of substantial change. A very particular substantial change awaits all living beings of nature, including ourselves—i.e., death. Reflecting on the fragility of life—and the sense of "nothingness" both before and after that an awareness of this fragility can induce—Maritain and Emonet (adapting the language of the twentieth-century phenomenologist and existentialist philosopher Martin Heidegger) speak of all natural being as "Being-with-Nothingness."[54] The being of our world, that is to say, is hemmed around with non-being; moreover, non-being would seem to be its destiny, in both its individual and its corporate character.

How, then, it must be asked, is it the case that even now, or at any particular moment, the nothingness of our kind of being is "overcome"? Even taken together, natural beings in their entirety do not seem able to account for the overcoming of non-being. Thus, according to the perennial philosopher, we begin to think in terms of "Being-without-Nothingness"—that is to say, Absolute Being, or Being hav-

---

54. See Jacques Maritain, *Existence and the Existent*, trans. Lewis Galantiere and Gerald B. Phelan (New York: Pantheon Books, 1948); and Emonet, *Dearest Freshness*, 70–72.

ing no trace of non-being, on which the beings of our fragile universe depend for their existence.

Regarding the second path, let us consider once again the transcendental and pure perfections. What can be the adequate explanation of the fact that the beings of our physical world actually participate, in their respective degrees, in these perfections? The last of the metaphysical principles outlined above is directly relevant here. Consider such qualities as being, truth, unity, goodness, beauty, intelligence, and freedom: to say that we and other finite beings "participate" in these perfections is to say that we do not exhaust their reality. It also is to say that our kind of being, in and of itself, does not manifest a "sufficient reason" for the presence of such perfections—either in ourselves or in other beings. (Here there might be contrasted our having a certain height, weight, and shape—which do follow upon, and thus are adequately explained in terms of, our being as natural and corporeal.) Reflection on the transcendental and pure perfections thus leads to the idea of Ultimate Perfection, or what would be the real synthesis of all these perfections in the highest, indeed infinite degree. Only such a Reality, it would seem, could be the adequate principle and cause of these perfections as we actually encounter them in experience.

In light of all this, it may be said that metaphysics in the tradition of St. Thomas Aquinas culminates in the recognition of an ontological Absolute. It does so, moreover, in a clearer and more direct way than was possible within natural philosophy, where, as we put it, we could only "gesture" toward, e.g., an ontologically first cause or originating intelligence.

As with the points suggested at the end of section 1.3, the present ones will be considered with greater logical rigor at the beginning of the third part of our book. But the reader who has grasped the present matters will begin to understand why some thinkers speak of the possibility of—and, indeed, the need for—a philosophical approach to God.

Responses to Initial Challenges

However the above-mentioned project may come to strike us, we at least are in position to develop critical responses to some of the challenges to perennial philosophy that were identified in the Introduction. Here at the end of part 1, let us focus on answering scientism and several associated views. It will be recalled that these views seemed, at first sight, to offer a profound test for the modes of thought encouraged by John Paul II. For they question the very possibility of a philosophical approach to understanding the being of the world.

As a primary example, the physical chemist Peter Atkins was quoted as propounding the view that "science is all-competent." Now, when he is asked about the basis for his view, Atkins says the following: "I base this belief on the observation that science has never encountered a barrier that it has not surmounted or that it cannot reasonably be expected to surmount eventually."[55] In evaluating this remark, let us first of all note that if the natural sciences can be said to encounter no insurmountable barriers, this is precisely because the only "barriers" recognized by Atkins and similar writers are ones arising along intellectual paths that practitioners of the natural sciences have chosen. This, of course, in no way is to disparage such paths. But it is to point out that science itself says nothing about other intellectual concerns and ways of knowing. In light of this, we may raise the following questions: 1) "What, precisely, for Atkins and his fellows, count as 'explanations'?" And, just as important, 2) "Are explanations that meet his criteria, whether taken individually or as a whole, completely and ultimately satisfying to the intellect?" To his credit, Atkins himself at one point seems to recognize that such questions are crucial. In a discussion of human consciousness, he says, "This, of course, is where some would wish to challenge, claiming that consciousness is irreducible; but then it comes down to what it means to give a scientific explanation."[56] Now, for the perennial philosopher, this issue goes beyond what is to count as a scientific explanation, at least as this is

---

55. Peter Atkins, "Purposeless People," 13.
56. Ibid., 20.

usually understood (i.e., as one that would be empiriological); rather, it encompasses every real factor that should figure in a comprehensive account of being and coming to be. And it would beg this very issue if Atkins, or another proponent of scientism, were simply to stipulate that only the types of explanation given in the modern positive sciences could figure in such an account. But Atkins gives the reader no argument for either the exclusivity or the potential completeness of explanations within the positive sciences, other than their success to date—which, of course, means their success to date along their own chosen paths. Thus, in light of the other modes of causality (especially formal and final causality) that we have elaborated in our exposition of speculative philosophy, scientism begins to appear simply as an intellectual prejudice—one that insists on ignoring any factors in being and coming to be beyond the material and mechanical.

To explore this matter further, let us consider scientism's rejection of dynamisms and ends in nature. Where the perennial philosopher of nature speaks of formal and final causality, those biologists who follow scientism (which, as we have stressed, is an opposed philosophy, not an instance of science itself) undertake to give complete accounts of the data in reductionistic fashion, i.e., by referring only to such factors as the operation of genetic programs in the context of a particular physical environment. According to such accounts, DNA—serving as a "recipe" for the constitution of bodies—exercises a primal causal force.[57] It should be noted, however, that other modern biologists have had a more expansive vision. Emonet quotes the French scientist Claude Bernard, who was a contemporary of Charles Darwin: "In a living seed, there is a creative idea, developed and manifested by organization. Throughout its existence, the living organism remains under the influence of this same vital, creative force. . . . Here, as everywhere, everything derives from the idea, which alone creates and directs."[58] As this point might be restated today, it does not suggest that DNA plays no important, indeed crucial role. But as noted in our

57. The most prominent purveyor of this type of account has been Richard Dawkins. See *The Blind Watchmaker* (New York: W. W. Norton, 1996) and *The Selfish Gene* (New York: Oxford University Press, 1990).

58. See Emonet, *Dearest Freshness,* 14.

earlier discussion of the four types of cause, this role can be seen to depend on the concomitant presence of a formal factor, namely, the nature of the seed in question. It is the latter that ultimately accounts for the type of actuality enjoyed by a being, as well as its tendencies toward specific acts and ends.

Regarding the related views known as materialism and physicalism, it will be recalled that they seek a complete account of being in terms of what is perceivable and changing, i.e., "marked-off" matter. Thus, whereas the Thomist school speaks of degrees of actuality, and of analogy in the forms of being, scientism and its variants tend to be "one-dimensional." Those who hold such views are skeptical of degrees of being (for these cannot, strictly speaking, be perceived); and they place their hopes in explanations that refer only to material complexities or summations of such complexities, rather than to formal factors. As we saw John Paul II express the matter in the Introduction, such views maintain that there is only "pure and simple facticity."

But again, even granting the important roles of such things as genetic predispositions, what is the argument for the physical as providing a complete account of reality? In section 1.3, we found reason to question whether such an interpretation can be adequate to certain things we know—e.g., the facts of evolution (including, especially, the evolution of human persons)—when these facts are fully and properly appreciated. Moreover, we noted other important questions that arise concerning natural being. For example, how is such being brought from states of potentiality to states of actuality? Such questions make it difficult to accept a purely physicalist or materialist account of reality.

Moreover, physicalism can be seen to be subject to the sort of critique Pierre-Marie Emonet makes against phenomenalism. It will be recalled that phenomenalists reduce all of reality to sensory data. Emonet cites the version of this view offered by the French philosopher Jean-Paul Sartre. Sartre holds, as we have seen, that "being is nothing but the closely joined series of its manifestations"; and, in light of this, that there is no such thing as substantial reality. But, says

Emonet, this view implicitly involves an "absurdity." For in the absence of substance one in effect would have to assert that what "joins" (i.e., what makes the manifold of sensory consciousness into discrete, continuing unities) is the same as "what is joined" (i.e., the manifold itself).[59] And, we may add, what holds for phenomenalism holds for physicalism as well. That is, at whatever level the physicalist philosopher chooses to refer to reality's ultimate and elementary "bits" (e.g., the level of molecules, or atoms, or subatomic particles, etc.), such bits themselves cannot be what makes our world into one of whole, integrally functioning beings.

If these other variants of scientism are rejected, there is little or nothing to support logical positivism, the view that any instance of language that cannot be tied to immediate experience is without cognitive meaning. In fact, we have explicitly undertaken in section 1.4 to establish the contrary position. That is, through our account of metaphysical concepts and principles by way of "eidetic visualization," and through our articulation of the philosophical theory of analogy, we have indicated a real grounding for terms whose meanings—although first recognized in connection with the empirical world—can be extended so as to apply across all the categories and modes of being.

To appreciate these critical points more fully, and to pursue the next phase in "understanding our being," we turn in part 2 to the main features of specifically human, personal reality.

SUMMARY

• Fundamental principles of metaphysics are the Principle of Identity, Principle of Sufficient Reason, and Principle of Finality. Other principles include one stating that a kind of "participation" by limited beings in transcendental and pure perfections is necessary for an explanation of their possession of these perfections in their respective and limited degrees.

• Metaphysics opens a gateway to Absolute Being via reflection along two lines: a) implications of the limited nature of finite being ("Being-

59. Emonet, *The Greatest Marvel of Nature*, 86.

with-Nothingness"); and b) implications of finite being's participation in transcendental and pure qualities (being, unity, freedom, etc.).

• Contrary to scientism and associated philosophies, the author has tried to show how there can be genuine knowledge about reality (and genuine expressions of such knowledge) which is not restricted to things as directly perceived.

QUESTIONS FOR REFLECTION (PART 1)

1. Why does the perennial philosopher stress a distinction between being in the logical sense and real being? Does such a distinction seem appropriate and necessary to the philosophy of being? Why or why not?

2. Regarding the natural sciences' approaches to being, does the characterization of them as "empiriological" (vs. "ontological") strike you as entirely correct? Why or why not? How helpful is Simon's suggestion that the difference is one of degree, i.e., that the positive sciences are to some degree ontological, and the philosophy of nature is to some degree empiriological? Discuss.

3. How does philosophy's account of the "four causes" of natural being and becoming relate to modes of explanation employed in the positive or empirical sciences? Some thinkers hold that these sciences demonstrate that there is no need for—or even room for—a genuine concept of final causality in nature. In light of suggestions in the text, explain why you agree or disagree.

4. Take one of our final, dialectical questions concerning natural being ("Could all being be limited by potency?" "How is it that things are really oriented to ends?" "Can the 'more' be explained by the 'less'?"), and consider whether a philosopher who is intent on restricting reflection to the realm of natural being could give an adequate response to it.

5. What does Maritain mean by "intuition of being"? How does a philosopher who follows Aquinas try to show that all of finite being is composed of the metaphysical principles existence and essence? Discuss whether there seem to be good grounds for saying that there is, in each finite being, a real distinction between "what it is" and "that it is."

6. Explain why perennial philosophers draw a distinction between "metaphorical" and "analogous" uses of language. Indicate a case in which

it might seem difficult or even arbitrary to characterize the uses of a particular term as one or the other. Does this case pose a threat to the perennial philosopher's view of the metaphysical significance of analogous language? Discuss.

7. Take one of the basic "transcendental" properties of being (being, unity, truth, goodness, or beauty) and show through examples how it is found concretely across various categories and levels of being. Discuss whether it seems plausible to say, with Aquinas, that such a property is shared more "purely" or "intensively" the higher the type of being under consideration.

8. Take one of the traditional metaphysical principles (Identity, Sufficient Reason, Finality, etc.), and consider how it might be defended against a professed skeptic. Do you believe that if the skeptic considers this defense in a rational way, he or she should (not necessarily will) concede the point? Why or why not?

9. Take one or more of the principles of metaphysics we have discussed and relate it, or them, to principles of a more particular discipline with which you are familiar (history, biology, mathematics, etc.). Does your discussion tend to support John Paul II's vision of philosophy as providing the "ultimate framework of the unity" of knowledge? Why or why not?

10. Take one of our critical discussions of a philosophical view opposed to the traditional account of being (i.e., scientism, materialism or physicalism, or positivism) and consider how a proponent of this opposed view might respond. Which side would seem to have better reasons for its position? Explain.

PART 2

OUR PERSONAL BEING

2.1 APPROACHES TO THE HUMAN

Common and Scientific Language

In this part of our book, general notions we have articulated about being (e.g., "substance," "form," "causality," "act" and "potency," etc.) are applied to the understanding of our specific type of being—namely, human and personal being. The reader will recall that we often referred to human reality and activity in our discussions in part 1. On reflection, this should come as no surprise. For, in spite of being's analogical generality, our acquaintance with it can come only by way of beings we actually know; and, it seems, the beings we in some way know best are ourselves. (As we shall see, however, a rational articulation of this knowledge requires much careful effort.) In *Fides et ratio*, John Paul II went so far as to say that "the person constitutes a privileged locus for the encounter with being, and hence with metaphysical enquiry."[1] We may expect, accordingly, that some of our metaphysical notions will become clearer—and their implications more sharply delineated—as we proceed through the second part of our book. For example, the notions of "subsistence" and "supposit" will be taken up again in our discussions of human soul or spirit.

Clearly, however, we cannot begin with such difficult matters. Rather, let us start by surveying certain terms commonly used in speaking of the human person, as well as images associated with these terms. Such a survey might provide a clue to whatever common sense understanding of our nature is available—and thus serve, in John Paul II's terminology, as "a reference point" for the philosophical efforts to follow. Such terms obviously would include "human being" and "person," but also "self," "mind," "soul," and "spirit."[2]

1. John Paul II, *Fides et ratio*, sec. 83.
2. The terminological notes summarized in the succeeding paragraphs are taken in part

The term "human being" may be regarded as most basic. It refers in a general way—i.e., apart from age, race, and other qualities or determinants—to any member of our biological species, *Homo sapiens*. (Interestingly, this species name includes the Latin word for "intelligent" or "wise"; the reader will recall that the related term *sapientia* means "wisdom.") As an initial point, then, we may say that "human being" picks out our specific kind of being—without, however, conveying any precise notion of what it is to be a being of our kind (although the Latin word *sapiens* in the species name perhaps can be taken as suggestive).

"Person" too is a basic term, one that in its primary meaning can be used of any human individual. However, it also conveys the image of an "inner" life, that is, a life characterized by personality or selfhood. Our English word "person" comes from the Latin *persona* (itself rooted in *per* plus *sonare*, "to sound through"). The characters appearing in a play often are listed in the program under the heading *"Dramatis Personae"* (literally "persons [i.e., roles] of the drama"). We might say that by "sounding through" their masks, garb, actions, etc., these players make their characters' inner lives known to the audience. Similarly, and more generally, those beings we call "persons" are ones that might reveal themselves to us in some way.

In its everyday use, the term "self" often refers to the whole individual person. However, it too carries a suggestion or image of "inner" life, as well as a sense of uniqueness—as in the expression "my true self." Moreover, a self, and only a self, can be an initiator of chosen actions, and accordingly ascribed moral responsibility.

Other terms are used somewhat synonymously with "self." Thus we speak of "subjects" in referring to human individuals who become the focus of biomedical research. Again, sometimes the word "heart"—which of course primarily designates a bodily organ—is used metaphorically for the self or the seat of moral character, as in the expression "He has a good heart" (when this is said by a moralist, not by

---

from the relevant entries in *Merriam-Webster's Collegiate Dictionary*, 11th ed. (Springfield, Mass.: Merriam-Webster, 2003).

a cardiologist!). "Heart" also can suggest a seat of perception and understanding, especially in matters of deep personal concern, as in "She knew in her heart that he would return." (Incidentally, the same metaphor is used in biblical Greek [with *kardia* as the word for "heart"]. In Luke 2, for example, we read: "Mary kept all these things, pondering them in her heart.")

Understanding, as related to matters of fact or theory, is most often expressed in terms of "mind." This word in fact conveys the whole complex of elements that we call "mental" acts or operations—e.g., perceiving, imagining, thinking, willing, and reasoning. Mind, too, often is thought of as an "inner," by contrast with an "outer" or publicly observable, dimension of the individual. In light of recent developments in psychology, many now speak of the "subconscious" and/or "unconscious" as well as of the "conscious" mind.

The word "psychology," it may be noted, comes from the Greek term usually translated as "soul"—that is, *psuche*. (Many other English words are derived from this same Greek root: e.g., "psyche," "psychic," "psychoanalysis," etc.) "Soul" is sometimes used similarly to "heart," as referring to a source of emotion, feeling, and personal understanding. But it has other, more philosophically significant meanings as well—e.g., "immaterial essence, animating principle, or actuating cause of an individual life" (the first entry under "soul" in *Merriam-Webster's Collegiate Dictionary*, 11th ed.). "Soul" also is used of the spiritual aspect or dimension of our being (and perhaps other beings), as this is understood in various religious traditions. Still, the question of how, precisely, we are to understand notions like "immaterial essence" or "animating principle" is left undetermined in standard dictionary entries; and it must be acknowledged that, at least in common usage, the word "soul" is both vague and ambiguous.

It also must be said that the words "soul" and, to a lesser extent, "mind" generate considerable controversy. Many people today see no real use for the word "soul," or even "mind," except as shorthand terms for human dispositions and activities which—in these people's view—eventually will come to be recognized as purely physical in nature. However, as we have indicated, others continue to use the word "soul" in one or more of several positive senses.

One of the positive senses we have noted points to the final term in our survey, i.e., "spirit." Sometimes this term is used synonymously with "soul"—and accordingly shares its vagueness and ambiguity. But generally "spirit" (and "spiritual") can be said to emphasize what are taken to be "immaterial"—sometimes even "supernatural"—aspects of a being (see, in this regard, *Merriam-Webster's* second and fourth entries under "spirit"). This linguistic fact—one that is represented in ancient as well as modern languages—in part underlies the distinction between soul and spirit sometimes made by biblical writers. (In Heb 4:12, St. Paul speaks of the word of God as "sharper than any two-edged sword, penetrating even between soul and spirit.") Not surprisingly, in an age marked by a tendency toward scientism, many people today reject this substantive, realist use "spirit" and "spiritual," as they also do of "soul."

As suggested earlier, linguistic notes such as the ones here assembled often are clues to an appreciation of common sense understandings. However, in the case of the human person, we must conclude that any such understandings are rather vague, and often ambiguous as well. There is little clarity or agreement about the terms to be used—e.g., "person," "self," "mind," "soul," and "spirit." There also is little clarity or agreement about relations between what these terms designate and the bodily dimension of our nature as human beings.

When we turn to scientific disciplines concerned with the human person, we find, unfortunately, a similar situation. Or rather, and more precisely, insofar as these disciplines—e.g., biology, psychology, sociology, and the rest—maintain what we have referred to as primarily "empiriological" perspectives (recall section 1.1), they have in fact reached considerable agreement; moreover, they have greatly enhanced our knowledge of facts about the human person along the lines in question. But the drive of the human intellect is to know the essences of things—which empiriological studies by themselves generally are ill equipped to articulate. It often happens, therefore, that a scientific account of human beings will implicitly incorporate one or more of the images fostered by common sense and common language. The overall result, once again, is confusion and division—as can be seen in the disputes among, e.g., cognitive psychologists, depth psychologists and psychoanalysts, behaviorist psychologists, psychobiologists, etc. What these diverse theorists and practitioners tend to lack is any explicit philosophical grounding for their respective, and competing, fundamental perspectives.

This confusion is only increased when we consider images of human reality represented in the arts, literature, etc. These cultural phenomena surely reveal in their own ways certain aspects of our nature as human persons. But what, precisely, do they reveal? Some novels and films suggest, for example, that our lives are full of meaning, whereas others suggest that they are absurd and meaningless. Moreover, whatever may be thought to be revealed by these media, how is this to be integrated within an overall account of human reality?

We come to see, therefore, that if we rely simply on common language, the positive sciences, and the arts, we are very unlikely to achieve a systematic, organized understanding of the human person—let alone one grounded in sound philosophical concepts and principles. Thus, while we should bear in mind the above linguistic summaries—as well as the contributions to our understanding made by both science and art—we now must press our inquiry about the human person to an explicitly philosophical level.

Can We Know the Nature of the Human Person?

In light of the above, it is reasonable to ask—indeed it is itself an important philosophical question—whether the ultimate natures of person, self, mind, soul, and spirit, as well as their relations with each other and with the body, actually can be known. In line with the theories of knowledge discussed in the first part of our book, a number of competing answers have been given.

Rationalists such as Descartes have tended to believe that these natures and relations can be known by direct insight or rational intuition. Those who hold to or are influenced by empiricism believe that the human person can adequately be treated as a physical and observable object—more "complex," to be sure, but not essentially different from other material beings, and thus in principle knowable by means of the positive sciences.

Skeptics are philosophers who hold that we cannot know the nature of the person, or of related realities like soul and spirit (if indeed there are such realities). In recent times, skepticism often is bound up—as it was in David Hume—with an empiricist approach to knowledge; the principal difference between skeptics and other empiricists is that the former tend to be less optimistic than the latter about the prospective achievements of disciplines that are rooted in sense observation. For their part, religious fideists agree with skeptics in one important respect: although they believe in the human soul and/or spirit, they hold that our views about the ultimate nature of the human person are strictly matters of faith, not ones that are in any way subject to the test of human experience, or reason and understanding.

Among those who believe we can know the nature of the person, ontological views—both historically and today—have tended toward two principal and opposed types. (Such an opposition indeed is already suggested by the linguistic and disciplinary facts noted above.) The first ontological view often is termed *dualism;* it holds that there are two fundamental types of reality—designated by "spirit" and "matter," "soul" and "body," or some similar pair of names. The second, opposed type of view often is called *monism.* According to this view, there is just one basic type of reality—generally held to be matter or the physical.[3] In monistic accounts, the image of the "inner" (a fertile source, as the student will appreciate, of dualism) dissolves in favor of what its proponents take to be a more consistent and plausible physicalism.

Historically, dualist views of human reality have been articulated

---

3. In principle, there could be a spiritual monism. This is at least suggested by the remark of George Berkeley, the seventeenth-century English-speaking philosopher quoted in section 1.1: "To be is to be perceived or to perceive."

by thinkers such as Plato and Descartes. In his famous dialogue *The Republic*, Plato likens the human soul to a group of people trapped and bound in a cave, able to see only flickering images of things on the cave's forward wall. Such people would be very far from recognizing the true nature of things—as indeed is the human soul in its current state, since it is trapped in and limited by the body. For Plato, accordingly, the soul's task is to free itself from the body and come to appreciate the ideal "Forms" of reality in their state of purity and transcendence.

In the second of his *Meditations*, Descartes overcomes an initial philosophical skepticism by realizing that he cannot doubt his own existence: "I am—I exist: this is certain; but how often? As often as I think." And this realization, he believes, in turn points to a conclusion about his fundamental nature: "I am therefore, precisely speaking, only a thinking thing, that is a mind [Latin *mens sive animus*], understanding, or reason."[4]

A well-known contemporary dualist is the British philosopher Richard Swinburne. He writes, "The soul is an immaterial thing; and the conscious life of thought, sensation, and purpose which belongs to a man belongs to him because it belongs to his soul." Moreover, for Swinburne, "the soul is the essential part of me, and it is its continuing in existence which makes for the continuing of me."[5]

Materialist monism was held by Plato's near contemporary Democritus, and by the Early Modern British philosopher Thomas Hobbes. According to Democritus, "Thinking consists ultimately of nothing more than the motion of atoms." Thus, according to one commentator, this ancient Greek philosopher can be regarded as "the first thoroughgoing materialist: the mind and all its reality are ultimately of derivative reality."[6] For his part, Hobbes, writing in the seventeenth century, pursues the materialist theme in connection with reflections

4. René Descartes, *Meditations on First Philosophy*, as quoted in Daniel Kolak, *Lovers of Wisdom*, 2nd ed. (Belmont, Calif.: Wadsworth, 2001), 245.

5. Richard Swinburne, "The Structure of the Soul," in Arthur Peacocke and Grant Gillett, eds., *Persons and Personality* (New York: Basil Blackwell, 1987), 33.

6. Kolak, *Lovers of Wisdom*, 70, 73.

on perception: "All . . . qualities called sensible, are in the object that causes them, but so many several motions of the matter, by which it presses our organs diversely. Neither in us, that are pressed, are they anything else, but diverse motions."[7] Moreover, since images and thoughts result from originating sensations, all that we understand as mind consists merely of "motions" of matter.

Today, the monist ontology typically is bound up with reductionism and physicalism, as these were discussed in the Introduction of our book. It will come as no surprise, therefore, that a prominent contemporary monist in his theory of the human person is Peter Atkins. In the essay from which we have already quoted, Atkins suggests that "the characteristically human capacities which we lump together for convenience of discourse as 'human spirit' or 'soul' are no more than states of the brain"; moreover, "consciousness is a manifestation of the brain, and on [Atkins's] model is no more than a fascinating property that depends on . . . the physical states of nerve cells."[8]

By contrast with all of the above views, philosophy in the perennial tradition, and in the school of St. Thomas Aquinas in particular, pursues a knowledge of the human person (along with soul, mind, and the rest of our objects of inquiry) in a way consistent with its overall approach to knowledge of natures. That is, this tradition applies the metaphysical principle, introduced in section 1.5, "The operations of a thing follow its being." According to this principle, we should try to understand a thing's nature or essence by way of its potentialities or powers; and these in turn can be grasped (to the extent that they can be grasped) in light of the thing's proper acts and operations—i.e., in light of what it does. And what it does we come to know through direct experience. Thus, by working backward from matters of experience we can come, by reflection, to know something of the nature of the being in question—in this case the human being or person.

As implemented by perennial philosophers, this approach gives

7. Thomas Hobbes, quoted in Kolak, ibid., 217.

8. Atkins, "Purposeless People," in Peacocke and Gillett, eds., *Persons and Personality*, 13, 20.

rise to an ontology of the human person that might be called a "modi-fied dualism." More fundamentally, however, it is an ontology rooted in the philosophy of natural being that Aquinas inherited from Aristotle. To come to appreciate this point, let us review key elements of that general perspective.

Hylemorphism and Soul in Perennial Philosophy

Earlier in this section we mentioned the Greek term *psuche,* commonly translated as "soul." The related term in Latin is *anima.* If we are to understand the perennial philosophy's notion of soul (and thus of the human person), it is crucial for us to see that "soul," *psuche,* and *anima* express what in part 1 was termed a "formal" principle.

It will be recalled that in Aristotle's "hylemorphic" understanding of substance, natural being is analyzed in terms of a material principle *(hule)* and a formal principle *(morphe).* The former is the "stuff" of a being or "that out of which" a being is composed (i.e., its matter); the latter is the specific type of determination that is given to this "stuff" (i.e., its form).

For Aristotle and the perennial tradition, a most basic distinction within natural being is that between living and non-living. That is, a most obvious fact of our experience is that while all natural beings are subject to movement by others, certain natural beings also have—but others do not—an ability to move themselves. Given this fundamental distinction, there must, Aristotle reasoned, be a corresponding difference between the types of formal principle that determine things to be of the one kind or the other. When Aristotle used the word *psuche,* he had this difference in mind. He said that *psuche* or soul is "the first grade of actuality [i.e., the primary, actuating formal principle] of a natural body having life potentially in it" (*On the Soul,* book II, chap. 1). We might expand on this brief account by offering the following definition:[9] *Soul* is the type of principle (substantial form) that organizes certain natural bodies so as to be living beings, and thus to

9. Elements of this definition derive from Emonet, *The Greatest Marvel of Nature,* 3.

have the power of initiating certain acts and operations from within (e.g., nutrition and growth, sensation and the conscious pursuit of objects, and reflective thought and decision-making).

One important and perhaps surprising implication of this definition is that if the perennial philosopher is asked, "How do I know that I *have* a soul?" the answer is likely to come in the form of a rhetorical question: Do you have signs of life—a pulse, digestive operations, sight and other powers of sensation, rational thought, etc.? That is to say, a person might as well ask, "How do I know that I have a pair of functioning eyes?" In the case of vital activities (i.e., activities of life) there must be a specific type of initiating formal principle; for the tradition of Aristotle, as developed by Aquinas and his followers, it is precisely this principle that is designated by *psuche,* or *anima,* or "soul." The above account, it should be noted, assumes the general philosophical framework elaborated in part 1, as well as the fundamental distinction, noted above, between living and non-living. Beyond these points, however, there is nothing remarkable—and certainly nothing "otherworldly"—about saying that we have or manifest soul. The real questions, as Aquinas himself noted, are: What is the nature of soul, and especially of human soul? Does human soul in some way involve spirit—i.e., the sort of being or reality that can exist apart from material conditions? These, as we shall see, indeed are difficult matters and ones that give rise to argument.

Let us again recall the general principle: "The operations of a thing follow its being." In the case of living beings, their natures will be distinguished by their sharing particular types of form or soul. Moreover, as is the case with all natural substances, the form will be knowable (to the extent that it is knowable) from a being's characteristic acts and operations. When we consider the range of the latter on display within the natural world, we gain a sense of the "hierarchy" of levels of being.

Within the realm of non-living substances, the question of ontological levels is somewhat obscure. In fact, as suggested in part 1, it may be wondered in the case of subatomic particles whether there is

enough stability to speak in terms of substances or central and specifying forms at all. Moreover, it was suggested by the twentieth-century Thomist Charles DeKoninck that throughout the purely (i.e., non-
living) physical realm all distinctions among types of substance are
primarily empirical and practical in their significance, and it is unclear
whether such distinctions have ontological correlates.[10] But it seemed
to DeKoninck, and to perennial philosophers generally, that the various realms of animate being, and thus of soul, manifest differences of
ontological significance. The following are traditionally identified:

    a) *Vegetative.* This realm encompasses types of activity, and thus
of soul, involved in the assimilation of nutrients, growth and development, and other basic changes implying an initiating principle that
is "internal" to the substance.

    b) *Sensitive.* This realm encompasses types of activity, and thus
of soul, involved in sensory knowledge as well as self-motion related
to objects of attraction and aversion. Such activities imply a "higher,"
or ontologically "richer," organizing principle.

    c) *Rational.* This realm encompasses types of activity (intellec-
tual knowledge and free choice, for example), and thus of soul, that
imply a still "higher" principle or substantial form. Indeed, as will
emerge from our inquiry, such activities suggest the presence of an
initiating principle that cannot be construed in physical terms alone.

    In the present day, certain complexities arise in assigning individu-
als and even species to this framework. But in principle such concerns
seem resolvable. For example, bacteria ordinarily are classified as living things. But if, for lack of nutrients, they enter a "quiescent state,"
they might be thought by some to be no longer alive (just as medical patients in a "persistent vegetative state" are thought by some to
be no longer alive). However, it seems more accurate to say that such
beings are not currently able to "actualize" or "use" their vital powers, rather than that they do not, in the fundamental sense, "possess"

---

10. As reported by Yves R. Simon in *Foresight and Knowledge,* 110n.

them. To take a different type of example, the plant called the Venus's flytrap might seem able to sense when a prey is present, and to close its teeth accordingly. But this behavior (which certainly mimics animal behavior) probably is better understood not as a matter of sensory awareness and conscious activity, but simply as a mechanical operation—and thus a process of merely vegetative life after all. Similar issues, as we shall see in succeeding sections, arise concerning whether non-human animals (e.g., the great apes) share in specifically rational activity.

It should be noted that the three levels of life and activity are cumulative. That is, beings of sensitive nature include in their powers those of the vegetative level; and beings of rational nature (at least as we know them from self-experience) include in their powers those of both the preceding levels of soul. Moreover, in keeping with the general philosophy of nature elaborated in part 1, things at higher levels of being should not be thought of as having "multiple" principles or souls. Rather, they have "unitary" souls (i.e., one formal principle animating each living being—rather than, say, both a vegetative soul and a sensitive soul animating a lion). These unitary souls in turn are the formal bases of these beings' progressively higher (and cumulative) powers and modes of activity.

This, in outline, is the perennial philosophy's understanding of soul, i.e., the formal principle of the human person (and indeed of living beings of whatever sort). We shall elaborate and discuss the implications of this understanding in the pages that follow. To anticipate, let us note two prominent types of activity that might be said to specify human nature: (a) taking the world in via the acquisition of knowledge, especially intellectual knowledge; and (b) responding to the world via diverse modes of affectivity, including the exercise of free choice. These respective types of human activity are discussed in the two sections that follow.

SUMMARY

• Both common and scientific language reveal ambiguity regarding the nature of the human person; accordingly, a philosophical approach is required if we are to have a full and well-ordered treatment of our specific type of being.

• Unlike both dualists and monists, perennial philosophers seek a unified, integral understanding of human personhood, one that recognizes the distinctive character of our nature.

• As used in the philosophical tradition of Aristotle and St. Thomas Aquinas, the word "soul" designates the type of substantial form that organizes matter so as to be, and to have the powers of, a living being.

2.2 LIFE OF KNOWLEDGE

What Is It to Know?

The above question can be understood in two ways. According to the first, we are concerned to develop criteria for knowledge, that is, proper indications that one really does know. (Much of the work of recent epistemologists has been devoted to proposing and assessing such criteria.) According to the second way of understanding the question, we are concerned with *knowledge* or *cognition* as such: we want to know what sort of activity knowledge is, how it relates to the being of the knower, and how it relates to the being of the things known. A "theory of knowledge" as developed in the perennial tradition is mainly concerned with questions of this latter sort. Such theorizing seeks to articulate key features of the human mind, in order to show the plausibility of the view we have termed "critical realism."

Let us begin with some elementary points. Most natural beings or substances, including minerals and plants, come into being, develop and grow (those that do), and exist as full instances of their types, without in any way sharing any other type of existence. But it is a privilege of certain living beings—animals and human persons—to exist in such a way as to be able to "become" the other, although not, of course, in just the way the other is in itself. This is what happens when an animal or human person engages in acts of knowing. The perennial philosopher accordingly says that knowing, i.e., being aware of objects in a sensory and/or intellectual way, constitutes a new type of being (i.e., a new type of actuality or perfection) in the knower. Thus, for example, to the extent that a student of geometry masters the Pythagorean theorem, a new reality comes to be in her or in him.

In accordance with the above, we now may distinguish two types of being: *entitative* being (i.e., being as it exists in itself, whether as substance or accident, as physical or mathematical, etc.) and *intentional* being (i.e., being as it exists in dependency on operations of a mind). Being known itself involves, for the object of knowledge, a distinctive type of being—although in coming to be known the thing as it exists entitatively does not undergo any real process of change. (The Pythagorean theorem may come to be understood well or poorly by the student, but in itself the theorem is not thereby altered.)

As suggested just above, there are two basic types of knowledge, "sensory" and "intellectual." Each represents, in its distinctive manner, the human search for truth—that is, the search for a grasp of "the way things are" that matches the intrinsic intelligibility of things. As we noted in section 1.4, such intelligibility (or "truth") is a transcendental quality, i.e., an analogically participated feature of all that is real.

Sensory Knowledge

Within the physical and temporal order, all knowledge originates in *sensation*. The powers of "external" sense (or the "external" senses)—through which living beings first become aware of realities other than themselves—are the familiar touch, sight, taste, smell, and hearing. Each of these powers operates through an organ or organs—the skin, eyes, tongue, nose, and ears, respectively—along with the relevant aspects of the nervous system and brain.

The external senses receive from things and communicate to the mind *sensible forms* or *species*. (The term *species* here is the Latin word used to translate Aristotle's Greek *eidos*, which, in this context, referred to a formal aspect of a thing insofar as it is available to mind.) All initial sensible *species* are discrete: this particular instance of color, that particular instance of sound, etc. The organs of sense, supposing they are in proper functioning order, are the means by which these discrete forms become objects of awareness. (Pierre-Marie Emonet in one place calls these organs "tools of the soul.")[11] Of course, a range of environmental factors—e.g., visibility as this is affected by air quality, sound ductility as a differentiating property within physical media, etc.—also play important roles in the successful communication and apprehension of sensible forms.

As originating elements in the process by which we come to know, these *species* (again, the term is Latin) have two aspects. First, while they are formally identical with related sensible features of physical things, they themselves exist only intentionally, i.e., as modifications of the awareness of animals or human persons. In terms of their ontological status, they thus fall within the Aristotelian category of quality (i.e., they are characteristics of particular minds), rather than the category of substance. Secondly, they function purely as a means of awareness of the forms of external things (in the Latin terminology developed by Scholastics, they function as a *quo* or "that by which," rather than as a *quod* or "thing which is"). We become aware of sensible *species* only by reflection, never by direct perception. In (successful) perception a person's object is an external substance or one or more of its features, not the form or *species* itself.

Although this basic philosophical account of perception can be stated rather clearly, there arise many concrete questions of great difficulty, both conceptual and empirical. For an exploration of some of these, the interested reader is encouraged to consult "An Essay on Sensation," by Yves Simon.[12]

In addition to the powers of external sense, there traditionally

---

11. Emonet, *The Greatest Marvel of Nature*, 12.

12. Yves R. Simon, "An Essay on Sensation," in Anthony O. Simon, ed., *Philosopher at Work*, 57–111.

have been recognized three "internal" senses: the central or common sense, the imagination, and the sense memory. Some authors, including Aquinas, also note an "estimative sense" (in Latin, *sensus aestimativa*), by which an animal or a human perceives objects as beneficial or harmful. Although this last topic might appropriately be taken up here, we shall defer treatment of it to the next section, which focuses on affectivity, because the estimative sense functions in service of our pursuits and avoidances.

With the powers of internal sense, animals (in something of a hierarchical order, according to the types and degrees of the powers they enjoy) come to the kind of awareness that culminates, in humans, in self-awareness. (An explicit judgment about one's being a self or a person requires acts of intellect as discussed in the next subsection.) With the internal sense powers there also occurs, at least at our human level, what Emonet calls the ability to "breathe above time."[13] That is, through the operations of central sense, imagination, and memory, human persons (and to some degree various other animals) become aware of things as existing wholes, with pasts, presents, and futures.

Like the powers and qualitative determinations of external sense, those of internal sense are apprehended only through reflection. The *central* or *common* sense comes to be recognized when we consider the fact that human perception (by contrast with mere sensation) involves the awareness of objects as "wholes"—this red sweater, that loud trombone, etc. If, as noted above, what comes to our awareness via the external senses is always particular and discrete, how is it that we perceive things as wholes? The answer is that there must be an internal sense that unifies or synthesizes the relevant data and thereby enables us to perceive and recognize things in an integral way. Thus we come to an awareness of the "common" or "central" sense.

The powers of *imagination* and sense *memory* depend on the synthesizing sense just described. Imagination is distinguished by its ability to put together "wholes" irrespective of their existence or non-

13. Emonet, *The Greatest Marvel of Nature*, 20.

existence in the entitative world (we can imagine, for example, the storybook animal called a "unicorn"—or "Jack's beanstalk" stretching high up into the sky—even though we do not believe that such things ever existed). Memory, on the other hand, insofar as it is accurate, has as its object an entitative reality. In this respect it is like perception. Of course, memory is unlike perception in that the object in question is a thing, person, or event from the past. Still there is an important parallel. The English word "memory," it may be noted, is ambiguous: it can refer either to the psychic power itself or to the object of this power (i.e., what is remembered). In the latter case, at least for the philosophy of critical realism, this object is not to be identified with the medium of remembering (i.e., the *quo* or "that by which"); rather, the object remembered is the past reality itself, whether or not the thing in question has entitative existence in the present. Thus, remarkably, when I remember Mrs. Frances D. Carlson, the object of my awareness is my mother (not an image or a phantom of my mother), even though she died over two decades ago!

Our appreciation of the above matters depends on our specifically human powers of reflection and intellectual knowing; indeed, the latter powers condition the very character of our sensory awareness. Many other animals manifest types and degrees (sometimes very high degrees) of sense powers. But they do not have an understanding of them—i.e., they do not know that they know in this way. It should be added that, while our knowledge of the world must originate in external sense, our various and complex acts of internal sense make it difficult to access any "pure" or "absolute" sensory data. (This, incidentally, poses a significant difficulty for any theory of knowledge of the sort identified as "empiricist" or "phenomenalist," according to which all that we know consists simply in additions to earlier, more basic layers of sensory data.) Moreover, the difficulty of directly "getting at" data of external sense is compounded by the influence of our intellectual operations. It is to an exploration of these that we now turn.

Intellectual Knowledge

This level of knowledge, as far as we know, exists within the realm of nature only in human persons. (We of course cannot preclude the possibility of "intelligent life" in other regions of the universe.) Such knowledge involves a new kind of (Latin) *species*, the *intelligible species* which is achieved by the mind through the activity we earlier called abstraction. Another name for "intelligible *species*" is *"concept"* (in the strict philosophical sense); insofar as it is a *universal* (i.e., related to all things that share the relevant intelligible features), the concept exists as a determination or modification of the person's intellectual (rather than sensory) awareness. As with sensible *species*, intelligible *species* or concepts function as pure means—in this case, means by which we come to know, at least to some extent, the essences of the things in question. This is the case whether the things known are in the category of "substance" or "accidents"—or indeed, as we have seen in the case of transcendental perfections, whether they cut across the various categories and levels of being. As with sensible forms, we become aware of intellectual forms or concepts themselves only by way of reflection.

Accordingly, let us reflect further on the results of abstraction, as well as the intellectual activity itself. As indicated just above, in this type of knowing the *species* (Latin plural) are generated and come to exist as modifications of a person's intellect. Scholastic philosophers—taking a cue from Aristotle (see *On the Soul*, book III, chap. 5)—have distinguished two aspects of this operation of intellect. The first they have called *agent* (or *active*) *intellect* (in Latin, *intellectus agens*); here the universal is formed ("abstracted") from the particular objects of sense, either as these are sensed in the present, or as they are retained in memory. (In the case of modern scientific concepts, various hypotheses, mathematical models, and other devices also can play a role in the process.) Once formed, the concept or intelligible *species* is then available to the second aspect of intellect, which is called *possible intellect* (in Latin, *intellectus possibilis*). Jacques Maritain had a picturesque way of describing the interplay of these two aspects. He spoke of there being in us an "'illuminating intellect,' a spiritual sun ceaseless-ly shining, activating everything in the intelligence, its light arousing all of our ideas . . . and penetrating with its energy all the operations of our mind."[14]

But, it may be asked, to what extent is the human mind actually able to abstract and then grasp the essences of things? This is a very proper and important question, one that lies at the heart of the "criti-cal" aspect of the philosophy of critical realism. Earlier in the book, we remarked that much of our knowledge, especially as represent-ed in the empiriological sciences, is knowledge "about" things (what Maritain called "perinoetic" knowledge), rather than knowledge of re-ality as it is in itself and essentially (what Maritain called "dianoet-ic" knowledge). It is the perennial philosopher's hope, as well as con-viction, that—aided in crucial ways by information developed in the natural sciences—humankind can come to some genuine knowledge of essence, including some knowledge of our own nature as human persons. This, of course, is not to say that such knowledge is easily achieved; clearly it is not.

A fuller account of intellectual knowledge would include detailed discussion of the distinction, and implications of the distinction, among "orders" of abstraction as introduced in part 1. It will be recalled that such orders, and thus the types of intelligible objects themselves, can be divided into three: 1) the physical, where the objects exist entitative-ly in matter and only in matter, and can be known only by reference to material conditions; 2) the mathematical, where the objects exist enti-tatively in matter in a "virtual" way, and are known through insight, mental construction, and/or definition apart from sensible matter; and 3) the metaphysical, where the objects can exist either in matter or im-materially, and are known and defined in the way of "transcendentals," i.e., apart from all conditions of matter. Of course, in most actual in-stances of human knowledge, including theoretical statements accept-

14. Jacques Maritain, *Creative Intuition in Art and Poetry;* as translated and quoted in Emonet, ibid., 39. For another excellent discussion, see Joseph Pieper, *Reality and the Good,* trans. Stella Lange (Chicago: Henry Regnery, 1967), sec. I.

ed by the natural sciences, we find a complex overlapping of types of concepts: the physical, the mathematical, and even the metaphysical (the last often implicit and reflecting the fact, noted earlier, that other types of concepts are "resolvable" into metaphysical ones).

Intellectual knowledge is said to have three "stages," the first of which is abstraction or concept formation as just articulated. The other two stages of our specifically human mode of knowledge are judgment and reasoning.

In *judgment*, the mind is said to "compose and divide"; that is, we declare that such-and-such is the case, or that such-and-such is not the case. In this way the mind in principle moves beyond essence, and affirms existence (or lack thereof): "This plant is healthy"; "Oak trees thrive in this environment, but palm trees do not"; "If the spring rains come, drought conditions will be much lessened this year"; etc. In judgment we employ universal concepts in declaring how things stand in reality, whether actually or potentially, whether in general or in the particular case, and whether in the past, the present, or the future.

In *reasoning*, the mind moves from one instance of knowledge (or what is believed to be or accepted as knowledge) to another, or to others. Two types of reasoning traditionally are recognized: *inductive* and *deductive*. In the former, we generalize on the basis of acquaintance with a range of particular instances. Typically, "laws" in the natural or empirical sciences—e.g., Boyle's Law regarding interrelations among the temperature, pressure, and volume of a gas—are developed through inductive reasoning. In the latter or deductive reasoning, certain statements are set down and, in light of logical relations that are discerned among these statements, another or others are judged to follow. Principal examples of deductive reasoning are found in the disciplines of mathematics (e.g., geometry, where theorems are established in light of axioms and postulates). Aristotle and his Medieval followers held out the hope that all scientific knowledge could be expressed in terms of this deductive model, with the primary and most general statements or principles known through a kind of intuition. As it turned out, this form of explanatory knowledge has proven very difficult to obtain; and modern scientific approaches to nature by and large have abandoned the deductive ideal. (A remnant of the ideal remains, however, in the so-called "hypothetical-deductive method," in which researchers deduce that certain phenomena should occur if relevant hypotheses and theories are correct; and in which these predicted results are then tested against experience.)

We have been speaking of intellectual knowledge as it operates in speculative matters—say, the natural sciences. At this point it should be mentioned that there also is "practical" intellect—i.e., understanding, judgment, and reasoning about matters to be done, especially moral matters. However, as with the earlier noted estimative sense, we shall defer treatment of this topic to section 2.3, when we discuss specifically human affectivity.

Above we said that among beings of nature only human persons are known to develop and display intellectual knowledge. But, it might be asked, what about so-called "smart animals"? A few years ago, a story by the Knight Ridder newspaper group stirred considerable interest. It reported on the findings of several researchers into animal brains and behaviors, especially in the great ape family and certain species of birds, e.g., parrots.[15] According to the writer of this story, it has been discovered that such animals "demonstrate a rudimentary self-awareness and can handle abstract concepts." A parrot named Alex, at the University of Arizona, can name more than 100 objects; moreover, says his trainer, Irene Pepperberg, Alex "now understands such abstract concepts as 'same,' 'color,' and 'how many.'" Similarly, Sue Savage-Rumbaugh teaches English words to chimpanzees at Georgia State University in Atlanta. Her conclusion is that, while her charges don't have vocal tracts, and thus cannot speak, "they comprehend very much the way we do." Finally, in light of studies making use of PET (positron emission tomography) and MRI (magnetic resonance imaging)—which show similar patterns of electrical activity in human and animal brains—the Harvard zoologist Donald Griffin be-

---

15. The story appeared in the *Omaha World-Herald*, March 25, 2001; its headline announced, "Scientists Finding Animals Are Smarter Than Expected."

lieves that "levels and types of intelligence in nonhumans form a continuum with those of humans."

In a similar vein, the *Washington Post* reported on a proposal by researchers on birds to change the official nomenclature applied to their subjects' brains, with the effect of bringing the avian descriptions more into conformity with those applied to humans. It has been discovered, for example, that "fully 75 percent of a bird's brain is an intricately wired mass that processes information in much the same way as the . . . human cerebral cortex."[16] One researcher quipped that, in light of these findings, calling someone a "bird-brain" is no longer to be taken as such an insult!

But now let us ask: Does Alex the parrot truly understand the number five? Does a chimpanzee manifest comprehension, or the possession of genuine concepts, by learning to respond to words in English? Our answer will depend in large part on how we take the terms "understand," "comprehend," and "concept." Recent research involving animals has produced some remarkable and hitherto unsuspected results. However, it may be that these results are fully interpretable in terms of the operation of sensory knowledge (including imagination and memory, which of course may be "tracked" via such methods as PET and MRI). Here the reflections of the Aristotelian Mortimer Adler are pertinent. Adler distinguished between "conceptual" and "perceptual" knowledge, and he pointed out that in certain species of animals the powers of perceptual "generalization" and "discrimination" are advanced to such a degree that some of their acts can be mistaken for ones involving genuine concept formation.[17] In keeping with this point, is it not reasonable to suggest that the birds and chimps mentioned above are exercising complex forms of sensory knowledge (and using signs—including words—in the process), but without any involvement of intellect strictly speaking?

16. Reprinted in the *Omaha World-Herald*, February 7, 2005.
17. Mortimer J. Adler, *The Difference of Man and the Difference It Makes* (New York: Fordham University Press, 1993), chaps. 7–11. See also Marie George, "Thomas Aquinas Meets Nim Chimpsky: On the Debate about Human Nature and the Nature of Other Animals," *The Aquinas Review* 10 (2003): 1–50.

A similar line of inquiry is appropriate regarding the anthropologist Penny Patterson and her multiyear interactions with Koko and two other gorillas (which, along with chimpanzees, are prominent members of the great ape family). An article in *Commonweal* magazine expressed some of Patterson's experiences, findings, and opinions.[18] For over thirty years she has worked with Koko to develop a facility in Ameslan, or American Sign Language. By the early 2000s Koko had mastered "at least 900 words" and could "link them up in statements of up to eight words." She even has expressed ideas about death. When asked about "her understanding of it," the gorilla responded, in sign language, "trouble," "old," "comfortable," "hole," "bye," "sleep." Now, no one would question that such a response is remarkable and creative. But the student of philosophy will want to ask: Does this linkage of words constitute a "statement" in the sense of an intellectual judgment? Are the various matters Koko associates with death indicative of the possession of abstract concepts; or do they rather simply involve familiar features of her perceptual environment? (It may be noted that Koko does not, for example, express a concern such as Pierre-Marie Emonet's about death as non-being, or about our status as "Being-with-Nothingness"—which indeed would indicate the presence of intellectual concepts.)

The Knight Ridder story cited above noted that certain researchers "remain reluctant to use the words 'think' or 'intelligence' in connection with animals." The present author would suggest that one source of difficulty concerning these issues is the ambiguity of the words in question. The term "intelligence" can be used as a synonym for "intellect" (Latin *intellectus*), as strictly and philosophically understood. But it also can be used—and, as we have seen, among psychologists and other scientists in fact often is used—to refer to complex behavioral phenomena, but with no implication of there having occurred genuinely intellectual acts as these were discussed earlier in this section. Koko the gorilla, Alex the parrot, and other animals dis-

18. Elizabeth Hanly, "Listening to Koko," *Commonweal*, June 18, 2004.

play intelligence in the behavioral sense. It is not at all clear that they display intelligence in the other, ontological sense—i.e., that they develop formal concepts, exercise intellectual judgments, or reason from one truth to another.[19]

We noted earlier that external sense powers clearly operate via organs (eyes, ears, nose, etc.). The internal senses, or at any rate what we termed the "central" sense, have been rather little investigated in empirical detail. This in fact indicates the need, already stressed in part 1, for greater cooperation between philosophers and natural scientists. Nonetheless, it would seem that all evidence so far available points to the fact that powers of internal sense also operate via an organ—or regions of an organ—specifically, the brain.

But what should be said in this regard about intellect? Does this power too, in its specific operation, work by means of an organ? To many people, it seems, the answer is "Obviously, yes." But is it known that this is the case, or does the answer in question perhaps reveal the influence of the philosophies called scientism and physicalism? In section 2.5, we shall discuss these contrary philosophies directly; at this point let us focus on what we have come to know of the human intellect's operations.

It indeed is true that for intellectual acts to take place the human brain must be in a certain condition or range of conditions. Certain types of brain damage can preclude such acts; and familiar disorders and conditions (depression, anxiety, drunkenness, etc.) obviously inhibit the effectiveness of a person's judgment and reasoning. But this is not to say that intellectual acts themselves are identifiable as brain processes. And, according to an argument proposed by Aquinas (see

19. In addition to the types of cases here discussed, one might note recent studies of "dolphin intelligence." See, e.g., "Dolphin Brains," on Science Update, March 2002 (http://www.sciencenetlinks.org/sci_update.cfm?DocID=76). However, there also have been expressions of skepticism within the scientific community about the significance of animal intelligence research. See, e.g., *The Clever Hans Phenomenon: Communication with Horses, Whales, Apes, and People,* Annals of the New York Academy of Sciences, vol. 364, ed. Thomas A. Sebeok and Robert Rosenthal (New York: New York Academy of Sciences, 1981). (For this reference and that to the article by Marie George in note 17, I am indebted to Steven C. Snyder.)

Summa Theologiae, I, q. 75, art. 5), the universal character of our concepts—according to which they express, as noted earlier, intelligible
features—implies that the process by which concepts are formed cannot itself, strictly speaking, be a physical one. Sensory images relate
to marked-off individuals; thus the process of their formation indeed
is limited by material conditions. But concepts or intelligible *species*
(the Latin term again) relate to realities that are strictly universal; how
could they, or their agent causes, be limited in this manner?

The question of whether intellectual activity is physical also arises in other ways. For example, consider our knowledge of the qualities we have termed "transcendental" and "pure" perfections. Such
qualities, supposing they exist, either can or must exist apart from
conditions of materiality. How could something that is through and
through material come to know—i.e., be related to by form and inten-
tionality—what is immaterial? Again, consider the nature of self-reflection: in such activity the person who undertakes it becomes both
"object" and "subject." How could the material as such "double back
upon" or cognitively mirror itself in such a complete (or nearly complete) manner? Finally, consider the fact that, as a matter of experience, the human desire for knowledge can never be fully satisfied; as
well as the parallel fact that the range of the intellect is, in principle,
without limit. In this regard, Yves Simon says of our power of knowing that it "provides an opening upon the infinite."[20] But whatever is
material is finite. How could an activity that is simply that of a physical organ (i.e., the brain) truly open us to the infinite?

What does all this tell us about the power called intellect? From
the empiriological perspective, the human brain is known to be more
complex than that of other animals. And this complexity doubtless
is part of the story of the genesis of intellectual knowledge. But the
above arguments suggest that this factor alone cannot ground an ad-

20. Yves R. Simon, *An Introduction to Metaphysics of Knowledge,* trans. Vukan Kuic
and Richard J. Thompson (New York: Fordham University Press, 1990), 39. For a recent re-
statement of these types of points by a scholar in the tradition of Aristotle and St. Thomas,
see Joseph M. Magee, *Unmixing the Intellect: Aristotle on Cognitive Powers and Bodily Organs* (Westport, Conn.: Greenwood Press, 2003).

equate formal explanation of the differences between sensory and intellectual knowing. Thus it would seem that the intellect, as a rational power, is somehow non-material. We shall explore this idea after considering the other main dimension of soul as it is treated in perennial philosophy—i.e., the dimension termed "affectivity"—and after discussing the nature and significance of specifically human, personal life in community.

SUMMARY

• Knowing is a new kind of being on the part of the knower: he or she comes to share in an intentional way the form (sensible or intelligible) of another reality.

• Sensory knowledge, which is shared by other animal species, involves participation in a quality that is apprehensible by either external sense powers (touch, sight, hearing, taste, and smell) or internal sense powers (the common sense, imagination, and memory).

• Intellectual knowledge—which, among natural beings, seems to occur only in human persons—involves participation in intelligibilities through concept formation, judgment, and reasoning.

2.3 LIFE OF AFFECTIVITY AND CHOICE

What Is Affectivity?

In keeping with a broadly Aristotelian and realist approach to philosophy, we are seeking in this part of the book to understand personal being by way of our characteristic activities. According to the "great tradition" spoken of by John Paul II, proper reflection upon these activities will enable us to gather indications of our nature or essence. We began by noting that we share with many other natural beings the property of being alive. The word "soul" (Greek *psuche*, Latin *anima*) traditionally has been used to designate the type of form that organizes bodies into such living wholes. Next, we considered a type of activity that we in part share with other animals—knowing.

In knowing, we might say, human persons "take in" being—the manifestations of and, ideally, the essences of things. In the operations that are gathered under the heading *affectivity*, we "respond to" and "reach out to" being. We are affected by and seek to affect the way things are. As in the case of knowledge, the realm of affectivity traditionally has been divided into two interrelated dimensions, the sensory and the intellectual. These are said by perennial philosophers to be two aspects of human "desire," or "appetite," or even "love" in the most general senses of these terms. To put the matter in another way, they are two dimensions of the human approach to being as good or desirable (or bad or undesirable)—just as sensory and intellectual knowledge are two dimensions of the human approach to being as true or intelligible. In our affective lives, the sensory dimension includes immediate responses of pleasure and pain, as well as various instincts, drives, passions, and emotions. By contrast, intellectual or rational affectivity involves the will and the exercise of free choice.

As we shall see, the category of sensory affectivity includes a wide range of phenomena, somewhat as did the category of sensory knowledge. The higher or intellectual modes of affectivity—like their counterparts in the cognitive realm—appear to be distinctive to personal beings.

Sensory Experience of, and Response to, Good and Evil

As noted in part 1, perennial philosophers hold that all beings by virtue of their very being seek certain ends or goods. However, they do not all seek these ends or goods in a way that involves psychic activity. Inorganic beings and even plants act in a more or less purely mechanical way—in spite of such phenomena as heliotropism and the operation of the Venus's flytrap. (Indeed it would seem artificial—or perhaps metaphorical—to speak in the latter cases of, e.g., an "awareness" of light, or a "psychic" response to the presence of an insect.)

As we suggested with regard to knowledge, so also with regard to affectivity, the threshold of sensory awareness appears to come at the ontological level of animal life. To use the language of Aristotle, it is with animals that "sensitive soul," here manifested in sensory affectivity, first makes its appearance among natural beings. Of course, precision in these matters—e.g., an answer to the question, "Which are the most elementary species that manifest animal or sensory affectivity?"—requires, in addition to philosophy, the application of information developed in the natural or empiriological sciences.

It seems clear that, in both animals and human beings, the most basic modes of affectivity consist in immediate responses to physical stimuli that induce pleasure and pain. That is, the elementary forms of goodness are matters of sensation—e.g., the sensation experienced in drinking a cup of hot chocolate on a chilly winter's day. As we may put it, *this* sensation, for *this* person *now*, is a source of immediate attraction and, as such, is a good. At the same level of experience, but in a contrary way, we also have an immediate apprehension of evil (and accordingly we respond with aversion) in the presence of painful stimuli—e.g., when one hits one's thumb while hammering a nail.

Beyond immediate responses of pleasure and pain lie many other movements of sensory affectivity. Some of these have been recognized throughout the ages; others have been identified and described (and perhaps in fact have occurred) only more recently. Further, the many different types of affective operations have been classified by philosophers and psychologists in a variety of ways, in part depending on the thinkers' overall theoretical interests. Such operations would include our sensory *appetites*, or *drives* or *instincts* (e.g., for warmth, food, and sexual relations), our *passions* (e.g., anger and the desire for acquisitions), and our *emotions* (e.g., fear and joy). In some cases these categories and the terms designating them seem rather sharply defined; in others there is considerable vagueness and ambiguity, as well as diversity, in accounts of the matters in question. For example, the term "feelings" is sometimes used very broadly, so as to cover the whole range of sensory affectivity (and even, although incorrectly, intellectual judgments and beliefs). At other times, however, this term is used more restrictively—e.g., as referring to movements of pleasure and pain, and/or to experienced passions.

Let us note in addition that it is characteristic of all modes of sensory affectivity to involve bodily manifestations in addition to states of psychic awareness. One can see, as we sometimes say, pain (or joy) on a person's face. And the various other instincts, passions, emotions, etc., also have typical "physiognomies"—i.e., bodily appearances and configurations that characteristically express, e.g., hunger, or anger, or hope. Of course, such observational cues are not infallible signs of the corresponding psychic states; for sometimes we are mistaken in our "reading" of bodily manifestations, and humans and perhaps certain other animals can dissemble.

Many forms of affectivity—hunger, desire for sexual intercourse, the instinct to protect and train the young, etc.—are shared, in respective ways, with other animal species. However, a higher emotion such as hope seems, strictly speaking, to be a distinctive feature of the affective lives of humans. Members of other species may experience and express something similar—e.g., a dog's anticipation, born of repeated experiences, of its master's return at the end of the day. But when we reflect on the character of what is correctly identified as hope—which involves the concept of a good that is at the moment absent, as well as a recognition that this good is one that might be obtained, although only with difficulty, or through luck, or as a gift—we see that it requires levels and modes of awareness found only in intellectual and personal life. Similar analyses would be appropriate regarding other "higher" emotions such as the love between parent and child and, unfortunately, the hatred between sworn enemies: in these terms' fullest senses they designate types of affectivity that are found, at least among natural beings of which we are aware, only in members of the human species. Hatred, for example, can occur only in the context of, and precisely in relation to, an understanding of the "other" as such. And the type of love mentioned above involves some comprehension of the significance of generational relationships.

Turning to a related matter, instincts and passions can be experienced in diverse degrees, due to a variety of internal and external factors: the length of time one has gone without food; the socially acceptable availability of an attractive member of (in most cases) the complementary gender; etc. Further, specific terms can mark differentiations along the line of intensity. Thus "sentiment" is sometimes used for an emotion that is experienced to a rather low degree; and "passion" is sometimes used for any affective response that is experienced to a rather high degree.

Variability in affective response also can range across species. (Similar phenomena in fact are to be noted regarding external perception, and internal sense—especially memory—as well.) For example, many animals acutely sense, and immediately recoil from, danger—much more so than do typical men and women, at least in modern Western cultures. This no doubt results in part from expectations engendered by the relative convenience and safety of life in modern society. (Recent trends involving terrorists, random snipers, and even campus crime may force us to redevelop and sharpen our "animal instincts.")

Two matters of special interest to the perennial tradition should be mentioned at this point. First, according to Ancient and Medieval writers—and those who follow them today in matters of detail—we should distinguish two general "spheres" of sensory affectivity or appetite: the *concupiscible* (from "concupiscence" or the instinct for pleasure, a generalized notion that is in some ways similar to that of "libido" in Freudian psychology); and the *irascible* (from "irascibility" or the instinct for aggressiveness). The former sphere relates to all matters of direct desire and aversion—food and drink, sex, security, anticipation of natural disaster, etc. The latter sphere involves a person's (or an animal's) psychic responses to difficulties that are encountered in achieving an object perceived as fulfilling, or in avoiding an object perceived as threatening. Examples of the latter type of sensory affectivity would be courage (i.e., the natural disposition so named), pleasurable anticipation, and fear.

The second special feature of perennial philosophers' understanding of affectivity involves what Aquinas termed the *"estimative sense"* (in Latin *sensus aestimativa*). Mentioned above in section 2.2, this is, strictly speaking, a cognitive sense. (Indeed, some Scholastic writers have referred to it, in humans, as the "cogitative [i.e., thinking] sense.") However, this sense—like the practical judgment and reasoning to be discussed below—is more or less completely at the service of affectivity. Thus, for example, it is by way of the estimative sense that certain animals can evaluate a sensible object (e.g., something that might be touched or eaten) with regard to its being beneficial or harmful. Differences in species involve differences in the levels of operation of this cognitive-plus-appetitive power. Our human abilities to "evaluate" objects include higher orders of consideration, as well as a wider range of standpoints, than are found in other animal species. Thus, for example, a person might recognize a particular meal to be sensorially desirable, but at the same time be wary of it because of concerns about dietary restrictions recommended by his or her physician, or because of concerns about safety or cleanliness in the meal's preparation. In us the estimative sense typically operates with some influence of reflective thought.

Certain recent Thomist philosophers—e.g., Pierre-Marie Emonet—have been impressed with the idea, originally developed by existentialist philosophers and psychologists, of what are termed *affective keys.* According to Emonet, these "involve the impregnation of the whole soul by a particular sentiment: gladness, sorrow, anxiety, anguish."[21] One who is operating in such a "key" finds that his or her whole affective life is colored by the sentiment in question. It is important to note that, by contrast with the general approach of the perennial tradition, existentialists typically regard such affective elements to be radically subjective; that is, one could not make any judgments about an affective key's objective appropriateness. As the German philosopher Martin Heidegger put it, "There is nothing determinate in the world over which the human being suffers [e.g.] anguish."[22] Whether the notion of such "keys" truly illuminates our affective life, and whether this

---

21. Emonet, *The Greatest Marvel of Nature,* 61.
22. Quoted by Emonet, ibid.

notion can be assimilated without compromising the realist orientation of the perennial philosophy, seem to the present writer important questions for further exploration.

As a final point in this subsection, we should note that in the case of persons elements of sensory affectivity sometimes overlap with and are interpenetrated by those of rational affectivity—our topic in the succeeding pages. Prime examples of this would be certain of the "higher" emotions. Consider, once again, love. As we have noted, the word "love" in its most general sense serves as a synonym for "affectivity." In another well-known sense it corresponds to the Greek *eros* and designates a complex of psycho-physical passions according to which a person desires to be with, even to "possess," another. But in its more excellent human form, designated by the Greek *philia*, love is a response to the other person whereby we will the good for him or her for that person's own sake—and we do so precisely because we recognize that he or she is another "self." To respond in this particular way (which requires concepts of "self" and "other," as well as of the "good") clearly involves an intellectual, not merely a sensory and emotional, mode of affectivity. Of course, the various modes and phenomena of love often are found together, and can be bound up in complex ways; but the present discussion shows how human emotional response can be elevated through its being bound up with rational nature.

To take another type of example, what we have identified as the estimative or cogitative sense can play an important, if subordinate, role in the formulation of concrete plans of action. The intellect can articulate general principles regarding, e.g., appropriate relationships involving sexual love, or the proper expression of justified anger. But the estimative sense plays a crucial role in a person's recognizing what is necessary, in his or her concrete circumstances, if that person is to develop a truly healthy and happy life related to such matters.[23]

23. See the discussion of the "cogitative power" by Herman Reith, C.S.C., in *An Introduction to Philosophical Psychology* (Englewood Cliffs, N.J.: Prentice-Hall, 1956), 105–7. The interested reader also may wish to consult the website of the psychologist Patrick DiVietri at www.familylifeinstitute.org, which discusses the respective roles of what we are calling

Earlier we stressed the need for enhanced relations between philosophy and the empiriological disciplines. We conclude this subsection by making our own—and indeed generalizing—a suggestion made by Yves Simon. Regarding the Scholastic terminology of "concupiscible" and "irascible" appetites Simon wrote: "I doubt that these names can stir any thoughts in people's minds today, and we shall be better off if we just describe what they stand for."[24] That is to say, many disciplines besides philosophy properly study human affectivity (as well as human cognitivity)—biology, psychology, anthropology, etc. And the shared goal of understanding surely calls for scholars to be prepared to set aside terminological differences—and to seek to learn from each other's approaches—whatever the peculiar conceptual features (often due to historical accident) of their respective branches of knowledge. Such is the case, we suggest, regarding knowledge of the human person, perhaps especially in the area of sensory affectivity.

The Will, Freedom, and Subjectivity

In discussing instincts, drives, and emotions, etc., we have been concerned with the good as apprehended in sensory and, more generally, psychic experience. We now turn to the good precisely insofar as it is understood and judged to be good. Affective responses at this level depend upon and are conditioned by activities of "practical" intellect—i.e., special modes of abstraction, judgment, and reasoning related to the ends of, and the goods achievable in, human action. Such affective responses are said to comprise activities of the *will*.

Here we come upon an order of responsiveness that is—or at least is said by perennial philosophers to be—specific to human, personal affectivity. Somewhat as in the case of lower levels of animal life (e.g., crustaceans), although the beings in question have an internal power to respond to direct stimuli, they seem to have no "estimative" sense enabling them to evaluate an object's potential benefits and harms, so

---

estimative sense and intellect in a person's coming to develop healthy and virtuous emotional states. (I thank Steven C. Snyder for calling this website to my attention.)

24. Yves R. Simon, *The Definition of Moral Virtue*, ed. Vukan Kuic (New York: Fordham University Press, 1986), 102.

in the case of all levels below rational life (i.e., all plants and animals with which we are familiar, other than ourselves), the beings in question seem to have no power by which they are moved to act by a genuine understanding of the good. Such an understanding and such a power of movement are, strictly speaking, intellectual in nature.

Aristotle puts the matter as follows. In human beings "thought gives rise to movement" (*On the Soul*, book III, chap. 10). In one place he even says that rational appetite or the will—i.e., the power that moves us in specifically human or personal ways—is "born" of the intellect. Let us consider how this metaphorical expression can be seen to be appropriate.

At the very beginning of human life, the intellect (in both its theoretical and its practical modes) is sheer potentiality for understanding. However, over the course of childhood, while our powers of sensory awareness are experiencing concrete goods of various sorts (pleasurable sensations, the satisfaction of desires for food and warmth, the loving attention of parents, etc.), our intellect is forming an idea or concept of good—that is (to recall our discussion of transcendentals in part 1), the idea of being inasmuch as it is desirable. (The young child, we come to see, is already a metaphysician-in-the-making!) Ultimately, there forms in our intellectual awareness the idea of *comprehensive good*—good that would be completely fulfilling of human desire. Such good (or, perhaps better, Good) can be called "the good as such"; it constitutes the formal and necessary object of specifically human affectivity. A sign of this is that when we have conceived such a good we realize that it is not possible for us *not* to desire it. The comprehensive good, accordingly, is the ontologically first or most basic object of will. And it is in the presence of this concept of the good as such that intellectual affectivity itself is "born"—or, more precisely, "activated."

But how does the emerging will focus on concrete, definite objects? Here the intellect can bring to the will's attention a range of basic human inclinations and needs, the fulfillment of which will constitute goods for persons, as individuals and as communities. For example, no individual can lead a truly fulfilled human life if he or she does not take an interest in personal health, in the development of nurturing relationships, etc. Again, no society can flourish if it ignores breakdowns in social order or clear threats from beyond its borders. Still, it seems quite beyond our powers to articulate a full account of the comprehensive good. But if this is so, then how (using Aristotle's expression) does "thought" give rise to any particular "movement" or action?

To treat this question, let us take a cue from Emonet and imagine a "conversation" between the will and the intellect.[25] (Needless to say, what follows is not to be taken literally: while there are two distinguishable powers of rational soul, the human person himself or herself is a true unity, not a combination of two "mini-persons.") As we might imagine the situation, the will is highly impressed with the intellect's ability to develop an abstract concept of comprehensive good; and it says, "Show me, please, where I can find such a good, in order that I may pursue it." The intellect, working in conjunction with the estimative sense, reviews a number of particular goods. Each indeed turns out to be desirable in certain respects, or from some particular standpoint. But each also has some undesirable aspect, or what today often is called a "down side"—even if this down side simply consists in the fact that, in wholeheartedly pursuing *this* concrete good, we would have to forego pursuing certain *other* legitimate objects of desire. Moreover, no human person has a natural experience of good that is comprehensive, or completely fulfilling of human desire; nor do we have any natural understanding of how such good might be achieved. Thus, ultimately, reason or intellect must say to the will, "Of whatever end or goal I actually conceive it must be said, 'This is good in such-and-such respects; *but* . . . .'"

Here we come to see that an ontological "deficiency" attaches to any concrete and finite good. When we make a particular choice, this deficiency must be made up by an act of will itself. That is, the will must freely select and attach itself to particular goods, although (and

25. Emonet, *The Greatest Marvel of Nature*, 71–72.

in fact because) it acts out of a natural orientation to the comprehensive good. Aristotle and his followers have termed this comprehensive good—the good to which all other goods are ordered—"happiness" (in Greek *eudaimonia*, in Latin *beatitudo*). The connection here implied between the good and happiness is not as clear in English as it is, for example, in French—where the word for "happiness" *(bonheur)* actually contains the word for "good" *(bon)*. However, we do sometimes say in English that a person is "staking his or her happiness" on such-and-such a good; and by this we seem to mean, as Simon remarks, that in such situations of human choice we "add to the [objective] desirability of a particular good . . . making it into an absolutely desirable good."[26] We do this because, in the final analysis, only what is taken as an "absolutely" desirable good actually moves the will to action.

As in the case of intellect generally, the operations of practical intellect traditionally are divided into three phases. The first of these relates to aspects of the good as it can be understood in its most general features—that is, overall values that can be achieved in, and general principles or norms that apply to, human action. Such moral considerations can be, and ideally are, implicit in (or "connatural" to)[27] human practical intellect. When we pursue an explicit knowledge of them, as in the discipline of ethics, they are seen to be grounded in common and basic human needs and thus in our natural ends or modes of fulfillment. (Recall the discussion of a natural "end" (Greek *telos*, Latin *finis*) in section 1.2). Whether the knowledge in question is explicit or implicit, our moral understanding comes to propose, and our rightly instructed will comes to order itself toward, a set of values and norms—ones which, although quite general, are known with a high degree of certainty. Following is a sampling of propositions expressive of such values and norms: "Human personal life is to be promoted and

26. Simon, *Freedom of Choice*, ed. Peter Wolff (New York: Fordham University Press, 1969), 148.
27. See the account of our knowing moral principles by "connaturality" in Jacques Maritain and William Sweet, *Natural Law: Reflections on Theory and Practice* (South Bend, Ind.: St. Augustine's Press, 2001). Another twentieth-century Thomist, Joseph Pieper, wrote similarly of the "primordial conscience." See *Reality and the Good*, sec. II.

protected." "We should guard the dignity of our personal sexuality." "Children are to be raised in such a way as to promote their becoming happy and successful adults." "Justice is to be pursued in human relationships." "We should seek to know, and to communicate, the truth."[28]

Rather clearly, however, such propositions by themselves do not dictate our selection of concrete acts. There are, for example, many ways to promote human personal life, or to pursue justice in human relationships. And the general norms in question do not tell us what those ways should be in particular cases. Thus, in one case personal life may best be promoted by undertaking a complex medical procedure (e.g., a heart bypass operation) because it offers genuine hope of success and the patient has no other major medical issues; while in another case such a medical procedure may rightly be deemed futile—or not worth the pain or expense—in light of the patient's overall condition. In the latter situation, personal life may best be honored by giving only "comfort care" to the patient (and by arranging grief counseling for his or her family) in the face of inevitable death. Here again the previously discussed estimative sense can play a crucial role in evaluating concrete circumstances and in assessing the likelihood of benefit or harm coming from alternative courses of action.

This leads to the second operation of intellectual affectivity, in which our judgment attains to a concrete good, and our will makes a determinate *choice*. Here we indeed come to genuine particularity; by the same token, however, we encounter variability in results and, at times, uncertain judgment. That is, while universal values such as those indicated above are always compelling, we may find it difficult to know precisely which act will best enable us to pursue a specific value; moreover, given the diversity of concrete circumstances, what is the best choice, or what is morally right, for one person may not

28. Compare Aquinas's discussion in *Summa Theologiae*, I-II, q. 94, art. 2. He points out that the very first—as well as most general and most certain—practical truth is, "Good is to be done and promoted, and evil is to be avoided." This, St. Thomas says, is comparable to the principle of non-contradiction in theoretical matters. (Recall our discussion in section 1.5.)

be the same as it is for another. (This point, it should be noted, does not involve our embracing relativism or subjectivism. Rather, it simply acknowledges that—as a matter of objective morality—judgments about concrete right and good in part depend on factors related to the respective individuals and situations.)

Strictly speaking, the term "choice" (in Latin, *electio*) applies only to this second phase or dimension. For to be oriented toward the good in its most general features is not so much a matter of choice as it is a more fundamental personal movement. That is, we naturally are "drawn" or "attracted" to, e.g., justice and the proper raising of our children. Moreover, while philosophers and others may help clarify the most general moral values and principles, they cannot, on their own authority, "establish" them. The tendency toward these values and principles is given with our sound natural affectivity.

Sometimes the correct moral choice can be intuitively seen—especially if one has developed what we shall come to identify as moral virtues. A virtuous person does not need to ponder whether, for example, he or she should help a friend in need or lie to a person in legitimate authority. At other times, however—as already suggested—the moral choice is not so obvious. Thus we come to the third phase of practical intellect, called moral reasoning or *deliberation*. Here, somewhat as in the case of theoretical reasoning discussed in section 2.2, we seek to discern intelligible relations among values and norms, as well as between these and specific types of moral situation. In this way, we are able to articulate rational justifications for our choices, both personal and communal. (Activities of community will be considered explicitly in the section to follow.) It should be obvious, however—given the variability and, often, the unpredictability of human circumstances—that conclusions of moral deliberation rarely achieve the clarity and certainty found in mathematics, or even in speculative philosophy.

Because the recognition of concrete good is rarely certain, and because the ability to do this can be reached only progressively (and/or, as will be suggested in part 3, with what is accepted as divine guidance), the operation of human choice should be protected by what we may call a "negative right" to *freedom*—i.e., a right, recognized by society, to follow the dictates of one's *conscience*, rather than be subject to moral coercion. That is, no person of good will who is competent to judge should be forced to accept, or to act upon, concrete views about the good that he or she does not find personally compelling. (The cases of children, as well as "psychopaths" and others of doubtful competence, are of course a different matter.) Moreover, no competent person of good will should be prevented from attempting to effectuate his or her authentic human choices. The only exceptions to these principles, the present writer would argue, relate to matters that are crucial for community survival and/or the maintenance of social order—goods upon which all persons rely and indeed should recognize that they rely. (This point will be explored more fully in the next section.)

Earlier we noted that the presence of reason or intellect conditions our affective experience. Similarly, what a person knows or believes about general features of the good can shape his or her experience of particular objects as things to be pursued or avoided. For example, recognition of the value of economic justice within society can, and normally does, temper an individual's desire for material wealth. Likewise, moral knowledge or beliefs can affect a person's reactions in situations that elicit strong instincts or passions. For example, recognition of the duty to protect young people—especially ones entrusted to one's care—can, and normally does, curb a teacher's sexual passions. But the reverse relationship also can obtain. That is, our passions and other affective movements can color our judgments about what is truly good or bad. Because of all this, the human person's right to freedom is accompanied by a very serious obligation—an obligation to develop what traditionally are called the *virtues*—that is, stable "dispositions" (Latin *habitūs* [plural]) of mind and heart that enable us to identify with relative assurance, and pursue with relative constancy, acts that genuinely promote human good, and to identify and avoid acts that would be evil.

We may approach this same point in a slightly different way. The right to, indeed the gift of, freedom—before which, St. Edith Stein says, "even God pauses"[29]—is an essential property of human persons. But even though it is basic, freedom must be developed if we are to approach the good in a truly human and effective way. Just as the understanding begins as pure potentiality or appetite for truth, so the will begins as pure potentiality or appetite for good. Thus we see, once again, that all human beings have a need to develop moral virtues—and especially the ones that, since ancient times, have been called the *"cardinal virtues"* (from the Latin *cardo,* "hinge"): prudence, justice, fortitude, and temperance. For on the presence of these virtues "hinges" the whole of an authentically human, personal life.

At this point, let us return to the notion of free choice, and use it in articulating a key notion in the philosophy of the person, namely, *subjectivity.* We humans speak of ourselves as "subjects" in at least two senses. According to the first, I, like any other being, am a thing that acts or makes a difference in the real order. (For some writers—e.g., W. Norris Clarke, S.J.—to be an "agent" is another transcendental property of being.)[30] But according to the second sense of "subject," I not only undertake certain real operations (as certain molecules interact in predictable ways, or as a trained animal performs tricks at its master's commands). Rather, genuinely human or voluntary acts arise from me in a quite distinctive way; they are a matter of my personal responsibility. I choose such acts and know that I choose them—or, as is sometimes said, I "own" them. Here we arrive at subjectivity, or "selfhood," in its deep philosophical meaning: to be the author of one's own acts.

To say that a person knows that he or she chooses calls to mind the remark made in section 2.2 that a person knows that he or she knows. Here, according to perennial philosophers, we have a basis for the claim that rational affectivity—or action undertaken from free choice—distinguishes our species from all others of which we are aware.

---

29. St. Edith Stein, as quoted by Emonet, *The Greatest Marvel of Nature,* 65.
30. W. Norris Clarke, S.J., *The One and the Many* (Notre Dame, Ind.: University of Notre Dame Press, 2001), 31–36.

But just as earlier we needed to consider the implications of recent research on "smart animals," so also here we need to take account of certain striking reports about affectivity in other species. It has been discovered that crows can learn to use hooks to retrieve bites of food, and even to bend wire so as to fashion hooks for this purpose.[31] Chimpanzees and other great apes have been known to stack boxes in order to achieve a position not otherwise available to them. Moreover, the story of Koko and her mates abounds with remarkable expressions of affectivity. For example, the male gorilla Ndume at one point is clearly moved by Penny Patterson's expression of pain associated with a migraine headache. According to the writer of the article, Ndume "chose" to stay with her, "even though he was free to move on to other rooms in the enclosure."[32] Now, we might well be impressed, even amazed by this display of affection. The philosophical question, however, is whether this display bespeaks what we have identified as a movement of intellectual affectivity. Are "being free" and "choosing" in Ndume's case really equivalent to the psychic activities involved in human action? Or is it not rather the case that here these terms are being used metaphorically, and that, when all is said and done, what is to be attributed to the gorilla is a complex of sensory (including emotional) factors, rather than any genuine process of choice in light of knowledge or belief about what is good? If, as it seems to the present author, the latter is the correct analysis, then the types of affectivity displayed by Ndume and other animals, while very impressive in their own right, do not involve acts of intellect or will.

Earlier we noted that affective reactions and movements (pain, joy, anger, etc.) have typical physiological expressions. It also is clear from personal experience, as well as common language, that certain modes of affectivity are felt in a bodily way. We sometimes speak, for example, of instincts and emotions as matters of "visceral" experience—from the Latin *viscus*, plural *viscera*, for "internal organ(s)." But now let us consider whether specifically intellectual affectivity, and thus

31. *Washington Post* story, reprinted in *Omaha World-Herald* (see n. 16).
32. "Listening to Koko," 17.

acts involving personal will, give signs of being more than, or being other than, physical or organic processes.

The exercise of free choice, as analyzed in the preceding pages, involves recognizing universal moral elements (e.g., values and norms) and reasoning about these elements' interrelations and applications. Further, we have stressed the need for a person to develop moral virtues, if choice is to be consistently well exercised. Now, concrete applications of norms, and concrete human choices, clearly involve a bodily or organic component: the sensory recognition of situations in which we find ourselves. Moreover, at least many virtues (e.g., fortitude and temperance) involve the modification of physical desires and reactions. However, the development and exercise of prudence (sometimes also called "practical wisdom")—by which we direct our moral lives, and undertake moral judgments—seem, like the counterpart elements of specifically human cognitivity, to require acts that cannot be merely physical or organic in nature.

Consider the following case, which may be familiar to readers of this book. Given concerns about traffic safety, there has been developed in this country a widely promoted program in which "designated drivers" are assigned when there are parties at which alcohol is served. The persons so "designated" decline alcoholic drinks that evening—and they do so, we might say, precisely in light of their judgments about a duty to keep one's promises and their commitments to the protection of their friends (and, perhaps, society at large). In at least many cases, it is reasonable to suppose, the decision to become a designated driver, and thus to abstain from alcoholic drinks for the evening, is made in opposition to the promptings of sensory appetite—which in most persons find alcoholic beverages to be appealing. Thus the moral thinking and choice involved in participation in the designated driver program go beyond any mere extension of sensory affectivity. Similar examples of choosing against sensory appetite no doubt will occur to the reflective reader.

Consider, as well, that many people recognize certain moral norms to be universal and exceptionless, that is, to hold always and in every circumstance.[33] Examples of such rules would be the ones against theft or murder—and in favor of working to establish a just society. If one truly understands and accepts such points of duty, one comes to see that, as a matter of principle, certain types of behavior are to be pursued or avoided—whatever the consequences for those involved, including oneself. How, we should ask, could such unconditional moral rules arise from purely physical affectivity?

Finally, let us consider what may be called the "universal reach" of conscience. Many take it as a sign of moral maturity that a person reflects on the goods, rights, and interests of all concerned before undertaking an action. Moreover, social issues such as poverty and hunger ultimately are without geographical boundaries. Thus, to borrow a phrase from Yves Simon, the person of intelligence and good will comes to have "a conscience as wide as the world";[34] that is, his or her moral vision will include countless individuals who are understood to be worthy of concern, but who never have been met, and never have appealed to one's visceral or emotional states. From all these lines of consideration, the perennial philosopher comes to propose that acts of will, or rational affectivity, operate beyond the limitations of the purely physical order—just as acts of intellect also operate beyond such limitations.

In concluding this section, let us return to the idea of the "comprehensive good." As we have noted, once we conceive and recognize this good, we have no choice but to pursue it. Moreover, we have suggested that in its most general features the human good is not a matter of human devising, but is, so to speak, "given" with our nature and its intrinsic needs. But, it may be asked, even with regard to these supposedly essential and universal features of the good, are we not free to embrace or reject them? Regarding any specific account of the good—

---

33. On the question of exceptionless moral rules and their counterpart, "intrinsically evil acts," see Maritain and Sweet, *Natural Law*; and Servais Pinckaers, O.P., *Morality: The Catholic View*, trans. Michael Sherwin, O.P. (South Bend, Ind.: St. Augustine's Press, 2001).

34. On the universal reach of conscience, see Yves Simon's discussion in *Freedom and Community*, ed. Charles P. O'Donnell, intro. by Eugene Kennedy (New York: Fordham University Press, 2001), 28–31.

even one said to come by way of a revelation from God—must not the human capacity to say "yea" or "nay" be recognized? (This seems, indeed, to be the point of the remark by St. Edith Stein noted above.) Moreover, even in the case of those moral matters about which, according to the perennial philosophy, we can be fairly clear (e.g., the value of personal life, the duty to promote justice in human relations, etc.), does not history attest, and does not introspection confirm, that it is possible for human beings to go against the authentic good? While a person cannot fail to pursue what he or she actually takes to be the good, an answer to the question of what that good *is* cannot be imposed on human affectivity, at least if it is operating in a specifically rational way. (Of course, a person can be forced to adhere to certain rules of behavior; but such forced or constrained action will not involve an exercise of free will.)

These points are not lost on authors we have been quoting. Thus Emonet speaks of a "metaphysical drama"—one according to which the human person, having discovered his or her freedom, must decide whether to accept the limits set for his or her own good by God. He alludes to the Genesis story of Adam and Eve in the Garden of Eden, with its tree of the "forbidden fruit" and the human temptation—which of course is actually followed—to set oneself up to be "as God."[35] For his part, Simon speaks of "the terrible possibility of [humans] falling away from the good."[36] That is to say, even though we are able to discover certain aspects of our genuine good, we seem ever in danger of committing ourselves to—or at least making choices under the influence of—things which, in the final analysis, lead in directions incompatible with authentic human fulfillment. A terrible possibility indeed—and also a terrible mystery.

With this, we must conclude our treatment of human affectivity. Table 1 draws together and represents the principal points discussed in sections 2.2 and 2.3 concerning our cognitive and appetitive powers,

---

35. See Emonet, *The Greatest Marvel of Nature*, 79.
36. See Simon, "Pessimism and the Philosophy of Progress," in *Freedom and Community*, esp. 176–91.

TABLE 1. Human Persons' Relations with Being

Mode of Awareness	Cognitive Object	Mode of Response	Appetitive Object
SENSORY			
External Senses: Touch Sight Hearing Taste Smell	Discrete, individual sensible forms (sights, sounds, etc.)	Pleasurable/ Painful Sensations	Objects producing pleasure/pain
Internal Senses: "Central" Sense Imagination Memory	Integral objects of sense, as perceived, constructed, or remembered	Other Sources of Movement: Sense Appetites, Instincts, Drives, and Passions; Emotions	Concrete goods/ evils, as experienced, anticipated, and viscerally responded to
["Estimative Sense"]	Things recognized as beneficial/ harmful	"Affective Keys"	Reality, as experienced via a dominating sentiment

KNOWLEDGE ——————————————————————————— AFFECTIVITY
(Cognition:
Relation to
Truth of Being)

(Appetite:
Relation to
Goodness of
Being)

Intellect (Reason)		Will (Rational Appetite)	
Abstraction/ Concept Formation: physical, mathematical, metaphysical	Intelligible forms (apart from individual matter, sensible matter, and all matter, respectively)	Self-Ordering toward: ends, values, principles and norms, etc. Justice	Goods (and evils) inherent in and achievable through human grasped (explicitly or implicitly) by practical/moral understanding
Judgment	Existence and nonexistence according to modes and categories of being		
Reasoning/ Systematic Knowledge	Intelligible relations within reality and as expressed in propositions	Choice	Concrete acts (personal and communal) as subject to moral judgment, sometimes after moral reasoning or deliberation
[Practical Intellect: Understanding, Judgment, and Reasoning]	Goods, norms, and situations, as grasped in themselves and in intelligible relations		

INTELLECTUAL

both sensory and intellectual, and concerning their relations with the order of real being. The reader also may find it helpful to look ahead to our expansion of the model of natural substance (from part 1) in the final section of this part. There we shall take up in a formal way the idea of human soul as a spiritual reality.

SUMMARY

- Affectivity is that dimension of living beings whereby they are drawn out of themselves, and are affected by and seek to affect the world around them.
- Sensory affectivity, which we share in various ways and degrees with other animals, prompts us to pursue goods and avoid evils as these are experienced through sensation and emotion.
- Intellectual affectivity, or will (which seems, among natural beings, to be distinctive of human persons), enables us to choose concrete acts in light of the intelligible structures of and interrelations among goods, moral principles, etc.

2.4 PERSONS IN COMMUNITY

Persons as Incommunicable, Yet Social

As suggested in the foregoing, a key element of human affectivity is the instinct for *community* life. This instinct, of course, is shared in various modes and degrees by other animal species. One thinks, for example, of colonies of ants, prides of lions, and pods of whales. But there are aspects and dimensions of the experienced desire for community that are distinctive to us as humans.

Let us recall that a feature of the metaphysical subject is "incommunicability." As noted in section 1.4, this characteristic is exemplified across a wide range, from the simple material incommunicability of copies of the daily newspaper to the profound personal incommunicability of individual members of our species. Yet, in spite of the deep sense in which no one else can share our individual being, human persons can recognize others as other "selves." And, with the recognition of other selves comes the possibility of developing interpersonal and social relationships.

In recent decades, such relationships have been studied intensively by the philosophers called phenomenologists and personalists. As mentioned in the Introduction, John Paul II—or Karol Wojtyła, as he was known during his pre-papal years—was one such philosopher. Let us consider some of the themes he developed—quite in consonance, as he would come to put it in *Fides et ratio*, with the "great tradition" that preceded him.

An initial theme has to do with the distinct, but connected types of relations we can develop with other persons. The first of these Wojtyła called "I–You" relations; the second he called "We" relations. He referred to these two types of relations as the "dimensions" or "profiles" of human community.[37] Unlike the existentialist Jean-Paul Sartre, for whom "the other" was seen as a threat to self, Wojtyła held that the only genuinely human response to the recognition of another person is love—i.e., as we expressed it earlier, willing the good of the other for the other's own sake. And the mutual recognition, along various lines, of our relatedness with other persons gives rise to the various "I–You" relations (e.g., mother-child, coach-player, elected official-constituent, etc.) and "We" relations (e.g., family members, teammates, fellow citizens, etc.) that make up the dimensions of human community. Here, it might be said, there emerges what in the Introduction we called "the basis of human meaning in the world."

Specifically human community arises from both cognitive and affective sources. As suggested above, many species of animals display traits of the general types in question: recognition of members of their

---

37. See Karol Wojtyła, "The Person: Subject and Community," in *Person and Community*, trans. Theresa Sandok, O.S.M. (New York: Peter Lang, 1993), 236–52. For earlier personalist discussions with which Wojtyła was familiar, see the works of Gabriel Marcel, e.g., *Creative Fidelity*, trans. Robert Rosthal (New York: Fordham University Press, 2002). For current personalist discussions by an American author, see the works of John Crosby, e.g., *Personalist Papers* (Washington, D.C.: The Catholic University of America Press, 2004).

own natural kind, the inclination to propagate the species, instinctual bonds that inspire acts of faithfulness (sometimes "heroic" in nature, such as those displayed in a moving way in the award-winning 2005 documentary *March of the Penguins*).

Although the instinct for community is shared in some way by all animals, distinctive elements are involved in our own case; for human life in community can be an expression of, and a vehicle for attaining, other and higher personal goods. One important type of personal good is that recognized by the perennial tradition as a *common good*. In fact, the various sorts of human communities can be defined in terms of the respective common good (or, usually, goods) they are oriented toward bringing about and/or preserving.[38] A truly common good is one that is a good for all members of the community, and at the same time a good in which each shares. Moreover, just as the benefit is common, it must derive, at least to some degree, from common action—and even common beliefs. For example, the maintenance of an effective system of justice in a civil society is a good for the whole of that society and also a good for each individual citizen. And the maintenance of such a system requires that all—or the great majority—contribute to it in relevant ways (e.g., through paying taxes to support the system, through generally obeying the law, etc.); it also requires that all believe that other citizens should—and that most do—contribute in these ways as well.

Obviously common goods, as here understood, are ideals; no actual society enjoys, e.g., a perfect system of justice. Yet without at least the shared intention to develop such a good, no genuine communion of persons—e.g., a family or a political society—truly exists.

Forms of Community

Some communities are products of specific human interests, modes of creativity, and choice—e.g., athletic teams, stage companies, and col-

---

38. For an excellent discussion of this topic, see "Common Good and Common Action," in Yves R. Simon, *A General Theory of Authority* (Notre Dame, Ind.: University of Notre Dame Press, 1980), chap. 2.

lege faculties. But other communities have forms that at least partly are determined by nature. That is, while these, too, in the particulars of their make-up, result from human choices, the fact that communities of these general sorts are necessary if central human goods are to be achieved is something about which no one deliberates or decides. In this way, they can be called "natural" forms. According to perennial philosophers, the most basic of these natural forms of community is the *family*.

Following a long tradition of Christian philosophical and theological reflection, but incorporating elements of his personalist approach, Karol Wojtyła/John Paul II proposed that family life is founded on the natural "complementarity" or "mutuality" of male and female, and the natural result of the special mode of love that expresses and enhances that mutuality (the "two-in-one-flesh" union of marriage)— i.e., children. To use the late pope's terminology introduced earlier, the family results from a special type of "I–You" relationship that matures into a "We" relationship (i.e., being spouses); and the latter, given its interrelated, intrinsic purposes—the good of the marital couple and the procreation and rearing of children—is naturally ordered to a broader "We," i.e., the family. It is through the family, spouses and their children, that the deepest bonds of human community are formed, the human race is most properly continued, and many elements of culture (including moral values) are most effectively communicated.

Of course, we are here speaking of an ideal—one which actual families approximate (and sometimes, unfortunately, miss by a rather wide margin). Moreover, it is clear from recent experience, and indeed from the whole of human history, that types of social arrangement from which one or more of the above elements are missing nonetheless can be vehicles for the goods in question. Every reader will be aware, for example, of adoptive families, single-parent families, and "blended" families in which these goods are—sometimes in the face of great difficulties—very admirably pursued. Still, for perennial philosophers, the "traditional" family stands as the natural model and ideal.

In recent decades issues have arisen regarding the precise meaning and normative significance of gender complementarity. Some have questioned whether such an ordering of the genders is a feature of nature at all, suggesting instead that (apart from obvious facts of biology) it is primarily a social "construct" maintained for the advantage of certain segments of society, notably, the male segment. By way of reply, Wojtyła and those influenced by him have sought to deepen and extend the perennial account of these matters. They have argued (in some cases, on religious as well as philosophical grounds) that gender is not simply an accidental and variable characteristic of human persons, and that it also is not incidental to the nature of authentic marriage and family life, as are people's heights, or levels of education, or races.[39] Neither, of course, are being male and being female to be regarded as marking two different species. Rather, according to Wojtyła, in our human case being male and being female are two distinct, yet fundamentally related, modes of being persons. Thus, again in our human case, procreation is not merely a biological phenomenon. Rather it is, both physically and in terms of its ultimate meaning, an organic extension of male-female, personal, spousal love. In turn, procreation—and the resulting project of family life—are significant enhancers of the mutual love between those spouses whose marriages are blessed with children.

Deepened through the insights of personalist philosophy, the perennial tradition stresses that certain human traits can be taken to be paradigmatically male or female. Typical male traits are said to include

---

39. The student may note that in times past matters of race and even ethnicity were, in fact, widely perceived as essential to proper marital relationships. This raises significant questions about how confidently a philosopher can appeal to "common human experience and reason" in developing the present argument, and about the possibility of its being influenced by homophobia—just as the views mentioned above doubtless were influenced by racial and ethnic prejudice. A full treatment of these matters would be pertinent to a book of moral philosophy. Here the author would note discussions, within the perennial tradition, of individual and social progress in ethical insight (see, e.g., Jacques Maritain, *Natural Law Reflections on Theory and Practice*, edited and introduced by William Sweet [South Bend, Ind.: St. Augustine's Press, 2001], 32–38). He also would suggest that, fairly read, the present pages adduce matters of experience that in principle are available to all, and they contain no indication of fear or prejudice related to sexual orientation.

leading, directing, and giving; typical female traits are said to include nurturing, caring, and receiving. Because of this fact (which in various ways affects a wide range of human relationships and undertakings), John Paul wrote that, in their particular modes of being and acting, spouses and parents "mutually confirm one another as persons."[40] Of course, since the two human genders are personal, and their relationships are interpersonal, their typical modes of being and acting interpenetrate one another. Thus, as the late pope put it, in forming the special bond that is the marital relationship, both male and female must make a "sincere gift of self" and be receptive to the gift of the other. Moreover, in light of the individual personalities that contribute to each marital "We," the actual exemplification of traits essential to spouses and parents take very many concrete forms. And, of course, depending on circumstances—e.g., the death of one's spouse—either male or female may be called upon in a special way to develop traits of leading and directing, or of nurturing and caring.

In connection with this perennial account, questions sometimes are raised about the precise meaning and normative force of the terms "natural" and "by nature"—and of their precise implications for an understanding of marriage and family life. This especially is the case in contemporary Europe and North America, where movements advocating the right of homosexual individuals to marry one another have gathered force. In considering such questions, let us note that the word "natural" has several distinct meanings. According to one meaning, whatever is found to happen in nature can be said to be "natural"—as opposed, say, to what is artificial on the one hand and what is physically impossible on the other. In this sense, as is well known, a certain incidence of homosexual orientation (often estimated at about five percent of the population) indeed is natural. However, according to another sense—one bound up with the philosophy of natural being developed in part 1—what can rightly be called "natural" is tied to the intrinsic ends of activities that types of beings undertake according to

40. Karol Wojtyła, "The Family as a Community of Persons," in *Person and Community,* 320.

their natures. In animals and human persons, sexual relations clearly constitute one type of such activity; and it is difficult to see how any serious account of its intrinsic ends could ignore the generation of new life.

Of course, in our human case sexual activity is not simply a response to biological instincts and passions; it also involves personal dimensions that are distinctive of our nature, such as love, mutual self-giving, and shared hopes and conscious choices regarding the future. Moreover, the wider society can be seen to have a stake in the success of human generation and development; thus it is that throughout history, and across cultures, requirements have been set for participating in marriage as a social institution.

Given the above accounts of complementarity and the natural, it will be apparent that the perennial philosophy would not support movements to legally recognize homosexual unions. Or, rather, to be precise, it would not support movements to treat such unions as being equivalent to spousal or marital unions. In fact, from the standpoint of the present tradition, a right to marry is enjoyed not by individuals, but by couples—in particular ones who, by virtue of their natural complementarity, are apt to engender and raise the next generation of society.

It is very important to add, however, that none of the above reflections would support the denial of basic human rights (e.g., to housing or employment) to any citizen, "gay" or "straight." To emphasize this point, let us recall from the preceding section that individuals' experiences and reflective choices in pursuit of their own and others' goods—as they themselves understand those goods to be—must be honored in a civil society, unless it is clear that the choices in question violate, or constitute a serious threat to, some aspect of that society's common good. Whatever the factors that contribute to fixed homosexual orientations, it would be hard to argue that consenting adults who act in line with them, especially in the context of sincere relationships, constitute any such threat.

We already have mentioned in passing the second main type of natural human community: *civil society*. This type of community is larger and more complex in nature. Besides the family itself (sometimes called the basic "unit" of society), it is made up of a number of other institutions, both formal and informal, that contribute to the common goods of the social order—goods such as peace, an educated citizenry, economic productivity, cultural awareness, proper patriotism, etc.

A civil society as formally organized for the pursuit of certain public goods—in particular, ones that could not effectively be pursued by smaller forms of community—is called a *state*. (It should be noted that "state" in the present sense applies to the United States of America, rather than to its fifty subunits.) The term "public" here is used in contrast with "private," a term that would apply to goods such as individual wealth or artistic creativity. Examples of public purposes that show the need for an organized state would be national defense, fair and effective regulation of the economy, and satisfaction of citizens' basic physical needs—including, as most perennial thinkers today would argue, basic health-care needs.[41]

At this point we should note the role within society of what are called "mediating" institutions or structures. Such institutions include churches, neighborhood associations, and organizations of a variety of sorts (educational, cultural, service-oriented, political, etc.).[42] None of these are operated by the state itself; rather, they "mediate" between the state (or smaller governmental entities) and individual citizens. This role can take a great many forms and can make use of informal, as well as formal, lines of authority and communication. Taken together, mediating structures promote the development of a strong and properly functioning citizenry; they also protect the individual citizen—who

41. For a recent exposition of this view by a philosopher and bioethicist of the perennial tradition, see Charles Dougherty, *Back to Reform* (New York: Oxford University Press, 1996).

42. To the best of the author's knowledge, the phrase "mediating structures" or "institutions" was first used by Richard John Neuhaus in *To Empower People* (Washington, D.C.: American Enterprise Institute, 1977). See also the more recent *To Empower People: From State to Civil Society*, ed. Michael L. Berger, Michael Novak, and Richard John Neuhaus, 2nd ed. (Washington, D.C.: American Enterprise Institute, 1996). It will be noted that churches are among the "mediating" institutions listed. This should not be taken to suggest that the human significance of these institutions is exhausted by their socially mediating role.

as a person constitutes an integral and self-conscious "whole," rather than a mere "part" of the general society—from overweening control by the state.[43]

An important principle that pertains to life in society is that of *subsidiarity* or *participation*. According to this principle, decisions about matters affecting the people (available services, regulations governing particular institutions, etc.) should be made at the level closest to the people themselves that would be effective in practice. Thus, while the raising of an army, or the determination of a tax system to fund national priorities, must be done at the federal level, decisions about marriage regulations, or the curricula to be followed in public schools, or, in some cases, the public health-care services to be provided ordinarily should be made at the state and local levels.[44]

In this way, ideally, a whole and integrally functioning civil society can provide for the needs of its members (insofar as this is possible); and it can do so while respecting both the legitimate authority of the state (and other public jurisdictions) and the crucial significance of mediating institutions and the family. Of course, as with our discussion of the family, we here are speaking of the state in ideal terms. No actual civil society has achieved the common good in a perfect way; in fact, a number of societies, and especially organized states, have

43. In relation to the point about an "overweening state," important questions have arisen regarding the relations between the goods of individuals and the common good. How are these relations to be understood? Are there ever genuine conflicts? If so, how are they to be resolved? These questions embroiled even perennial philosophers during the middle of the past century. Jacques Maritain tended to emphasize, as has the present writer, the significance, indeed the inviolability, of the human person. Certain of his followers claimed that, in light of this point (and no doubt also in light of twentieth-century experiences with totalitarian regimes), the good of the individual person is to be favored over the common good. But one of the Thomists mentioned in part 1, Charles DeKoninck, pointed out that such a view would be incompatible with clear statements by Aquinas himself. Maritain maintained a respectful silence about the issue, but the debate raged on for some years. Finally, Maritain's student and colleague Yves Simon developed what he termed a memo of "perfect accord" between upholders of the person and upholders of the common good: when the beings that constitute an organic unity are themselves persons, there will, in the nature of the case, never be a real conflict between the two orders of goods. For an account of this episode, along with Simon's solution, see Michael Novak, *Free Persons and the Common Good* (Lanham, Md.: Madison Books, 1989), 30–35.

44. For a recent discussion of subsidiarity, with special reference to providing for people's health-care needs, see Charles Dougherty, *Back to Reform*, 129–30.

turned out to be quite bad. Nonetheless, the author hopes, the general character and features of a well-functioning society can be gathered from the present account.

It should be noted that states have been organized in various ways—from benevolent kingships to representative forms of government to pure democracies. In view of the characteristics of an optimally functioning society, each of these forms has "pluses" and "minuses"; moreover, each can be most suitable for a given set of circumstances, and each also can be abused by persons in power. Still, it may be said that in a "normally" developed society—i.e., one that has matured according to nature-based norms of personal and communal self-determination—there is at least a tendency toward forms of state in which citizens are directly involved in their own governance. The modes of such involvement must be worked out in light of circumstances—levels of education among the citizenry, economic conditions within the society, the need for a strong principle of unity in times of external threat, etc. But recent perennial philosophers such as Maritain and Simon have argued with great force that representative democracy is the form of government most in keeping with our human, personal nature as ideally perfected.[45]

At this point, let us compare and contrast the above account of life in community with that offered by the political philosophy known as *liberalism*. There are, in fact, several varieties of liberalism, but one belief typically held is that, when it comes to fundamental perspectives on the human person, genuine knowledge that would be suitable for grounding public policy is, in principle, unavailable. That is, contrary to the account developed in these pages representing the perennial tradition, theorists called liberals usually are non-cognitivists (and in fact often are relativists) about questions of ultimate meaning

45. See especially Yves R. Simon, *Philosophy of Democratic Government* (Notre Dame, Ind.: University of Notre Dame Press, 1993). Here, it should be noted, we find an especially clear case of the perennial philosophy (in Maritain's phrase) "growing and renewing itself" in keeping with the needs of the age. Without in any way forcing the matter—indeed by reflecting more deeply on the tradition's profound insights about human nature—perennial thinkers today are able to develop much needed intellectual support for the principles of democratic government.

and value in society. Thus, while they support many of the freedoms articulated in our presentation, they ground them in a different way. Our account has stressed a person's need—indeed obligation—to seek the good as he or she conscientiously believes it to be. But individual choices, as we have seen, are subject to many impulses, some of them unlikely to lead to genuine good; thus such choices sometimes are rightly constrained by well-considered traditions of the community. However, on liberalism's philosophical account the individual is sovereign; thus its notion of freedom would support the legal recognition of all decisions and preferences of competent adults, as long as these produce no clear harm to others. In short, while perennial thinkers may make common cause with political liberals on a variety of concrete issues, they hold to a realistic, nature-based foundation for civil society that is missing from typical liberal accounts.[46]

Is There a Genuine Global Community?

We noted above that, on the traditional understanding, a complete political society is one that is able to provide for all the genuine needs of all its citizens. However, it seems clear and in fact ever clearer—in light, e.g., of advances in communications and the globalization of the market economy—that no contemporary state in fact can provide for all such needs. Even the most highly evolved nation-states, such as the United States of America, are far from being entirely self-sufficient. World events affect our economy; we are to a large degree dependent on foreign oil supplies for energy; as a wealthy consumer nation that imports many goods from cheaper labor markets, we have amassed a huge trade deficit; etc. And while our military power is unparalleled, recent applications of that power have brought decidedly

46. The best known of recent liberal political philosophers is John Rawls. See his *Political Liberalism* (New York: Columbia University Press, 1993). For critical discussions of liberal philosophies from perennial and specifically Catholic points of view, see R. Bruce Douglass and David Hollenbach, eds., *Catholicism and Liberalism* (Cambridge: Cambridge University Press, 1994). For a recent articulation of certain "liberal" themes from within the perennial tradition, see Christopher Wolfe, *Natural Law Liberalism* (New York: Cambridge University Press, 2006).

mixed results. In light of such facts, the perennial philosopher recognizes the reality, at least in principle, of a global or world community, as well as the need for some appropriate form of world governance.

Beyond the insufficiencies of individual nation-states, other considerations ground the idea of a global community. One of these involves what perennial thought (especially as represented in Catholic tradition) has come to call "the universal destination of goods." That is to say, the goods of this earth are not ordained to this or that individual or group—nor even to a particular state. Rather they are ordained to all people of the earth, so that, ideally, all may live a fulfilled life. This point ties in with one articulated by Yves Simon, as noted earlier: the person of moral maturity has "a conscience as wide as the world"; thus, even if his or her own individual needs are fulfilled, such a person cannot be happy while realizing that others' needs go unaddressed.

Moreover—as world events continue to impress upon us—there can be no sure or lasting peace among nations unless there is some sort of world order. (The early Christian writer St. Augustine offered a definition of peace that reflects this very point: peace, he said, is "the tranquility of order.") Until, and unless, the war-generating ambitions and fears of individual nations are kept in check, peace on earth will remain a mere ideal.

Can we—and should we—realistically hope for a world-state? Over the past century, there have been, and continue to be, comprehensive organizations of states. At the regional level, entities such as the European Union and the Organization of American States (the latter less formal and less juridical than its European counterpart) have emerged. At the global level, there should be noted the League of Nations and, of course, since 1948, the United Nations organization. But can any such body truly have governing authority? To many perennial philosophers, the rationale for such governance is clear: the need to secure common goods (peace, the equitable distribution of resources, etc.) at the international level, goods that very likely cannot be secured in any other way. But perennial philosophers, it will be recalled, are "realists"—and no realist thinker would maintain that the United Nations, as currently constituted, is adequately structured to serve these global purposes. A most important and difficult practical question therefore remains: How, until such an adequate structure comes into being (via evolution of the United Nations or development of some new structure altogether) should nations, mediating institutions, families, and individuals—especially the most powerful among these—conduct themselves? To take just one area of concern: How, if at all, and by what governmental or non-governmental entities, can the globalization of the market economy be managed, so as to promote continued growth but at the same time an equitable distribution of goods? Recent studies by social scientists whose work has some affinity for the perennial tradition (e.g., John Gray and David Held)[47] propose models that deserve further exploration.

Let us now ask, as we did at the ends of the two preceding sections: Do features of community as we experience it provide intimations that human personal life is more than merely physical or organic? We should ponder the significance of the fact that incommunicable personal wholes can develop "I–You" relations, and that some of these are transformed into relations marked by a lasting "We." Further, we should notice that, as in the case of individual values and duties (e.g., keeping a promise to abstain from alcohol for the evening), so also at the community level, some moral elements are not subject to legitimate compromise (e.g., the maintenance of justice, the concern for basic human needs, etc.). Moreover, the idea of a "global community" suggests that each of us as individuals, and we together as a nation, must recognize common goods that extend to persons we have never met and do not know as the concrete, existing persons they are. If such goods, and associated moral obligations, are more than mere abstractions or matters of sentiment, does it not seem that interpersonal and communal life must be more than merely physical? Considerations

47. See John Gray, *False Dawn: The Delusions of Global Capitalism* (London: Granta, 1998); and David Held, *Democracy and the Global Order: From the Modern State to Cosmopolitan Governance* (Stanford, Calif.: Stanford University Press, 1995). (I am indebted to Tony Smith for calling these works to my attention.)

such as these, combined with parallel results from sections 2.2 and 2.3, lead to the culminating topics of this part.

SUMMARY

- The incommunicability of personhood does not preclude, but rather provides the basis for, a recognition of other subjects or selves; such, in fact, is the natural and necessary condition of specifically human forms of community.
- Various types of community—especially the family and civil society—are defined and ordered in terms of the common goods achievable only by their means.
- Given advances in communications, as well as the global reach of economic systems, it seems quite proper—but difficult in practice—to think in terms of a genuine world community.

2.5 HUMAN SOUL AS SPIRITUAL

Soul and Spiritual Reality

Let us return to the concept of "soul" (Greek *psuche*, Latin *anima*). It will be recalled from section 2.1 that this concept, as understood by the perennial tradition, designates one of the two principles of natural substance in a living being. Specifically, it designates the formal principle that organizes matter so as to give rise to a being that undertakes vital activities from within—growth, sensation, the affective pursuit of objects, etc. In light of this, it will be noted that soul, just as such (i.e., just as fundamental formal principle in plants, animals, and humans), is not itself a "thing" in the full metaphysical sense. That is, soul is not a being that instantiates a complete essence; all natural beings (including human persons) are composites, whose essences also involve matter—i.e., that which is organized by soul, or by some other, non-animating formal principle. However, as was suggested in our survey of common language ("human being," "person," "self," etc.), the word "soul"—and, even more so, the word "spirit"— very often are understood as designating a being, or an aspect of a being, that somehow is independent of matter. We now must consider whether, and to what extent, the philosophical school of Aquinas can support such an understanding of human soul.

The reader will recall our general method of philosophical inference: from acts or operations, to potentialities or powers, to the nature or essence of the type of being in question. The reader also will recall that Aquinas, following Aristotle (but unlike Plato), was not a strict dualist. Still, in developing the perennial tradition's account of human activities we have expressed points suggesting that a soul of our specific type, although not strictly a substance or an instance of a complete nature, is (as Aquinas put it in his *Disputed Question Concerning the Soul*) in some way "itself a thing" (Latin *res ipsa*). Let us pursue this difficult and important topic.

Regarding activities of human life, two main dimensions have been explored in sections 2.2 and 2.3, respectively: knowledge and affectivity. Further, the desire for community, a central element of human affectivity (and one partially rooted in our intellectual nature), has received its own extended discussion in section 2.4. Traditional arguments, including Aquinas's, for the human soul's being "itself a thing" have focused on the implications of recognizing specifically intellectual powers of knowledge and specifically rational powers of affectivity. The present writer believes that such arguments can be supplemented by reference to specifically personal aspects of our human orientation toward community. Let us recall the relevant points from our earlier discussions.

In our study of the life of knowledge, we saw that concepts or intelligible *species*, insofar as they are universal in their formal objects, cannot themselves be physical qualities or characteristics. This perhaps is most obviously so in the case of concepts whose formal objects are transcendental in nature, namely, "being," "goodness," "unity," and so on. For the latter not only apply to indefinitely many physical things; in principle they extend to things that are not themselves material. Moreover, we suggested that the human intellect's special ability to reflect upon itself, and its desire to know all that is, also indicate that this power is not simply a physical one. The intellect's successful operation obviously requires certain states and processes of the brain; however, those operations themselves (i.e., abstraction, judgment, and reasoning) cannot literally be said to be instances of organic activity. Thus here—by contrast with the operation of the external and internal senses—the soul acts in an immaterial way.

As in the case of our cognitive life, so also in the case of rational affectivity or the will, reflection on the power in question points to the judgment that human soul acts beyond matter and the physical. Unlike the "estimative sense," the emotions, and other sensory movements, manifestations of truly rational affectivity—e.g., the orientation toward knowable values and norms, and the exercise of moral reasoning—relate to universals (in this case, "moral universals"). In all activities involving the will, concepts and judgments about the good (not simply feelings or other acts of sensory appetite, which are related to particular sensory stimuli) are necessarily involved. Indeed, as we have seen in discussing "designated driver" programs, moral commitments can be made and followed that go against the inclinations of sensory appetite. Similar results are suggested by reflecting on our recognition of "exceptionless moral rules," as well as of the global reach of human conscience.

At this level of moral values, principles, rules, etc., we are in the realm of moral essences. Thus here there arise considerations about soul similar to those noted in the cognitive realm. If we accept that certain types of acts, just as acts of those particular types, should be commended and pursued (e.g., the promotion of justice), whereas certain other types of acts, whatever the circumstances, should be condemned and avoided (e.g., genuine cases of murder), then such examples of moral awareness—being strictly universal—must have as their associated psychic power one that is immaterial in nature.

Finally, just as our desire for truth cannot be satiated in this life, neither can our desire for good. In fact, nothing that might be pointed to or concretely imagined—including religious pictures of a "life to come"—can be grasped by us as totally fulfilling of our natures, and thus be intrinsically compelling to our wills. Therefore, since its formal object (the "comprehensive good") outstrips all powers of human experience and imagination, rational affectivity must operate in a way that goes beyond matter.

Reflection on the specifically human desire for life in community (a subdivision, so to speak, of rational affectivity) suggests the same result. As members of communities, we all participate in certain goods—e.g., living, ideally, in just and well-ordered societies—that are not simply reducible to physical and sensible elements. Moreover, these goods, precisely as common goods, relate equally to all members of the community; thus to desire such goods for oneself necessarily involves desiring them for one's fellows. Indeed, in its fullness, the human desire for community requires recognizing that one's own genuine good in part depends on the good of all human beings without qualification. Thus we develop, in Simon's phrase, "a conscience as wide as the world"—a mode of affectivity stemming from universal (i.e., intellectual) judgments, rather than being limited to goods to which we incline by our sensible and emotional nature (such as the physical welfare of our families and local communities).

Taken together, the above points can be seen to argue that all the specifically personal powers of human soul are immaterial in their operation. But if this is the case, then human soul itself—as the source of these powers—also must be immaterial or, what means the same in the present context, *spiritual* in nature. Thus in our type of natural substance, soul turns out to be an instance of spirit. Of course, it is a spirit of a very distinctive sort—one which (by contrast with the type of being called an angel, a purely spiritual being) also functions as form of a natural (human) body, and thus one which is essentially oriented toward composition with matter. (See *Summa Theologiae*, I, q. 75, art. 7.)

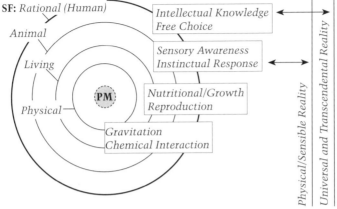

Note: "SF"= "substantial form;" "PM" = "primary matter"

Figure 2. Model of Human Person

At this point, let us recall our model of a natural substance from section 1.3. Here we expand this model by adding an outer circle (see figure 2).[48] The new circle represents the specifying and substantial form, together with its associated powers, of human personhood. The distinctive character of our personal powers (intellect and will) are indicated by the double arrows that connect them, as well as their sensory counterparts, to their respective types of objects—namely, transcendental reality, and physical reality, respectively.

We now are in a position to answer the question Aquinas mentioned earlier: Is human soul "itself a thing"? Like other instances of soul (i.e., in plants and animals), human soul is essentially oriented toward matter, but it also can operate independently of matter. Therefore, in light of the metaphysical principle that a being's acts follow from its essence—or, in the case of a natural being, that its typical operations and powers follow from the character of its substantial form—the perennial philosopher concludes that human soul in principle can

48. Here again I adapt a model from Wallace, *The Modeling of Nature*.

exist apart from its role as form of a human body. (Of course, in its present mode of being and activity, it does not actually exist in such a way.) Recalling additional metaphysical terminology from part 1, we now also can say that human soul, although not itself a substance, nevertheless "subsists," or enjoys "subsistence." (See *Summa Theologiae*, I, q. 75, art. 2.) In this precise sense, then, the human, personal soul indeed is "itself a thing."

Implications of This Understanding of Personhood

The position at which we have arrived can be characterized as a modified dualism—not the strict dualism of a Plato or a Descartes, but one that recognizes human soul to be in principle separable from matter and the physical condition. However, even such a modified view must face a very important question concerning the unity of the human person. We experience ourselves, surely, as unified wholes. Indeed, it is a common argument against all forms of strict dualism that such views are unable to account for our integral nature. Let us consider whether perennial philosophers can respond to this difficulty. Can the human person actually be both soul and body?

The key to answering this question results from reflection on the technical term "supposit" (Latin *suppositum*). As will be recalled from section 1.4, this term refers to the metaphysical subject, i.e., the subject of existence. In the context of the human person, we now are in a position to say that the primary supposit, or subject of existence, in fact is the rational soul; and that the whole person—i.e., the composite of soul and matter—enjoys existence by way of the soul, which, once again, is metaphysically primary. This means that the very nature of our organs, precisely as human organs (whether these are related to nutrition, sensation, emotional reaction, or intellectual function), depends on the fact that immaterial, subsistent soul organizes matter in appropriate ways. Thus, while the account developed in these pages may be considered a modified form of dualism, it takes the integration of body with soul to be complete. That is to say, there simply is no living body, in the human or any other case, apart from the presence of soul. And the integration in question remains complete as long as the individual person is alive.

At this point, let us consider the precise mode of existence of the "pure" perfections discussed in part 1. Although these perfections—e.g., intellectual operations, freedom of choice, developing and exercising virtues, etc.—are features of certain natural beings (i.e., ourselves), they do not, strictly speaking, inhere in a material substance as in their metaphysical subject, i.e., the subject of their existence. Rather, strictly speaking, these features inhere (or can come to inhere) in that immaterial and subsistent soul which also functions as the animating form of the human body.

Here, obviously, we are testing the limits of human comprehension. But additional implications about the human soul can be seen to follow from the above account. Let us consider some of the most significant—and, as it happens, most difficult and philosophically controverted.

First, if the human soul subsists as a spiritual being, it must by its very nature be *immortal*. It may be noted that the term "mortal" (along with "mortality," etc.) comes from the Latin *mors,* meaning "death." We say, accordingly, that for a natural being to be mortal is for it to be able to die—and (what soon enough follows death) to fall apart or corrupt or disintegrate. But in the case of spiritual souls, unlike the composite physical beings they serve to actuate, there are no literal parts—and thus there are no literal possibilities of "falling apart" or "corrupting" or "disintegrating." (Of course, psychiatrists sometimes speak of the "disintegration" of a personality; and moralists sometimes warn against a "corruption" of our virtue. But these expressions are to be understood metaphorically, rather than literally; they express, by way of images, the kinds of "undoing" that are possible for beings of a spiritual nature.) In short, in the case of human souls, there is no real possibility of death.

Let us now ask, What could be the "adequate cause" or "sufficient reason" of an immaterial soul? In the case of the life-principles of plants and other animals, there seems to be no reason to suppose that any forces beyond those of physical nature are immediately operating. (Moreover, when the plant or animal dies its soul or animating form simply no longer is.) But in the case of spiritual soul, the question of an adequate cause or sufficient reason clearly comes to the fore. Could any natural, physical being—or any combination of such beings—adequately account for the type of reality in question? The answer, we would suggest, is No. (Compare our answers to somewhat similar questions posed in section 1.3.) Here, indeed, we see a clear exemplification of the principle that although what is ontologically "more" might historically follow what is ontologically "less," it cannot literally be caused by what is less, in the sense of the latter's providing a fully adequate explanation of its actual existence. Immaterial being—including human soul as we have concluded it to be—can come only from some other and higher type of immaterial being.

We indicated above that the human soul is not liable to die. But could it nonetheless go out of existence? Here the philosophical answer would seem to be, "In principle, yes." For although it is an instance of immaterial being, the human soul is a being that is contingent, a being that happens to be, or, as we earlier expressed it, a "Being-with-Nothingness." That is, the human soul cannot account for its own traversing from non-existence to existence—nor can it preserve itself from the opposite type of change. Rather, it would seem that the human soul (like all other finite beings) ultimately must be "held" in existence by "Being-without-Nothingness." And if it is "held" in existence, could it not in principle also be "dropped" from existence? Of course, as noted above, there is no natural tendency in the human soul toward non-existence, although there is such a tendency in the whole human individual as an instance of natural being, i.e., as a composite of soul and matter.

Can philosophy speculate on the human soul's condition after physical death when it is separated from material conditions? For obvious reasons, such speculation in and of itself provides only a very thin picture. Granted that we have reason to suppose that personal soul does not go out of existence, what basis is there for conceiving its postmortem "state" or "activity"? Here, it might be suggested, we can draw a rough analogy with the condition of "quiescent" bacteria (recall our mention of such bacteria, from which all sources of energy have been removed, in section 2.1). The condition of the "separated soul" may seem to be such that it has no natural basis for or object of activity (i.e., no bodily sensations, sense memories, emotions, etc.); thus, somewhat like bacteria that have nothing from which to draw energy, it may seem destined to be "quiescent" or "dormant." (One may note that the word "dormant" comes from the Latin *dormire*, "to sleep"—and that many religious writers, including those of the New Testament, sometimes speak of the dead as "asleep.") Moreover, from the standpoint of what can be known philosophically, we have no reason to affirm that a human soul in this condition would receive any external stimulation (i.e., that some other being would act directly upon it). Thus, from a purely natural and philosophical point of view, the activity of our souls after death may seem restricted to simply existing—a pale and perhaps unattractive prospect. It is precisely here, of course, that Christianity (as well as other religions that are compatible with the perennial philosophy) can intervene to propose fuller pictures of the "next life"—including, in the case of Christianity, God's granting of the "Beatific Vision" and a sharing in the life of the Trinity, and, ultimately, bodily resurrection and the reintegration of the whole human person in a state beyond all death.[49]

Finally, let us consider whether we can mark in a precise way the ending—and the beginning—of a human life. To take the latter point first, there would seem to be no natural reason to suppose that any human soul "pre-exists" the actual human person. Philosophically, at least, it is more natural to suggest that a human soul begins to be when the actual human person begins to be. But when, precisely, is that? This question has raised considerable controversy, even among

---

49. For a discussion of this topic, see Adrian J. Riemers, "Epilogue: God, the Person, and the Afterlife," in his *The Soul of the Person: A Contemporary Philosophical Psychology* (Washington, D.C.: The Catholic University of America Press, 2006). This book in fact sheds light on all the topics of the present section.

followers of St. Thomas Aquinas.[50] Moreover, its answer can be seen to have implications for many other issues—including public policy issues concerning practices such as embryonic stem cell research. The present writer holds with those who maintain that the most reasonable contemporary application of the perennial philosophical analysis would mark the beginning of human life at the completion of successful fertilization, when a new individual being with its distinctive genotype begins to function on its own.

With regard to the "moment of death," it perhaps should be said that this is an instance of what is termed a "legal fiction." Of course, if it is a fiction, it is a very important one for a range of practical purposes, from the assignment of responsibility in the case of a homicide, to the transfer of property and the removal of viable organs for medical transplant. Moreover, the idea of a "moment of death" has a foundation in reality. For at some point in the overall dying process personal integration is no longer present, and the human body is no longer operating as a unified whole. Indeed, it now is a "body" only in an attenuated, perhaps even metaphorical, sense, for its tissues no longer can function in a truly organic way. When that point has arrived, the human person no longer is alive—that is, human death has occurred. (We say "human death" to distinguish it from complete tissue and cellular death, which typically follows the death of the organism by a period of minutes or hours.)

Turning to another matter—one of special interest in light of evolutionary biology—it may be wondered whether the emergence of human life is the historical endpoint of the process of species development. Some have suggested that there could be (or even that inevitably there will be) further natural evolution, i.e., evolution beyond the human species. In fact, the newspaper story on "smart animals"

50. Some Thomists (as well as many other recent thinkers) have adopted a kind of "delayed" or "progressive hominization"—whereby the human zygote-embryo-fetus takes on a succession of actual forms until the being's matter is "apt" for receiving the spiritual form that is specifically human soul. See, e.g., Jacques Maritain, *Untrammeled Approaches*, trans. Bernard Doering (Notre Dame, Ind.: University of Notre Dame Press, 1997), 91–110. As indicated just below, however, the present writer sees no philosophical reason not to regard the entity as a human being from the time of successful fertilization.

to which we referred in section 2.2 concludes with a quote from one researcher who speculates, "It is possible that we humans are just another step in the continuity of the evolution of mind."[51] Here it becomes crucial to distinguish between empiriological and ontological approaches. Regarding the former, it indeed could turn out to be the case that, for their own quite legitimate purposes, biologists might come to mark a difference between *Homo sapiens* and what they see as a newly developing species. (But of which species would the biologists themselves be members?) However, from the latter or ontological point of view the issue appears to be rather different. For any future biological developments would remain within the realm of rational animality, and thus would involve the same general type of essence or nature as is found in the case of human beings—although in a state that in some way is more advanced than that which characterizes our reality at present.

Whatever the future may hold regarding further evolutionary development, only human persons (among beings of nature as we so far are aware of them) have an understanding of truth precisely as truth; and only human persons find themselves called to seek such truth— including the truth about human nature, its activities, and end—and to embrace it as their own. Further, only human persons understand the good precisely as good, and find themselves called to develop virtues of soul in order to pursue the good without fail. These characteristics of our nature—which can be fully appreciated only through an ontological, rather than a purely empiriological approach to the human person—can be regarded as the natural grounds of our specific dignity and worth. Moreover, the actual achievement of truth and virtuous action might be called "proximate" ends of our nature as humans. (That is, these are ends that we can, and should, directly and consciously pursue.) The question of whether we can specify our "ultimate" end involves difficulties that will be discussed at the end of the present section.

Let us conclude this discussion by noting a pertinent passage from

---

51. *Omaha World-Herald*, March 25, 2001.

our book's epigraph page, taken from *Fides et ratio*, sec. 90. According to John Paul II, when we appreciate the "ground of human dignity" (specifiable, we have suggested, in the manner indicated above), we are able to see that "the countenance of man and woman" reveals "marks of their likeness to God." Of course, in order to "see" all this, we must recognize our proper nature as human persons—i.e., as beings in which spirit informs matter.

Responses to Further Challenges

We now should turn to a further consideration of views we have grouped with scientism, especially physicalism and materialism. In the essay "Purposeless People," Peter Atkins develops his remark about the "omnicompetence" of science and applies it specifically to a philosophy of the human person. As we noted in section 2.1, Atkins, as a contemporary monist, holds that "the characteristically human capacities which we lump together for convenience of discourse as 'human spirit' or 'soul' are no more than states of the brain."

Here we should note the great difference of understanding between Atkins and perennial thinkers on the very meaning of the words "spirit" and "soul." Atkins in effect claims that these words, strictly speaking, do not admit of what we have termed a designative use. Instead, "spirit" and "soul" (accompanied, we may suppose, by various movements of the imagination) function simply as linguistic tools by which we gather together and discuss specifically human, but nonetheless physical and behavioral, traits. That is, these terms have no genuine ontological significance; in a philosophically conscious use of them, we will not even try by their means to pick out a specific type of reality.

How different is this understanding from that of Aristotle and the tradition of thought that follows him! For the latter, as we have seen, the disciplined use of the word "soul" leads us to apply it to the type of formal principle that animates all living beings. Moreover, "spirit" finds its proper use (in the context of a study of natural being) only with the realization that specifically human soul is immaterial and subsistent. All of this Atkins simply ignores. Of course, this in itself does not show that Atkins's view of these matters is mistaken; but it does show that his view depends on an understanding of key terms that, to say the least, is not universally shared and need not be accepted at face value.

We also have seen that for Atkins "consciousness is a manifestation of the brain." He elaborates this point by saying that consciousness "is no more than a fascinating property that depends on, and is the non-linear summation of, the physical states of nerve cells."[52] By "non-linear" here Atkins seems to mean that we should not expect a one-for-one relationship between every datum of consciousness and some state of a nerve cell (or vice versa). Nonetheless, on his reductionistic view, everything real is physical; thus the data of consciousness (including concepts, intentional decisions, etc.) would merely be what sometimes are called *epiphenomena*—that is, they would have no genuine reality of their own (not even, as in the account given by perennial philosophers, as qualitative determinations of human soul). Rather, such data would be incidental features of human experience that somehow arise from underlying activities of the brain—which, for materialists, are the only "real things" in question.

Let us note some strange uses of language into which Atkins's views lead him. For example, in discussing the "self," he says, "I do not see that there is anything particularly odd about a brain treating its nerve endings as its boundaries"; and in another passage he speaks of the "brain's true power of understanding."[53] Here it may be said that Atkins is talking about the brain as if this organ were itself a person! But this surely goes against common sense and common usage—which, as we have urged, should not be abandoned unless there

---

52. Atkins, "Purposeless People," 20. For similar physicalist accounts, more fully and technically elaborated, see Patricia Churchland, *Neurophilosophy: Toward a Unified Science of the Mind/Brain* (Cambridge, Mass.: MIT Press, 1990); Daniel Dennett, *Consciousness Explained* (Boston: Little, Brown, 1991); and Paul Churchland, *The Engine of Reason, the Seat of the Soul: A Philosophical Journey into the Brain* (Cambridge, Mass.: MIT Press, 1996). These authors sometimes are said to promote "eliminative materialism," the view that the whole of "folk" psychology, which uses categories referring to the mental, eventually will give way to a scientific psychology that uses only categories referring to the physical.

53. Atkins, "Purposeless People," 20, 21.

is compelling reason to do so. But so far from offering a compelling reason in this case, Atkins simply assumes that at some future point in time common sense will be shown to be wrong. Moreover, the present author would suggest that the perennial philosophy's account—according to which it is the whole, integrated person (not the brain as such) that "treats" things in certain ways, and exercises acts of "understanding"—offers a reflective philosophical approach that is more realistic than that of Atkins, as well as one that better squares with common sense.

In a related set of remarks, Atkins says: "I claim that the principal activity of the brain, that of sustaining a sense of consciousness through a lifetime, is open to explanation in terms of its physical structure . . . and its chemical activity." Again, he says: "[T]he brain . . . can be perplexed; moreover, armchair brains can avoid unnecessary exercise by adopting easy explanations."[54] As with his remark about "the brain's true power of understanding," such language strikes the present writer as highly metaphorical—or, if it is taken literally, as asserting something that is simply implausible in light of the facts of experience as we have come to understand them. For while the brain's physical structure and chemical activity may be a necessary condition for consciousness, consciousness itself is a property of persons (and other cognitive beings), not of brains. Again, it is persons, not brains as such, who experience perplexity and seek to develop explanations. Moreover, the physicalist account seems in no way to recognize, let alone properly explain, the true character of what we have called human "subjectivity"—i.e., that in terms of which we are able to be "selves," and to operate freely and thus responsibly.

As before, the above points in and of themselves do not demonstrate that Atkins's view is mistaken; but they do place the argumentative burden squarely upon him. And, as indicated in section 1.5, Atkins and his fellows seem to address this burden simply by assuming the ultimate correctness of scientism, reductionism, and physicalism—views

54. Ibid.

which, we have suggested, appear to be rooted in intellectual prejudice rather than careful, reflective analysis.

But if these views bespeak an intellectual prejudice, it is one that is very pervasive and influential. In fact, it should be noted that even some religious thinkers (especially in the United States) have come to embrace materialism and physicalism, as if these views were entailed by the progress of the modern natural sciences, especially brain physiology. Thus, in a volume titled *Whatever Happened to the Soul?* a group of Christian theologians and scientific researchers articulate what they term "non-reductive physicalism"; and they try to show that this account is compatible with orthodox Christian faith. A leader of this group of thinkers, Nancey Murphy, holds that "no new kinds of ingredients need to be added to produce higher-level entities from lower . . . no immaterial mind or soul is needed to get consciousness [from processes of the brain]."[55] Thus her overall view (at least regarding the human person) is clearly a kind of physicalism or materialism. But she contrasts this view with the "reductive materialism" expressed by Peter Atkins, Paul Churchland, and others. (See the works mentioned above in note 52.) On the latter, "reductive" views, the elementary physical components (atoms, molecules, etc.) are all that is "really real"; and organisms, including human beings, have no reality other than that of these components. Whereas for Murphy, the human being or person is a distinct "configuration" or "organization" of material components; and our distinctive mode of organization entails that the human person is, in one important sense, more than a mere assemblage of material parts. In particular, we humans have consciousness and mental states that "supervene" upon our basic physical reality. Thus, while Murphy "denies the existence of a nonmaterial entity, the mind (or soul)," she insists that her type of "physicalism" can provide the religious philosopher with a theory that is compatible with Christian beliefs.[56] For, on her account, the genuine distinctive-

55. Nancey Murphy, "Non-Reductive Physicalism," in *Whatever Happened to the Soul?* ed. Warren S. Brown et al. (Minneapolis: Fortress Press, 1998), 129.
56. Murphy, "Non-Reductive Physicalism," 130–31. For views in some ways similar to

ness of human persons is preserved; and it even is possible that such persons will be "reconstituted" at the end of time (in accordance with Christian belief in the resurrection of the body).

Now, as will be appreciated from our earlier discussions, the perennial philosophy also wishes to assimilate the results of the empiriological sciences, including psychology and brain physiology. However, from this perspective, it seems quite unnecessary—indeed, wrongheaded—to accept the radical assimilation proposed by Murphy and other contributors to *Whatever Happened to the Soul?* For the follower of Aristotle and Aquinas regards soul not as some foreign "ingredient" or "entity" added to the body (as in the strict dualism of a Plato or Descartes); but rather as the first principle or act of the living body, whereby that body is able to carry out vital activities (including specifically mental activities, which are understood as qualitative determinants of the soul).

Moreover, it seems to the present writer that the approach of Murphy and similar thinkers is inadequate from an orthodox religious standpoint. For a purely physicalist account of human reality, even one as carefully developed as Murphy's, makes no room for the continued existence of human soul beyond death; rather, on such an account, the word "soul," if used at all, refers simply to the configuration or mode of organization of material elements that constitute a human being—one that clearly ends with organic death. Could such a "configuration" go out of existence and then, at the end of time, literally (i.e., in its original identity) be "re-created"? On what basis could the newly created person be said to be "identical" with—rather than simply a replica of—the original?

At this stage of our book, we also should consider the contrary

---

Murphy's, compare William Hasker, "Thomistic Dualism" and "Critique of Thomistic Dualism," in *The Emergent Self* (Ithaca, N.Y.: Cornell University Press, 1999), 161–70. For a more nuanced view that tries to accommodate a type of physicalism while making room for the position of Aquinas, see Eleonore Stump, "Non-Cartesian Substance Dualism and Materialism without Reductionism," in *Faith and Philosophy* 12, no. 4 (October 1995): 505–31; and the same author's *Aquinas* (New York: Routledge, 2003), 212–16. In the end, Stump challenges the adequacy and exhaustiveness of the dichotomy between "materialism" and "dualism"—somewhat as the present author has done in section 2.1.

views introduced as historicism or progressivism and secularism. According to the first pair of views, later forms of thought always and perhaps even inevitably supersede earlier ones, to the general benefit of humankind as it proceeds through history. In just this sense, the later forms of thought can be said, according to historicists, to be "truer" or "better" than the earlier ones.

Now, it is important to recognize that there is a kernel of truth in historicism and progressivism. Our scientific (primarily empiriological) knowledge of the world, and the technological control of processes and events that such knowledge makes possible, indeed has steadily improved. Natural philosophy itself, while it focuses on speculative rather than practical matters, has made certain parallel advances partially under the tutelage of the positive sciences. (Several such advances were mentioned in part 1—e.g., an improved understanding of the types of causal factors involved in processes of sense perception and the transmission of heat.) Moreover, we should recall Maritain's general characterization of "perennial philosophy" as "involv[ing] a fundamental need, inherent in its very being, to grow and renew itself." In light of this, we should expect our knowledge, including our philosophical knowledge, to manifest a "progressive" dimension.

However, as John Paul II and the "great tradition" would insist, knowledge or understanding also requires a secure anchor in being. And insight into being as such is considerably less subject to change with the times than is insight into empiriological matters. Hence, at least within the school of St. Thomas Aquinas, new expressions of fundamental themes (e.g., Maritain's discussions of the "intuition of being") are matters of growth and development—or of more accurate and more illuminating articulation—rather than matters in which earlier claims to knowledge are rejected and replaced.

The idea of an anchor in real being is precisely what is missing in historicism and progressivism. In light of this, a line from *Fides et ratio* that appears on our epigraph page seems especially relevant: "It should never be forgotten that the neglect of being inevitably leads to losing touch with objective truth. . . ." (sec. 89). Now, a relative lack of concern for objective truth may be acceptable in some areas of rational thought (e.g., in making use of alternative models involving "waves" vs. "particles" in interpretations of the physics of light); however, such an attitude clearly is unacceptable in speculative philosophy. For in this discipline, as will be recalled, the aim is precisely to articulate "how things ultimately are."

Regarding secularism, let us first recall that this view is to be distinguished from recognition of the proper secularity of the temporal order, as takes place in American and other forms of government influenced by modern European thought. Such recognition entails, in particular, that public policy proposals be discussed in terms that are available to all, regardless of their religious beliefs or lack thereof. (Of course, there sometimes arise debates as to whether particular discussions—e.g., concerning legislation to restrict the practice of abortion—in fact do turn on religious perceptions.) But secularism, properly so called, holds that there simply is no place in human thinking for belief in a non-material and non-temporal order; and that the focus of all should be restricted to what is called the "real world"—i.e., this temporal world.[57] Such a secularist view will seem overly narrow to one who has profited from an encounter with the perennial tradition; for, while it recognizes the intrinsic, natural sources of interpersonal and community relations, this tradition nonetheless regards those sources as stemming in the final analysis from an order that transcends this world. For this reason, the type of political freedom or liberty supported by perennial philosophy is not an unlimited one; rather, as noted in section 2.4, it is ordered to and at times constrained by the society's common good. This latter in turn is a participation in a higher good.

Earlier we noted that no object that is concretely imaginable can satisfy our profoundest desire for the good. Recognition of this fact leads to a consideration of questions about the "meaning of life" and our ultimate human "destiny"—questions that, throughout the ages, have occupied philosophers and religious thinkers, as well as produc-

57. See, e.g., John R. Searle, *Mind, Language, and Society: Doing Philosophy in the Real World* (New York: Basic Books, 1998).

ers of literature, film, and other genres within popular culture.[58] (Recall the discussion of the latter in section 2.1.) According to the perennial philosophy, we in fact can specify certain most general features of our good, e.g., the pursuit of truth, and positive participation in community. Moreover, we can see that certain values, e.g., a respect for persons, are such that we cannot achieve the ultimate good without them. And we can see that other values—or, rather, disvalues, e.g., a lack of concern about the effects of one's actions on other people—are incompatible with authentic human fulfillment. However, when we seek to move beyond such general understandings, we must ask: Does human experience provide a basis for confidence about our ability to know and successfully pursue the "ultimate" good? Is it not rather the case that, from a purely natural point of view, our final end or goal seems both impossible adequately to specify and doubtfully attainable in fact? Moreover, what are we to make of the persistent human tendency, noted by Emonet and Simon, to choose against what we understand to be genuinely good?

The upshot of our discussion is that, while we have offered a rather thorough elucidation of the human person, and in particular of human soul or spirit, certain ultimate questions are, finally, matters of deep mystery: What is the nature of the comprehensive good, or of our final end as human persons? How are we to articulate the transcendental properties (goodness, intelligibility, unity, beauty) as these are present in our specific kind of being? What sort of reality must be enjoyed by a being capable of bringing into existence spiritual souls? What, if anything, provides ultimate significance to human life; and how, if at all, is it possible for us to achieve our final end? These mysteries, it should be emphasized, are "natural" ones; that is, they arise from purely philosophical reflection—i.e., reflection that makes use only of resources that in principle are available to all human thinkers. Of course, Christian philosophers (as well as philosophers from certain other religious

58. See, e.g., the anthology *The Meaning of Life,* ed. E. D. Klemke (New York: Oxford University Press, 1999). For reflections from the standpoint of the perennial tradition, see Joseph Owens, C.Ss.R., *Human Destiny: Some Problems for Catholic Philosophy* (Washington, D.C.: The Catholic University of America Press, 1985).

traditions) believe that these natural mysteries in the end are supplemented by "supernatural" ones—i.e., ones that break in upon us, so to speak, from "outside" the realm of natural human thought. Supernatural mysteries, of course, can be recognized and accepted as such only as matters of faith, and as coming by way of some sort of revelation from what we have termed "Absolute Being."

Thus, as we conclude our reflections on human, personal reality, we once again are led to the question of God—and, indeed, the question of a possible communication from God. It is to these large and difficult questions that we shall turn in part 3.

SUMMARY

• Discussions in the preceding sections support the view that rational soul is immaterial; moreover, if such soul is immaterial, it is spiritual in nature and not subject to mortality.

• Regarding the ultimate state of the human person, religious visions—e.g., of resurrection and a life to come—can, for the person of faith, supplement what otherwise is a very thin philosophical picture.

• Physicalism has been argued to be inadequate to a philosophical reflection on experience; similarly, progressivism and secularism, while being influential cultural movements, lack an intrinsic intellectual grounding.

QUESTIONS FOR REFLECTION (PART 2)

1. In the Introduction, we noted John Paul II's opinion that there is a common sense or "implicit" philosophy, which includes "the concept of the person as a free and intelligent subject." What evidence would seem to count for or against this opinion of the late pope? Do you think there is a common sense philosophy about our nature as persons? Explain.

2. Explain the perennial philosophy's concept of soul (Greek *psuche*, Latin *anima*). To what extent does the soul/matter (i.e., form/matter) distinction of Aristotle and his tradition seem similar to or different from the dualistic soul/body distinction of Plato or Descartes? Would some sort of

materialism seem to be the only real alternative to strict dualism; or does the perennial philosophy provide a genuine middle ground? Discuss.

3. Is it obvious today that there is a fundamental ontological distinction between the living and the non-living? Does it seem correct to say that natural being manifests three general levels of life (vegetative, sensitive, and rational), and that therefore we should recognize three levels of life-principle? Explain.

4. How, for the Thomist school, is the act of knowing an enhancement of a person's being? Explain, with examples, the distinction between "entitative" and "intentional" being. Some might argue that this approach to knowledge requires the use of a single term (English "form," Latin *species*, or Greek *eidos*) to designate two different types of "thing"—the form or nature in the external being, and the form or nature as expressed in the concept. *Are* these different types of thing? Discuss.

5. According to the perennial philosophy, what is the distinction between sense knowledge (including knowledge as organized by the internal senses) and intellectual knowledge? In light of recent research on "smart animals," discuss whether acts reliably attributed to other species suggest that some of them in fact should be thought to share in intellectual knowledge.

6. How do Aquinas and his followers mark a difference between the whole range of acts of "sensitive" appetite, and those of "rational" appetite or will? Does it seem correct to say that every human person by nature has the power of freedom, however much or little it has been developed? Does it seem correct to say that no other species of our acquaintance manifests this power? Why or why not?

7. Explain the notion of common good, by contrast with individual good. What does it mean to say that there is a natural basis for certain forms of human community? Take one of the following projects and discuss whether the perennial philosophy can make a positive contribution to it: a) articulating the nature and significance of family life, while maintaining the dignity of all persons, regardless of sexual orientation; b) identifying the basis for, as well as the prospects for implementing, the idea of a world community.

8. Explain the Thomist argument that the soul is "itself a thing" and in fact subsists as a spiritual form. In light of our metaphysical account of

subsistence in part 1, discuss how well the proper unity of the human being can be accounted for on this approach.

9. Imagine a discussion on the nature of the human person between a perennial philosopher and Peter Atkins. How would the former challenge Atkins's statements about "soul" and "spirit," and how well could Atkins respond?

10. In what ways might the perennial philosophy draw on themes from progressivism; and in what ways must it oppose this movement? What would a secularist philosopher say about the account of human reality outlined in section 2.5—and how might a perennial philosopher respond? Which side would seem to have the better of the argument? Explain.

PART 3

GOD — BEING'S SOURCE
AND END

3.1 REASONING TO GOD?

Nature and Possibilities of Demonstration

Near the end of each of the preceding parts, lines of thought related to traditional ideas of God suggested themselves. In section 1.5, we came to the idea of Absolute Being, which might provide an ultimately satisfactory explanation of the being of our experience. In section 2.5, we speculated about a Being that (or Who) might answer the deepest mysteries of our human, personal being. At this point in our inquiry, questions about God become the formal subject matter of our investigation. As a preliminary exercise, let us follow our practice of considering certain points about language. In particular, let us clarify a number of terms used in discussions of belief in God, or in gods. These terms are "theism," "monotheism" and "polytheism," "pantheism," and "deism," as well as "atheism" and "agnosticism."

"*Theism*" (from the Greek *theos*, for "God") refers to any position holding that there is a God of the general sort referred to in the classical religious writings of the West: that is, a creator and sustainer of the universe. For the traditions of Judaism, Christianity, and Islam, this God is also a personal God Who enters into communication and other relations with humankind. It should be noted, however, that philosophers who profess no religious faith also can be theists; the latter typically hold to the "creating" and "sustaining" aspect of theism, but not to the "communicating" or "relating" aspect.

Theism is sometimes divided into *monotheism* and *polytheism*, with the specifying elements stemming from the Greek words for "one" and "many," respectively. Thus "monotheism" is a more spe- 1 god cific term for "theism," as we have characterized it above, whereas "polytheism" means a belief in many gods—a belief quite different

185

from those of the principal Western traditions, but represented (or so it appears at first sight) in, e.g., Hinduism.

"*Pantheism*" and the closely related "*panentheism*" refer to positions that differ from standard forms of theism in the following way: whereas theists hold that God exists independently of the world, pantheists and panentheists in some way identify God with the world, either by saying that the whole world just is God, or that God exists in and through the world.

The philosophical view called "*deism*" typically refers to a vague belief in a creator, along with an assumption that, having initiated the world, this God now has no direct relations with it. (It is of interest to note that, while a number of the founders of the American republic were devout Christians, a number of others—including, apparently, Thomas Jefferson—were deists.)

"*Atheism*" and "*agnosticism*" refer, respectively, to the position that there is no God, and to the position that the question of whether there is a God simply cannot be addressed in such a way as to warrant either belief or unbelief.

Now let us ourselves take up the question of God's existence and, more particularly, the question of whether God's existence can be brought to light philosophically—that is, by rational reflection and argument rooted in common human experience. In order to pursue this difficult matter, we need to consider certain points of logic—specifically, points about the nature and possibilities of rational proof, or what technically is called "demonstration."

We begin with the notion of an *argument*. An argument is a process of reasoning whereby a conclusion is proved or rendered probable on the basis of other propositions—ideally ones that are better grounded. As noted in section 2.2, processes of reasoning can be divided into two broad categories: inductive and deductive. In the case of inductive arguments, the supporting propositions are well-formulated summaries of experience. Here one begins with individual cases and generalizes to probable (perhaps increasingly probable) statements. In the case of deductive arguments, the supporting propositions (called *premises*) are ones said by proponents of the argument to lead to the conclusion necessarily; that is, it is claimed that if the premises are true, then, by proper reasoning, the conclusion also must be true. The premises themselves may be accepted on a variety of grounds: e.g., as resulting from prior deductions, or as known or believed on the basis of *experience, insight,* and/or *definition.* (In this context, "experience" refers to sensory data and other matters of direct awareness; "insight" refers to the result of a philosophical inquiry into the essence of a thing; and "definition" refers either to the adequate formulation of an essence, sometimes called a "real" definition, or to an account of a term that is acceptable for practical purposes but does not attempt to express an essence, sometimes called a "verbal" definition.) Alternatively, the premises may be treated as hypotheses or simply "accepted for purposes of discussion"—that is, they may be accepted for the sake of seeing what, if anything, can be deduced from them.

Typically, and regularly within the perennial tradition, arguments for God's existence are deductive in form, and their premises are arrived at via what is claimed to be genuine insight or real definition.

In assessing a deductive argument, two factors need to be considered: (1) the quality of its premises, and (2) the supposed relationship between its premises (taken together) and its conclusion. To begin with the latter, if the conclusion logically follows from the premises—that is, if it is the case that if (all) the premises are true then the conclusion must be true, the argument is said to be "valid." (*Validity*, in this technical sense, is thus a formal matter: it depends on logical relations between premises and conclusion, or logical relations among the terms appearing in premises and conclusion, rather than on any aspect of propositional content.) If, in addition, the premises indeed are true, the argument is said to be "sound." Thus *soundness* involves success on each of the two counts and is the goal of deductive reasoning: having both validity and true premises, a sound argument yields a conclusion that is, of necessity, true.

The idea of formal *demonstration*, as understood in philosophy, relates to a species of sound deductive argument. Such an argument will be a genuine demonstration, or a strict proof of its conclusion, if its form is actually seen to be valid, and if its premises are actually known to be true (not, for example, simply believed or accepted as hypotheses, or grasped on the basis of prior deductions—unless the premises of those prior deductions themselves ultimately are rooted in insights into essence).

The possibility of achieving demonstrations indicates the power—at least in principle—of deductive argumentation. If something is demonstrated or proven in the strict sense, the conclusion expressing it both is true and is known with certainty to be true.

Since the Middle Ages, logicians have distinguished between demonstrations of two types: *"quia"* demonstrations, and *"propter quid"* demonstrations. The former establish with certainty the truth of a conclusion, without displaying the ontological reason for this truth; the latter demonstrate both the truth itself and the related ontological reason. ("Ontological reason" here means the reason for the being of the thing, not the reason for our knowledge of it.) A little reflection will show that—and why—any demonstration of the existence of God would have to be of the *quia* sort: a *propter quid* demonstration of God's existence would require direct knowledge of God's "sufficient reason"; and this in turn would require a direct acquaintance with or intuition of God's essence—something that no one, at least no one in the perennial philosophical tradition, claims to have. (However, certain "properties" or ways of speaking about God can be deduced as "corollaries" from the content of conclusions arrived at by demonstrations *quia*; this point will be explored in section 3.2.)

Let us now consider what should be said in the case of a deductive argument that is not sound, or in a case in which we are not sure whether the argument is sound. Here we cannot know demonstrably—or, rather, we cannot know demonstrably by means of the argument in question—that the conclusion is true. Notice that the fact that a deductive argument is not sound does not entail that the conclusion is false. For the conclusion may be subject to proof by some other rational argument; or it may be accepted (as, after all, the great majority of everyday statements are) as a matter of belief or faith. (The nature and status of statements accepted on the basis of specifically religious faith require special treatment, which will be undertaken later in this part.)

We also should consider the possibility—indeed, in this area of concern the likelihood—that people will disagree as to whether an argument is sound, or whether it constitutes a strict demonstration. Here again certain notions developed in the Medieval period remain helpful today. Aquinas spoke of propositions *per se nota* or "knowable through themselves"—i.e., knowable through an understanding of the essences represented by the terms in the proposition. Such propositions ultimately guarantee all demonstrative knowledge. But Aquinas also distinguished between a proposition's being per se knowable "in itself" *(in se)* and per se knowable "to us" *(quoad nos)*. Propositions knowable in themselves may, for a variety of reasons, not be known to or appreciated by us; or, more frequently, such propositions may be known to, or appreciated by, only certain individuals—those who have made sufficient progress in the relevant discipline (mathematics, say, or—as in the present case—speculative philosophy).

In light of the above, we come to see that an argument may be sound—indeed it may constitute a demonstration—although it can be seen to be sound by only a few. Of course, for us to responsibly claim that we have demonstrative knowledge requires that we be confident that the stringent conditions for proof are fulfilled in our own case. On the other hand, unless one can see that, and why, a particular argument is not sound, the fact that it does not constitute a proof for that person does not mean that it cannot genuinely be a proof or demonstration for someone else; for the other may have deeper or more accurate insight into the relevant matters. Many people find this point to be a source of consternation; however, for better or worse, such is the actual condition of human reasoning.

Catholic tradition historically has maintained that God's existence in fact can be demonstrated. In the nineteenth century, Vatican Council I (alluded to in John Paul II's *Fides et ratio*)[1] clearly affirmed

1. See John Paul II, *Fides et ratio*, secs 8–9 and notes 6–7.

this. And no document of Vatican Council II or of the recent pontificates has implied that the teaching is to be set aside. Interestingly, however, the Catholic Church has never declared that any particular argument in fact is a genuine proof of the existence of God. Rather, it simply maintains that such a demonstration is possible for the human mind, and then leaves it to interested philosophers and philosophically minded theologians to articulate and assess individual arguments—knowing that, in a matter of such theoretical difficulty and personal significance, it is unlikely that all (or even very many) will fully appreciate and embrace any such reasoning, even if it in fact is sound.

The "Poverty" of Natural Being

We noted above that a demonstration of the existence of God will need to be of the *quia* sort. That is, such an argument will have true premises and will validly lead to the conclusion that God exists, but it will not attempt to disclose the ontological reason for God's existence. This, and indeed all matters regarding the nature of God, must remain shrouded in mystery—except insofar as God should choose to reveal something of them to us. (Even then, as we shall discuss in section 3.5, the points revealed would occupy the realm of specifically religious mystery.) But how are we to begin what might constitute even a *quia* proof of God?

We saw in the Introduction that John Paul II pointed to common sense as a "reference point" for formal philosophical inquiries. And, in the present area of inquiry, common sense provides helpful suggestions. Yves Simon articulated the matter as follows: "Genuine metaphysicians . . . recognize, in totally unsophisticated reasonings, the essence of [genuinely demonstrative] reasonings." In such cases, common "images . . . can be used as symbolic of ontological concepts," and they can express in a moving if imprecise way the essential content of a philosophical understanding. By way of example, Simon referred to an "old sailor" who "used to say that at sea, far away from any land, man knows that he is a very small thing, and thinks of God." Here the "image of . . . smallness symbolizes the insufficiency of the things of this world."[2] For the philosopher it is the latter term, "insufficiency," that more accurately expresses the key insight, one that needs to be disengaged from the imagery of common sense. However, even in this disengaged state, the philosophical understanding retains a link to that of common sense.

In a somewhat similar vein, Pierre-Marie Emonet spoke of the "'ontological' poverty of things."[3] The term "poverty" here refers to the common status of all limited beings precisely insofar as they are limited. This common status, as we shall see, is manifested through a variety of real features of the world of our experience. In reflecting on these features, the philosopher—who of course is a limited being himself or herself—begins to think of Being that is Unlimited.

When one reads through the imagery or symbolism involved in people's common sense musings about the world and God (e.g., a sense of our smallness, or of our relative inability to control the forces of the universe, etc.), it is precisely this concept of the insufficiency or poverty of natural—including human—being that most accurately represents the substance of those musings. As Simon put it, the "logical structure" of the various reasonings, in common sense as well as in philosophy, is the same. "It all boils down to an experience of a reality so unachieved that it would be foreclosed from existence if it were not given existence by a Being whose plenitude both corresponds to whatever plenitude is found in this reality and contrasts with its unachievement."[4]

The above discussion may recall to the reader's mind the term "Being-with-Nothingness," which was introduced at the end of part I. In coming to realize that all of finite being might be construed under this concept, we also began to speculate in terms of the contrasting concept, that of a Being that would not be insufficient in this way. As we now might put it, one of the "poverties" of finite being (our spe-

2. Simon, *Freedom of Choice*, 88–89.

3. Emonet, *God Seen in the Mirror of the World*, 1.

4. Simon, *Freedom of Choice*, 90. (Simon died at age 58 and did not complete a treatise on the philosophy of God. But remarks such as the one just quoted indicate the direction of his thinking—a direction we are seeking to follow.)

cifically personal finite being included) is that such being is unable—is insufficient in and of itself—to account for its own existence, and thus that it is, at any moment, liable to go out of existence. As Emonet remarked, "(natural) beings have nothing in themselves, in their own essence, to draw them up from nothingness and thereupon to sustain them above it."[5] Here we come upon a very deep philosophical fact, reflection on which can lead reason to conclude to the existence of another type of Being altogether—a type of Being that is not liable to go out of existence, and a type of Being on which the relatively impoverished beings of our world utterly depend as Source of their being. Such Being would rightly be thought of as "Being-without-Nothingness."

As we shall see in the pages that follow, reflection of this sort (if not in these specific terms) is to be found in the work of St. Thomas, who used it in developing brief sketches of five arguments for the existence of God.

Aquinas's Specific Arguments for God

For St. Thomas, the proposition "God exists" is per se knowable in itself, but it is not per se knowable to any human being. That is, if anyone truly understood God's essence, he or she would see by way of that very essence that God exists, and indeed exists of necessity. But, says Aquinas, no one—at least in this life—understands the essence of God. Thus he rejects as impossible all efforts of the sort called "ontological arguments" for God, such as were developed by St. Anselm in the eleventh century, and by a number of other thinkers down to the present day.[6] Anselm in particular had argued that our idea of God can be expressed as "that than which nothing greater can be conceived," and that on this basis alone we can come to see that God must exist. For anything, even if called "God," that does not exist would be such that a greater *can* be conceived—i.e., a being, perhaps just like the first, except that it does exist—and this latter being, in fact, will be

5. Emonet, *God Seen in the Mirror of the World*, 4–5.
6. For Anselm's argument, see *Proslogion*, parts I–III. For Aquinas's critique, see *Summa Theologiae*, I, q. 2, art. 2; and *Summa Contra Gentiles*, book I, chap. 11. Recent proponents of the ontological argument include Norman Malcolm and Alvin Plantinga.

God. Among other difficulties with this argument, it should be noted that the distinction (discussed earlier in this section) between "verbal" and "real" definitions powerfully undercuts it. That is, the expression "that than which nothing greater can be conceived" is, at best, a verbal definition of God. For the school of Aquinas, we in fact can achieve no real definition in this case. Thus there can be no foundation of an "ontological" sort—which would have to rely on such a definition—for a proof of the (real) existence of God.

From all of this we may draw two points. First, the perennial philosophy, as an integral part of the Christian intellectual tradition, is quite serious in seeking a demonstration of God's existence. But second, this philosophy is equally serious in assessing the quality of arguments proposed. As Aquinas realized, if we were to base our belief in God on what is an unsound argument, this would bring ill repute to the whole structure of our religious beliefs; and this is something that no Christian philosopher or theologian would want to have happen.

Aquinas nonetheless was convinced that we could develop demonstrations *quia* for the existence of God. These are represented in his famous "Five Ways," which are set out near the beginning of the *Summa Theologiae*.[7] All of these "ways"—i.e., paths by which the human mind can come to be demonstratively aware of God's reality—are best read, we believe, as expressing what we have called the "poverties" of natural being, as well as the ways in which the human mind, reflecting on these poverties, is led to conclude to a Being with a contrasting "plenitude," a Being, therefore, that can rightly be called "God," as God is spoken of in the theistic traditions of Jews, Christians, and Muslims, as well as certain other religious peoples.

Below we will offer an articulation of the common logical structure of Aquinas's Five Ways. But first we should say a word about aspects of these arguments' content. As might be expected of arguments developed in the thirteenth century, they contain in their original ex-

7. *Summa Theologiae*, I, q. 2, art. 3. (It is suggested that the reader access these arguments, or argument-sketches, which cover only two pages. They are widely available in both print and online versions. See the Bibliography.) For additional relevant argumentation by St. Thomas, see his *Summa Contra Gentiles*, book I.

pression allusions to certain supposed facts that now are known not to be the case, or at least are no longer part of a modern view of the universe. For example, Aquinas's Third Way contains a line of speculation about beings that have "necessary existence," but have it from another. This very likely alludes to the Medieval theory of "quintessence"— according to which the heavenly bodies were made of a kind of element that, unlike the four terrestrial elements (earth, air, fire, and water), is not liable to be mixed with others, and according to which the heavenly bodies are thereby rendered everlasting (as they seemed to observers at the time to be) rather than subject to decomposition. Again, the Fourth Way speaks of the element "fire" as what is highest in the category of heat, and as what is responsible for the respective degrees of heat in the bodies that contain it. Here, Aquinas embraces for purposes of illustration a theory of heat that has been thoroughly replaced by modern theories of thermodynamics. Fortunately, from the standpoint of the perennial philosophy, such outdated scientific references turn out to be incidental to the content, as well as the form, of the respective arguments.

Aquinas's Five Ways have been variously analyzed and interpreted in the centuries since their composition. Following is a schema, or outline, developed by the present writer to express the deductive structure common to all five arguments, with "P_1" and "P_2" representing the first and second premises in each case, and with "C" representing the conclusion:

P_1: Beings of our experience manifest feature x.

P_2: But natural beings, even taken together, are insufficient to account for their having or being x (there is in this respect a poverty in their being); indeed, no finite or limited reality could account for x.

C: Therefore, there must be, beyond nature and finite reality, Being that has (or is) the relevant and contrasting Sufficiency or Plenitude, which alone can account for x. This Being the religious traditions call "God."

Table 2. Aquinas's Five Ways of Reasoning to God

Way	Feature of Natural Being (x)	Insufficiency (Poverty)	Being of Contrasting Sufficiency (Plenitude)
1	Change ("motion"); coming-to-be	Must go from potency to act, through the agency of another	First Agent ("Unmoved Mover"); Pure Act or Actuality
2	Exercise of agency, efficient causality	Must itself be actuated, through ontologically prior efficient cause	First Cause (absolutely independent of any other)
3	Being/existence	Contingency (possible to be or not-be)	Necessary Being (having necessary existence of Itself)
4	Transcendental and pure perfections	Shared only in degrees; participated in by, rather than properly belonging to, beings of nature	Absolute Perfection (Plenitude of Being, Goodness, Beauty, etc.)
5	Actions, orientations toward ends	In general, no intellect by which things might direct themselves	First Intelligence, Orderer of the Universe

Now let us consider, in terms of each of Aquinas's arguments, a) what is to be filled in or instantiated for the natural feature x; b) the type of insufficiency or poverty in each case; and c) the contrasting Sufficiency or Plenitude. These elements are represented in table 2.

Reading across each of the five rows, and keeping the above schema in mind, we arrive at a comprehensive grasp of the Five Ways as these are presented in the *Summa Theologiae*.

We would mention a key feature of the present approach to these classical arguments for God. It seeks accurately to represent the Five Ways' overall contents and structures, while at the same time enabling attention to be focused on issues that most often divide those who comment on the arguments' soundness and status as demonstrative. Specifically, the author hopes that the overall form of the argument-schema (i.e., that P_1 and P_2 together entail C) will be judged by the reader to be valid; further, he believes that the five instantiations of P_1 are, at least arguably, all factual (although they are not, as Aquinas himself noted, equally "manifest"). If these points are accepted, then the focus of attention in each case will be on the complex proposition represented by P_2. If this proposition is true, then, given that the overall argument is valid and that the first premise is arguably true (because factual), the argument as a whole is arguably sound. And, of course, if the argument is sound then the conclusion necessarily is true—that is, there indeed exists a Being that can be identified as the God of religious tradition.

Moreover, if the premises of the arguments can be known to be true—from direct experience and correct insight or real definition— then the arguments will count as demonstrations; that is, not only will their conclusions be true, but they will be known with certainty to be true. Of course, regarding the truth of these premises (and even regarding the validity of the arguments), we must distinguish, within the per se knowable, what is per se knowable in itself and what is per se knowable to particular persons. It clearly is not the case that all per se knowable propositions (especially within the realm of metaphysics) are per se knowable to all—or even, explicitly, to very many. In the end, after reading our exposition of the five classical arguments, the student himself or herself must undertake to judge the truth of the propositions represented by P_2.

Properly understanding the Five Ways involves directing our attention to the whole universe or cosmos (from the Greek *kosmos*, for all of natural being taken as a whole). As an aid to doing this, we offer the diagram in figure 3 as representing a contemporary scientific picture of the universe. For obvious reasons, we sometimes shall refer to it as our "cone" diagram.[8]

The point of the cone, on the left, represents the "Big Bang," the beginning of our universe, hypothesized by contemporary scientific cosmology to have occurred some twelve to fifteen billion years ago. The concentric "slices" represent units of space-time as the universe has developed—through the congealing of the basic elements, the for-

8. Although the author believes that his use of this diagram in relation to reasoning to God is original, the general idea of such a representation of the cosmos is not. See, for example, the similar image on the website Cosmic Evolution maintained by Eric J. Chaisson, at http://www.tufts.edu/as/wright_center/cosmic_evolution/docs/splash.html. For the actual construction of the present diagram, and the two related diagrams in section 3.3, I am indebted to Andy Jaspers, S.J.

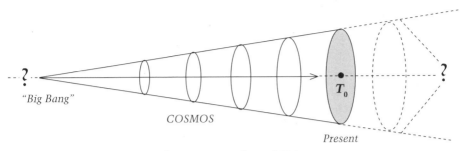

Figure 3. The Cosmos, or Physical Universe

mation of galaxies, the emergence of life on earth, etc. It will be noted that on this model—by contrast with Early Modern scientific pictures of the cosmos (e.g., that of Isaac Newton)—with the passage of time, space itself has expanded. Slice T_0 represents the present along time's unidirectional line; that is, this slice is intended to capture all of natural being at the current moment. (Of course, our model represents in a two-dimensional way what in actuality is a three-dimensional expanse.) The hashed lines extending the cone to the right represent the anticipated future of the universe—a future which, according to contemporary cosmology, will come to an end either in a dead-flat expanse, or in a crushing together of all matter and energy into an incredibly small and intense "ball" (indeed, another point). Another hashed line extends to the left from the "Big Bang," signifying that we simply do not know—scientifically or philosophically—whether any physical reality preceded it.

It will be noted that all of Aquinas's arguments rely on the Principle of Causality or—more strictly and metaphysically—Sufficient Reason. (The student may wish to review our discussions of these principles in part 1.) Let us consider how the relevant philosophical concepts are applied in each case.

In the First and Second Ways, which deal with change or coming-to-be and efficient causality, Aquinas is concerned with what traditionally have been called "essentially subordinated causes"—that is, causes whose effects, even if they occur in a series, occur and must occur together. (This, as opposed to causes that are serial, but whose effects take place separately across time—as is the case, for example, with successive generations of human persons and members of other living species.) Essentially subordinated series, says Aquinas, cannot actually "proceed to infinity," with each member depending on another, for if they were supposed literally to go on without end there could be no satisfactory explanation of the actual coming to be of the members of the series we encounter in experience. It should be noted, therefore, that when Aquinas speaks of a "First" Agent or "First" Cause—as he does at the ends of the first two ways—he is referring to absolute ontological priority, rather than to temporal priority. In fact, as already suggested, and as Aquinas goes on to make clear in the Third Way, he does not believe that it can be established by philosophical or scientific reasoning whether there is an absolute temporal origin.

It may be wondered whether the idea of a series of essentially subordinated causes, at least within the physical cosmos, is not another outdated Medieval notion. This idea has had a place in traditional philosophies of nature, but it does not seem to be reflected in the structures and modes of explanation currently employed in the natural sciences. Thus it may be the case that today the crucial notion of "essential subordination" should be reinterpreted to apply to physical change and becoming in the cosmos taken as a whole, with the First Cause acting without any intermediary.[9] The argument then would reduce to proposing that a world in which actuality must continuously be brought forth from potentiality is a world that must depend on sheer Actuality.

Regarding the Third Way, we should note that it alludes to the hypothetical notion of an infinite past. Aquinas's argument is that even if the world of contingent or "possible" being were to stretch back in-

It has to BEGIN at some point in order to exist

9. It may be noted that many followers of Aquinas, including both Maritain and Simon, speculate about an intermediary role in the development of the physical world for (finite) pure spirits or angels. (In fact, an alternate interpretation of the Third Way's "necessary beings that do not have necessity of themselves" would take these words to refer precisely to angelic beings—which, once in existence, have no tendency to go out of existence.)

finitely in time, we still would need to posit a Being that has necessary existence, and indeed has such existence of Itself. Here, as already suggested, Aquinas recognized—unlike some authors of both his day and our own[10]—that there is no compelling physical or metaphysical argument to the effect that <u>there must have been a first moment of time</u>. As a Christian believer he in fact accepted that there was a first moment of Creation; but as a philosopher he could not make use of this point of faith in his argumentation. Hence what may seem to be the peculiar mode of elaboration of the Third Way. It will be recalled, moreover, that this argument seems to involve (but not essentially to depend upon) an outdated scientific notion of necessary but natural beings (i.e., the heavenly bodies)—beings that have "necessary" existence, but cannot be supposed to have it of themselves. In the contemporary scientific context, some might suggest that the cosmos itself— or the whole of the mass-energy complex—should be regarded as such a necessary natural being. However, just as in the case of Aquinas's thirteenth-century reasoning, a question must arise as to the cause of this necessary being—for clearly it cannot be said to have the reason for its existing, let alone existing of necessity, within its own ontological structure. Recognition of these points actually enables us to simplify the logical pattern of the Third Way; that is, now the reasoning is simply from the order of beings that can not-be (or, if this whole order itself is regarded as having a condition of necessity, then an order of being that has its necessity in a dependent way) to Being that cannot not-be and that has Necessary Existence of Itself.

The <u>Fourth Way</u> focuses on those qualities or perfections that were introduced in part 1 as "<u>transcendentals</u>"—being, <u>goodness</u>, <u>unity</u>, etc. (By parity of reasoning this argument also may be taken to include "pure" perfections such as freedom and the operation of intellect.) Supposing these indeed are real properties encountered in the

---

10. That we can reason to a first moment of time was held by the *kalam* school of Medieval Islamic theology. For contemporary statements of this view, see various writings of William Lane Craig, e.g., "Philosophical and Theological Pointers to Creation *ex Nihilo*," in *Contemporary Perspectives on Religious Epistemology,* ed. R. Douglass Geivett and Brendan Sweetman (New York and Oxford: Oxford University Press, 2002), 185–200.

natural and human world, and supposing they are genuinely transcendental (or, in the case of some, pure), they are not inherently limited
to the physical realm; neither are they subject to adequate definition
or explanation in purely physical terms. Rather, these qualities call
for an application of our metaphysical principle related to "participation." Thus, disregarding the unfortunate allusion (already noted) to
the purely natural property of heat—which Aquinas and his contem-
poraries wrongly believed also should be explained by participation—
we are led to affirm the existence of Absolute Perfection. Such Perfection will be the principle and cause of certain participated qualities
(i.e., those of a transcendental or a pure nature) that we are aware of
through common human experience.

The Fifth Way originates in the recognition of natural beings' orientation toward ends. (In the version of this argument in the *Summa
Contra Gentiles*, cited in note 7, emphasis is placed on the ways in
which things of diverse species cooperate in the production of a natural world order.) Now, things' being really oriented toward ends (or
toward a world order) is a sign of an intellectual cause at work. Since
our own intellectuality—although real—is limited, it certainly does
not extend to the governance of all physical reality. Indeed, it does not
seem that any finite intellect (or combination of such intellects) could
perform the requisite ordering function for the whole, potentially infinite cosmos. At this point someone may object that evolutionary biology—which does not appeal to any intelligence at work—provides an
account of the order within the physical, or at least the living world.
And in fact such concepts as "random variation" and "natural selection" have given scientists a fruitful structure for investigating and
explaining many phenomena of life. However, as already noted in section 1.3, what stands out philosophically about the succession of biological species is that some appearing later in the temporal series have
a higher degree of actuality than their predecessors. In particular, human beings—as measured by our intrinsic, active potencies—have a
higher degree of actuality than all other natural beings of our acquaintance. Thus, while on the plane of material causality, the accounts

developed by evolutionary biologists are very suggestive—and may continue to be progressively refined and confirmed—these accounts cannot be complete or comprehensive, for they do not address the precise question of greater actuality, which is a question that calls for an account in terms of formal causality. From the standpoint of the latter, it simply makes no sense to suggest that what has less of actuality literally can "cause" (i.e., be an adequate explanation of) what has more of actuality. Once again, accordingly, we must conclude to an ontologically First Being or Actuality, One that also will be the Primary Intelligence and Orderer of processes (including evolutionary processes) within the natural world.[11]

As here discussed, and as represented in our earlier table, each of the five arguments has its own starting point in human experience. However, many contemporary students and followers of Aquinas regard the Third Way as the deepest or most fundamental.[12] As perhaps can be gathered from the above discussion, the present author agrees. For the argument from "possibility" or "contingency" focuses on the very being of finite reality, and in particular on the very being of that order of finite reality we call the natural world. Moreover, as we saw in our earlier discussion of metaphysical principles, all other ques-

11. It should be noted that Aquinas's Fifth Way, here interpreted as a metaphysical argument, is not to be confused with what some contemporary writers propose as the theory of "intelligent design." The latter often is presented as a natural science theory of origins in competition with the theory of evolution. See, e.g., Michael J. Behe, *Darwin's Black Box* (New York: Simon and Schuster, 1998); and William A. Dembski, *Intelligent Design* (Downers Grove, Ill.: InterVarsity Press, 1999). As we have emphasized in part 1 of this book, the theory of evolution—properly understood as a scientific and empiriological theory—is supported by an overwhelming body of evidence. For a fuller discussion of this matter that complements our own, see Owen Gingerich, *God's Universe* (Cambridge, Mass.: Harvard University Press, 2006).

12. See, e.g., James V. McGlynn, S.J., and Sister Paul Mary Farley, R.S.M., *A Metaphysics of Being and God* (Englewood Cliffs, N.J.: Prentice-Hall, 1966), 124–44. See also Joseph Owens, C.Ss.R., *An Elementary Christian Metaphysics* (Houston, Tex.: Center for Thomistic Studies, 1985), 335–52. And consider the following remark of Herbert McCabe, O.P.: "Aquinas's Five Ways, as I read them, are sketches for five arguments to show that a certain kind of *question* about our world and ourselves is valid: 'Why the world, instead of nothing at all?' This is a question, in Aquinas's jargon, about the *esse* of things. . . ." *God Matters* (Springfield, Ill.: Templegate Publishers, 1991), 40. Finally, see the commentary on the Five Ways in the edition of *Summa Theologiae*, I, q. 1–13, prepared by Brian Shanley, O.P. (Indianapolis, Ind.: Hackett, 2006).

tions about "what is" ultimately are resolvable into questions immediately related to being. Thus, in spite of its placement in the middle of the Five Ways, this third argument in effect serves as the basis of and model for them all. It links them to one another and expresses their common insight—namely, the ontological insufficiency of natural and finite being.

Do the Five Ways, as here represented, constitute genuine demonstrations or proofs by the stringent standards outlined above? If, as we have suggested, these arguments are valid, and if the initial premises in each case are true, then—as indicated earlier—our attention is directed to the second premise in each case. Recalling our schematic formula P_2, we thus are led to ask: Is it true that natural beings—with regard to their coming to be, their exercise of efficient causality, their actual (but contingent) existence, their sharing in transcendental qualities, and their being oriented toward ends—are "even taken together . . . insufficient" to account for the properties in question? And again: Is it true that "no finite or limited reality" could account for these properties? Further, supposing that these statements are true, can we clearly see that they are true? The seeing of such things obviously requires mastering the insights and formulations of metaphysics. And, without doubt, these insights and formulations—among all those in speculative philosophy—are the most difficult, and they continue to generate controversy.[13] But the author hopes that the perennial modes of reasoning to God now have been properly articulated and defended; and that (in line with Simon's story of the old sailor) they have been shown to agree with, while at the same time purifying, the image-based thinking of common sense.[14]

---

13. Among contemporary scholars of Medieval thought there are, not surprisingly, a number who question the soundness of Aquinas's arguments. See, e.g., Anthony Kenny, *The Five Ways: Thomas Aquinas's Proofs of God's Existence* (Notre Dame, Ind.: University of Notre Dame Press, 1980). Even among Thomists, certain scholars of significance demur in whole or in part. See, e.g., John F. Wippel, *The Metaphysical Thought of Thomas Aquinas* (Washington, D.C.: The Catholic University of America Press, 2000), chap. 12. However, Wippel, at least, is writing primarily as a historical scholar, and his questions focus on the Five Ways in their original formulations, not as presented here.

14. Throughout the centuries there have been numerous variations on the types of ar-

Supposing the conclusions of Aquinas's arguments are accepted, how is God to be represented in relation to our cone diagram? As will be explored more fully in section 3.3, the Being concluded to in the Five Ways may be represented by a single point, placed outside (or "above") the cone, with lines representing ontological dependency stretching from each slice of space-time to this point (see page 216).

SUMMARY

• Instances of reasoning to God must be of the form that logicians have termed *quia* demonstrations—i.e., sound deductive arguments that bring to light the reality in question, although not the reason *(propter quid)* for the reality.

• Aquinas's "Five Ways" of reasoning to God can be understood as following a common pattern: stating features of natural and finite being, then arguing that these features, as they are made known to us in experience, are ontologically insufficient and thus require a Being with Plenitude to explain their actual presence in the world.

• Recent scholars—with whom the present writer agrees—have tended to regard the "Third Way," focusing on the very existence of natural and finite being, as the most fundamental of the ways of reasoning to God.

---

guments recognized and sketched by Aquinas. Contemporary anthologies typically have sections on the "Cosmological Argument" (compare the first three Ways), the "Teleological Argument" (compare the Fifth Way), and sometimes the "Moral Argument" (compare the Fourth Way)—as well as the "Ontological Argument" (which, as we have mentioned, Aquinas rejected). It also should be noted that Jacques Maritain developed what he called a "Sixth Way" to God—one rooted in the spiritual nature of the human person. (See Maritain, *Approaches to God* (New York: Harper and Brothers, 1954), 72–83. And recall our own section 2.5, above.) This argument perhaps can be assimilated to Aquinas's Fourth Way; however, it is helpful to set it out in its own terms.

3.2 KNOWLEDGE OF GOD: NEGATIVE AND ANALOGICAL

The "Negative Way"

Aquinas and the perennial tradition recognize the desire of the human mind—and the human heart—to know something of the nature of God. But they also recognize that, as a matter of principle, great difficulties attend any attempt to gain such knowledge. Indeed, in one place Aquinas flatly states: "(W)e can know what God is not, and not what God is." (*Summa Theologiae*, I, q. 3, prologue.) Accordingly, in exploring what can be said of God, we should begin with what is called the "negative way" (in Latin, *"via negativa"*).

Aquinas's views on this matter were influenced by those of the great twelfth-century Jewish thinker Moses Maimonides. So strict was Maimonides's position on the issue that he proclaimed that anyone who tried to say "what God is" not only would fail in this task, but also would fall unwittingly into atheism or idolatry. He writes: "(H)e who affirms that God, may He be exalted, has positive attributes . . . has abolished his belief in the existence of the deity without being aware of it."[15] That is to say, any positive conception of God that we might form would be based on ideas coming from knowledge of this world; accordingly, if we were to take such a conception seriously as representing the essence of God we in fact would be worshipping an idol, not the true God. Now, as a Christian thinker, Aquinas just as much as his Jewish predecessor was anxious to avoid idolatry; accordingly, he himself vigorously pursued the possibilities of the negative way. Following his example, let us do the same.

We can develop at once an initial "corollary" of the Five Ways. Let us note that the content of the conclusions of those arguments was expressed as, e.g., Pure Act, Perfect Being, and Absolute Intelli-

---

15. Moses Maimonides, *Guide of the Perplexed*, trans. S. Pines (Chicago: University of Chicago Press, 1963), book I, chap. 60.

gence. Thus here in the very language of the conclusions there is implied an identity of God's existence with God's activity, God's perfection, God's intelligence, etc. In no being of this world could we say
that its very existence is identical with its perfections. However, we
come to realize that in God the situation must be otherwise: God's
perfections cannot be conceived as "coming into act," or as emerging as an addition to a temporally prior existence. Rather, these perfections must "already" belong to God's very being. In light of this,
the perennial philosopher comes to say: "In God, unlike things of this
world, essence and existence are not distinct." Note that this follows
what we are calling the negative way: we do not here know—or claim
to know—what it is for essence and existence to be identical; we simply know that in God being is not actually distinguishable into essence and existence, as it is in natural and finite beings. (If we sometimes talk as if there were such a distinction in God, we must realize
that this is due to the limitations of our human ways of thinking and
speaking.) There can be no real distinction between What God Is and
the fullness of God's Existence Itself. As Emonet says, "In God there
is no composition, only an absolute simplicity."[16] And this simplicity extends to what we humanly conceive as the "principles" of God's
Being.

Other "negative" characterizations of God follow from specific aspects of the five individual lines of reasoning. Thus, the First Way can
be said to conclude to the existence of an "Unmoved Mover"—i.e.,
an Agent that does not have any ontological predecessor in the essentially subordinated causal series. Similarly, the Second Way concludes
to the existence of the First Cause—i.e., One that does not depend in
any way on another; and the Third Way concludes to the existence of
an absolutely Necessary Being—i.e., One that is not merely "possible"
or contingent (nor even "necessary" while having its existence in a
dependent way). Notice that in each of these cases, there may be the
appearance of something positive (First Agent or Cause, or Necessary
Being); but the philosophical content, at least as this can initially be

16. Emonet, *God Seen in the Mirror of the World*, 48.

understood and explicated, is negative ("has no ontological predecessor," "does not depend on another," "is not merely possible").

Other statements derivable from the conclusions of the Five Ways
also can be seen to be essentially negative. Thus, because God is fully Act, God is said to be "Infinite"—and here the meaning grasped by
our minds is "not limited or bounded." Similarly, as we shall discuss
in more detail in section 3.3, God is said to be "Eternal"—and here the
meaning, at least as initially grasped, is "not subject to temporality,"
by contrast with all things of the natural world.

Medieval writers sometimes called the results of reflections such
as the above *"docta ignorantia"*—"learned (or well-instructed) ignorance." And we now can see that the classical tradition of philoso-
phizing about God is able to develop quite a few rationally grounded
expressions to convey "what God is not." (The reader may wish to impress his or her friends by explaining just how ignorant he or she has
become by this point in the course!) Here it should be emphasized that
docta ignorantia is not the equivalent of agnosticism; the latter holds,
as we noted in section 3.1, that the human mind cannot know anything about God—whether God exists, what God's characteristics may
be or not be, etc. On the contrary, a person of *docta ignorantia* knows
a great many things that should be said of God, and indeed knows why
these things should be said. However, in articulating such knowledge
he or she is always saying something about what God is not, rather
than about what God is. Moreover, it should be noted that this mode
of articulation, although negative, bespeaks a fullness of Being. As
Aquinas points out, "we refuse to ascribe [certain attributes] to God
not as if God lacked them, but because God is too far above them."
(*Summa Theologiae*, I, q. 12, art. 12.)

Application of Theories of Metaphor and Analogy

Although Aquinas was intent, as was Maimonides, on not falling
into idolatry, he could not accept the strictly negative account of religious language his Jewish predecessor had set out. For it seemed to
him obvious, and in fact inevitable, that humans seek to say positive

things about God—things that, unlike the term "infinite," cannot be reduced to a negative form. Surely, for example, when religious believers say "God is good," they do not simply mean "God is not bad"; and when they say "God is intelligent," they do not simply mean "God is not stupid or unintelligent"; etc. But if God is infinite and beyond all human understanding, what philosophical account can be given of this "positive" language about God? And would such an account be consistent with Aquinas's remark, noted earlier, that we cannot actually know "what God is"?

In responding to these questions, a first task is to distinguish metaphorical and symbolic from literal or designative language. The word "metaphor" comes from the Greek *meta,* meaning "beyond" or "after," and *pherein,* meaning "to carry." Thus *metaphorical* language can be said to involve a term's being carried beyond its original or normal context, i.e., its being used in a new, non-literal, or specially constructed sense that the user—and, it is hoped, the hearer or reader—relates to the original one. By contrast with such a use of language, it should be said that in general—except for the role of theoretical "models" in the positive sciences—the disciplined studies of reality, both scientific and philosophical, strive to avoid reliance on metaphor. That is, these studies seek to be literal in their use of terms, by designating real features of being through the application of concepts expressive of those features. (Here the student may wish to review the matters discussed in section 1.4 under "Analogous Language as a Tool of Metaphysics.")

As a reader of the Hebrew and Christian Scriptures, and as a participant in liturgies and other religious practices, Aquinas was well aware of the importance of metaphor in the life of faith. No doubt Maimonides was aware of this as well and intended his strictures against positive language to apply only to what we are calling "designative" language. Thus, for example, the ancient Psalmist says, "The Lord is my rock, my fortress, and my deliverer, my God my rock in whom I take refuge . . ." (Ps 18: 2). Further, God is spoken of in Scripture—and in various religious practices based on Scripture—as a shield, a shepherd, an eagle, a lion, etc. Aquinas and Maimonides before him were well aware that such statements are not to be taken literally. As Absolute and Immaterial, God's Being *could* not have any of the characteristics indicated, for all of them can be seen to imply limitations and material conditions. Thus, if one did try to affirm these characteristics literally of God, or say that the terms in question apply directly to God, one would be making statements that are simply false—and idolatrous as well! Similarly, a non-literal or non-designative interpretation is required when God is said to perform acts of a physical nature. Aquinas writes: "'Approaching' and 'withdrawing' are acts attributed to God by Scripture; but this is a matter of metaphor." Comparing such language to that whereby we say the sun "enters" or "leaves" a room, St. Thomas points out that just as in the latter case we say these things according to the presence or absence of the sun's rays, so also "we say of God that he approaches or withdraws from us according to whether we receive the influence of his goodness or are deprived of it." (*Summa Theologiae*, I, q. 9, art. 1 ad 3.)

Related to the notion of metaphor is that of *symbol*. The symbolic character of much religious language has become a staple of modern theological discussion. As elaborated, for example, by the twentieth-century Protestant thinker Paul Tillich, language that is symbolic serves to bring to our awareness a reality of such depth or mystery that it cannot be expressed in literal or designative language. Therefore, says Tillich (in response to critics), "symbols are not used in terms of 'only' but in terms of that which is necessary, of that which we must apply."[17] That is to say, we must use symbolic modes of expression if we are to enter into the heart of religious mysteries.

The above might be taken to suggest that symbolic language, at least about God, is superior to, or more revelatory of its object, than is designative language. And indeed, such is Tillich's view. However, Aquinas was convinced—and the "great tradition" to which John Paul II referred remains convinced—that at the basis of religious language

---

17. Paul Tillich, "The Nature of Religious Language," in *Philosophy of Religion: Selected Readings*, ed. Michael Peterson et al. (New York: Oxford University Press, 1996), 364.

(and indeed of cognitive language generally) must lie terms that genuinely express conceptual content. And, in fact—to return to our earlier examples—is it not the case that in expressing such propositions as "God is good," "God is wise," "God acts freely," etc., religious people seek to use language in a way that directly designates God—and in doing so provides an anchor for the range of metaphors and symbols that also are used? As a theologian Aquinas thought it clear that this indeed is what religious people seek to do; and as a philosopher he saw—rightly, in the opinion of the present author—that there needed to be an account of precisely how the statements in question, understood precisely as literal or designative, are possible for the human mind.

The key to developing such an account lies in the distinction among types of literal meaning. Here let us recall from section 1.4 Aquinas's account of the three categories of designative terms: the univocal, the equivocal, and the analogous. Terms (or uses of terms) falling into the first two categories are such that they express entirely the same thing or entirely different things, respectively. (Thus "man," or *homo sapiens,* is used univocally, whereas "bank" is used equivocally.) By contrast, terms or uses of terms called "analogous" are partially the same and partially different in their meanings; or they have distinct but similar or related meanings. Importantly, in genuine analogy the relationships holding among the term's meanings are rooted in relationships among the realities thus designated. (Recall our discussions of the terms "healthy" and "good.")

It should be clear from our explanations that terms designating both things of this world and God cannot be taken as univocal. For if they were, we would be saying that God is on the same "level" as things of the world (and vice versa), and this indeed would be falling into idolatry, just as Maimonides had warned. On the other hand, terms such as "good," "wise," and "free" also cannot be construed by the philosopher of language about God on the model of the equivocal. It would be futile, for example, to try to clarify one's meaning by simply noting, "When I say 'God is wise,' I mean something completely different from what I mean when I say a particular man or woman is wise." Such an approach works well enough in the case of the two different and unrelated senses of "bank"—because we know the alternative meanings in each case. But it already has been agreed that we do not understand the essence of God, and thus we cannot directly know how "good" or "wise" or "free" apply in the case of God.

The remaining alternative—that terms applied to God and to the natural and human realms are analogical in character—seemed to Aquinas to provide the basis for a proper account. For all positive, literal statements about God will involve the attribution of what we identified as "transcendental" and "pure" perfections; and reflection reveals that the language of such perfections follows the logic of analogy, specifically what we called the analogy of "proportionality." Thus we may say, for example, "God's Goodness is to the essence of God as human goodness is to the essence of human personhood." Moreover, since God is the absolutely First (i.e., ontologically Primary) Cause, from which all instances of perfections in finite things derive, there also is involved what we called the analogy of "attribution." That is, God is said to be "good," "wise," "free," etc. by way of causal relations, according to which God is the ultimate source of these perfections within the order of finite being. And it can be seen that—since these perfections (unlike the "mixed" or physical perfections representing color, shape, size, etc.) have no internal limitations—the ultimate source of the perfections must share in them, indeed must constitute them, to an infinite degree.

In light of the above, it can be said that the development of literal or designative language about God involves a threefold "process"—or, as Emonet put it, a "triple leap."[18] The first step, suggested just above, relates to causality. As Ultimate Source, God must share in all real perfections that are not intrinsically limited, i.e., all those that are not by their essence bound up with matter or other limiting conditions. The second step involves negation. Since God's mode of enjoyment of the transcendental and pure perfections is infinite, this mode is decid-

---

18. Emonet, *God Seen in the Mirror of the World*, 74–75.

edly not the same as our mode of enjoyment of them. Finally, the third step is called *eminence* or *supereminence*. In saying that these perfections do not exist in God as they do in our world, we are not saying that they do not exist. Rather, we are saying that, in God, the mode of existence of goodness, beauty, wisdom, freedom, and the rest is beyond anything we can attain through our limited imaginations and intellects. Indeed, as is implied by our prior discussion, in God these various types of essence, infinitely exemplified, are identical with God's very existence. As Thomists have put it, God's Act of *Esse* (to Be) is such as to comprehend all transcendental and pure perfections.

It is sometimes said regarding terms expressing these perfections that God is their "primary analogate." The question of primacy within analogy can be posed either from the standpoint of being itself, or from the standpoint of our knowledge of being. Obviously, in terms of our knowledge, "good" and related words come to be learned in the context of many other things before they are applied to God. Thus, to say that God is the primary analogate in the formula "*X* is good" is to say that the perfection designated is present in the highest, indeed infinite degree in God, and that it is present in various finite degrees within the realm of created being.

Some readers of this text will be familiar with the Islamic writings called Hadith (meaning "Traditions"). These contain sayings of and stories about the Prophet Muhammad—as distinct from what faithful Muslims accept as a revelation of God that was received by the Prophet and set down in the Koran. One section of the Hadith concerns what are called the "Ninety-nine Most Beautiful Names of God."[19] Here are set out what in fact do number ninety-nine expressions for God (or "Allah," the word designating God in Islam). In light of our discussion of positive language about God, the present writer would suggest regarding certain of the Muslim expressions (e.g., "Just," "Wise," and "Loving") that a philosophical account in terms of analogy seems appropriate; and he would suggest regarding others (e.g., "the Watcher"

19. See "Appendix: Selections from the Hadith," in *Anthology of World Scriptures*, ed. Robert E. Van Voorst (Belmont, Calif.: Wadsworth, 1994), 335–36.

and "the Beginner," i.e., the Originator of the cosmos) that a philosophical account in terms of metaphor seems appropriate. Here, it may be noted, we come upon very interesting parallels among the world's religious traditions—as well as an indication of how philosophy might be used to facilitate a mutual appreciation of such parallels. (We shall explore this matter further in the Epilogue of our book.)

At this point, it may be asked: Does the above account of positive language by way of analogy (including causality, negation, and supereminence) genuinely move us beyond the strictures of Maimonides? This is truly a question to ponder. Our account appears to go beyond that of the twelfth-century writer, and Aquinas and his close followers think that in fact it does so. But we might imagine a follower of Maimonides responding, "With the point about 'negation' in your account of analogy the appearance of an essential difference is given back. What is being articulated here is no more than a sophisticated variation on the 'negative way.' Moreover, did Aquinas himself not say that 'we do not know what God is, but only what God is not'? Thus, in the end—beyond the 'negative way'—there can be no literal or designative language about God."

It may be noted in response that Aquinas also wrote (in the context of truths about God), "A little knowledge of the most sublime things, even though it is poor and insufficient, is a source of the highest joy." (*Summa Contra Gentiles,* book I, 8.) Our discussion in the immediately succeeding pages seeks to articulate the context and basis for this sentiment. Perhaps it also will be seen to shed additional light on the present issue—and even to suggest a perennial philosophical reply to our imagined follower of Maimonides. However, further explicit consideration of this matter must be left to the reflective reader.

God as "The One Who Is"

Now let us consider what, for the "great tradition," should be regarded as the most profound of the names of God. In the Introduction to our book we noted John Paul II's idea that the philosopher can be inspired by religious faith—e.g., by finding certain themes for reflection suggested in the Scriptures. Such is the case regarding the present issue, for early Hebrew revelation contains a story specifically portraying God's own act of Self-naming. In the book of Exodus, God calls to Moses from a burning bush. Moved by this awe-inspiring experience, Moses is prepared to be God's messenger; but he is apprehensive regarding the Israelites' reaction to his words. He thus inquires: "If . . . they ask me 'What is his [i.e., God's] name?' what shall I say to them?" In reply, God says: "'I AM WHO I AM' . . . Thus you shall say to the Israelites, 'I AM has sent me to you.'" (Ex 3: 13–14.)

We believe that this religious story coheres perfectly with—and can inspire the philosopher to recall, gather together, and apply—a number of the preceding points about God.

First, let us recall that, to many students of Aquinas, the Third Way (leading to "Necessary Being") is the most fundamental of his five arguments for God. It is most fundamental because, while the other four focus on various features of natural being, this one focuses on the very reality of natural being itself. Moreover, as Aquinas emphasizes, the Necessary Being concluded to in the Third Way not only exists necessarily, but also has, or is, necessary existence of Itself. This Being, that is to say, is Absolute Being, One that in no way is dependent on any other.

Connected with the above points is the perfect identity of God's essence and existence. Reflection reveals that to be God just is to Be, although in a mode—which lies utterly beyond human understanding—that includes all the other transcendental and pure perfections to an infinite degree.

The point just noted recalls to our minds that among the transcendental perfections—that is, perfections found among all the categories of things that are—being is the most fundamental. (Remember that Aquinas at one point calls the others "inseparables," i.e., perfections that are inseparable from being.)

Again, we might approach the question of how best to name God from the standpoint of God's activity. When we do so we note, with Emonet, that as "self-subsistent being," God is uniquely able to communicate existence; and indeed that "God's first effect in all things is existence."[20] That is, God gives to all things their very being, by which they might pursue their respective fulfillments according to the types of things they are.

Similarly, from the standpoint of our own knowing and naming of things, let us recall that, as Maritain put it, it is through the "intuition of being"—the analogical grasp of existence in all its amplitude—that we arrive at our most fundamental concept. As such, this concept ("being" or "existence") will apply most perfectly—although again in a manner utterly beyond human understanding—to the Absolute, i.e., to God.

Moreover, we have seen that God shares to an infinite degree the pure as well as the transcendental perfections. That is, God is supreme Intelligence, Wisdom, Freedom, etc. Accordingly, God is supremely Personal and is properly thought of as a "Who," not just a "What."

Finally, philosophical reflection leads to the conclusion that God is uniquely One Being. For, as St. Thomas reasons, "if there were more than one God, they would have to differ in something"; and, this being the case, "some perfection would be lacking to one or the other," so that one "would not be absolutely perfect"—and accordingly would not be God! (*Summa Theologiae*, I, q. 11, art. 3.)

Putting all of these philosophical points together, and applying them to the question of the most proper name for God, we arrive at a result that precisely corresponds to—and in fact elucidates the meaning of—the "I AM" or "THE ONE WHO IS" of Judeo-Christian revelation in the book of Exodus.

Of course, the reflective reader must consider whether the philosophical results really do come together in the way we have suggested. But, supposing they do, it can be appreciated that for one who philosophizes in the context of Christian faith, there scarcely could be a more important, or more precious, outcome.

Of the above confluence of positions, philosophical and theological, Jacques Maritain wrote as follows: "(T)his shows how philosophy

20. Emonet, *God Seen in the Mirror of the World,* 77. See also p. 50.

can be reinforced and enhanced in its proper order . . . in better than ever accomplishing its work of natural wisdom, through faith." He adds that—to bring the relationship full circle—St. Thomas's philosophy has "whispered" the "most sacred metaphysical truth" (i.e., that God is Subsistent Being Itself) "in the ear of his theology."[21]

SUMMARY

• The primary mode of developing concepts about God must be negative—that is, such concepts will indicate what God is not.

• Perennial philosophers and theologians also apply positive terms to God; insofar as these terms ("good," "free," etc.) are used literally or designatively, they must follow the pattern of analogous language and involve relations of causality, negation, and supereminence.

• From the philosophical standpoint (which coheres remarkably with the account of God's Self-naming in the Hebrew Scriptures), the most fundamental expression for God is "the One Who Is."

3.3 THE WORLD AND ITS CREATOR

Transcendence and Immanence

The ontologically first effect of God's activity is, as we have seen, the very existence of things. Another word for this effect is *"Creation."* We also might speak of God's "Conservation," that is, God's maintenance of the universe through the continual coming to be of things of nature. But how are we to conceive these relationships between the world and God? Here let us recall that we are operating within what

---

21. As quoted by Emonet, ibid., 54; see also his discussion on 84–86. (To the present account it may be objected that New Testament writings—e.g., 1 Jn 4:16—emphasize that God is Love. But the two points are not incompatible. Philosophically, the most fundamental expression is "the One Who Is," while religiously, "Love" indeed has a certain priority—although, of course, God could not *be* Love unless God exists as a Personal Being.)

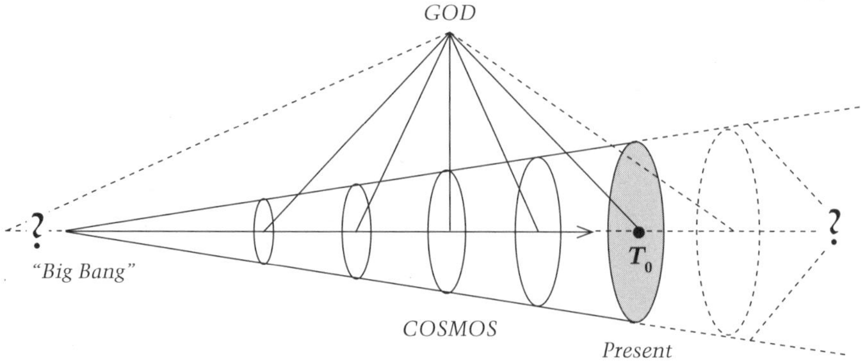

Figure 4. Relations between Cosmos and God

we have termed the "third order of abstraction." That is, the objects of our thought—God and the world's relations with God—are devoid of all matter. Thus they are incapable of apprehension via the senses and imagination. Still, we hardly can avoid wanting to think about these relations. And, as human thinkers, we hardly can avoid trying to represent the relations in some pictorial way. Let us consider whether this is at all possible.

We might begin by recalling our "cone" diagram. At the end of section 3.1 we suggested that God could be represented by a point "above" (that is, outside) the cone, with lines representing ontological dependency extending from each slice of space-time to this point. (We would emphasize that, while the point in question might be placed above the cone, there is no suggestion here of directionality. All genuine matters of direction—"up," "down," "before," "after," etc.—are to be located within the cone itself.) In this way, the whole cosmos, the whole realm of natural being, is represented as depending at each moment and in all essential respects on the Pure Actuality of God. Figure 4 gives our expanded diagram.

The representation of God by a point outside the cone also expresses what traditionally is called God's *transcendence,* that is, God's complete otherness from the world. In addition to indicating onto-logical dependency, the quasi-vertical lines can be taken to symbol-ize God's *immanence,* that is, God's intimate presence to the world. Accordingly, the idea represented is that God is both completely other than and intimately present to the physical cosmos. This idea seems to involve a paradox; it may even seem to involve a contradiction. Let us see whether further reflection in terms of our diagram can give us a clearer understanding of these matters.

Notice first that in picturing God as a point "above" we are not suggesting that God occupies a position somehow isomorphic with any point along the cosmos's timeline. As indicated earlier, all spatial and temporal relations are represented within the cone (and its pro-jected extensions). Indeed, it should be said that, from the standpoint of cognitive content, the idea of God's transcendence itself follows the "negative way": God's complete "otherness" at least initially and pri-marily conveys simply that God is not like the beings of the natural universe. (To accentuate this understanding, and to diminish the ten-dency to mistakenly conceive God as "up," we might think of the di-agonal lines as expressing another dimension—e.g., picture them as "folding out" from the printed page.)

But why, for the perennial philosopher, must God be conceived as completely other? To answer this question is to move closer to the paradox of transcendence and immanence—and also to a resolution of it. We noted above that, as self-subsisting Being, God is uniquely able to give existence. Now existence is given to the whole of natural be-ing; that is, it is an effect that is universal. But if the effect is univer-sal (that is, shared in by all things, past, present, and future), the cause also must be universal (that is, able to act on all things, past, present, and future). Therefore, unlike causes operating within natural being, this Cause is not to be identified with, or limited to, any particular region of space or any particular period of time. That is to say, once again, God is transcendent.

But if God is utterly different from things of this world, God also is utterly "near" to them. As Emonet puts it, "God and created things—

an abyss separates them, and yet without there being any distance between them."[22] This leads us to a consideration of God's immanence.

Etymologically, to be "immanent" is to "remain in" (from Latin *manere*, "to remain"). This can be connected to Emonet's point about lack of distance. Consider, with regard to natural or physical beings, that while they exercise agent causality in relation to one another, they remain separate from one another. For example, while the rays of the sun warm natural beings on earth, the sun itself is ninety-three million miles away. A natural cause is at a distance—whether large or small (perhaps only the distance consisting of the "space" between exterior membranes, as in the case of one physical being pushing another)—from the effect. But in the case of God, Whose universal and primary effect is the very existence of things, the situation is completely different. As the spiritual writer Dom Vermiel puts it, "When God arouses a new reality, first, He acts not 'upon' things—or 'against' them (as we are obliged to do)—but 'in' them."[23]

It of course must be remembered that in speaking of God acting "in" things, we are using the language of metaphor. Alternatively, we might say, as suggested above, that God is "intimately present to" things—to all finite beings, throughout all periods of time. In fact, both phrases are used by Aquinas himself, and sometimes in a single passage: "As long as a thing possesses being, God must be present to it, and this in the manner in which it possesses existence. Now, existence, in each thing, is what inheres in it most intimately and most profoundly. . . . (T)hus . . . God is in all things, in an intimate manner." (*Summa Theologiae*, I, q. 8, art. 1.)

But now let us note that if God is thus said to be "in" all things, God also must be completely other than those things. God must completely transcend the world in order to be present to it universally and immanently. Thus, so far from their leading to a contradiction, the notions of God's transcendence and immanence turn out to be necessary complements of one another.

22. Ibid., 51.
23. Quoted in Emonet, ibid., 52.

Eternity vs. Everlastingness

Now let us return to our diagram and focus on a feature mentioned earlier—that the "point" representing God would not be isomorphic with any point along the horizontal line running through the cone, the line that represents the passage of time. Indeed, God's own Being, according to classical philosophers and theologians, is not to be conceived as temporal (or as conditioned by time) at all. Rather, God's being is said to be *eternal.*

God's eternality is connected with God's fullness of actuality and changelessness. The great Patristic figure St. Augustine wrote: "You have already said, Lord, with a strong voice in the ear of my soul, that you are eternal. . . . For you change neither in form nor in movement, and your will does not vary according to moments." (*Confessions,* book 2, 11.) Being fully actual—that is, beyond movement or change—God also is beyond temporality.

Another key figure in the development of the traditional account of this matter was the early Medieval thinker Boethius (fifth–sixth centuries). In his work *The Consolation of Philosophy* Boethius turns to questions of temporality and eternity, i.e., of the modes of existence of the world and of God; he discusses them as follows. "Now, eternity is the complete possession of an endless life enjoyed as one simultaneous whole"; by contrast, "whatever is living in time proceeds in the present from times past to times future; and nothing existing in time is so constituted as to embrace the whole span of its life at once, but it has not grasped tomorrow, while it has already lost yesterday."[24] Someone might ask: What if it were the case—as Aristotle in fact held, and, as a number of people seem to suppose today (in spite of the fact that we are unable to establish scientifically whether anything temporally preceded the Big Bang)—that physical reality is co-extensive with a projected infinity of time? Even such reality, according to Boethius, "could not rightly be held to be eternal. For even granted that

24. Boethius, *The Consolation of Philosophy,* in Peterson et al., *Philosophy of Religion,* 122.

it has an infinite lifetime, it does not embrace this life as a simultaneous whole; it does not now have a grasp of the future, which is yet to be lived through."[25] Thus, according to this view, we must distinguish two different modes of existence: the one called "eternal," and proper to God alone; and the other called "temporal," and proper to all natural and thus changing being.

This view has been enormously influential in the history of reflection on God and the world's relations with God. Aquinas in particular followed Boethius in insisting that God be conceived as eternal. It should be emphasized, however, that to be eternal is not to be without duration. In fact, this mode of existence, according to the perennial tradition, involves duration in its highest form—life and actuality possessed, in Boethius's words, "as one simultaneous whole." We come to see, accordingly, that the term "duration" is still another instance of analogy. It applies differently, but with likenesses and relations, both to the world's mode of existence and to God's mode of existence. In the case of things of our world, duration requires a succession of states; in the case of God—Who is Existence complete and actual—duration is what might be called an "all-at-once present" involving no stages or successions.

Here it is instructive to recall our earlier discussion about identifying a "primary analogate." When considered in terms of our knowledge, primacy among the two types of duration goes to temporality; but when considered ontologically, that is, in terms of the being of things, the primary analogate would be eternity. For God, to recall Boethius, has—or just is—"complete possession of unending life"; and God imparts to things of this world such life as we have, with ours involving a form of duration that requires approaching completeness of existence in stages (and, at least in terms of our purely natural resources, always by way of approximation).[26]

What about the question of the coming into existence, or temporal beginning, of the universe? As a Christian theologian, Aquinas be-

25. Ibid.
26. On this point, see Simon, "On Order in Analogical Sets," 168–71.

lieved in a Creation "event," as symbolically represented in the book of Genesis. Thus he disagreed with the claim of his philosophical mentor Aristotle that the world has existed through an infinite passage of time. But Aquinas's judgment was that Aristotle's view could not be shown to be false by reflection on common experience alone. Thus, although important theologically, the supposition of a Creation "event" could not be used in a philosophy of God. As may be gathered from our earlier discussions of "Big Bang" cosmology, the present writer would argue that Aquinas's judgment on this matter remains true today.

In view of all these considerations, the diagram constructed above also can be taken to represent God's eternity (as well as Creation and God's transcendence and immanence). By contrast with the temporality of the cosmos—however long its span of time, and whether or not it was preceded by a precursor or precursors—God's mode of duration is represented simply by a point. But such a point, we might say, would be infinite in "density" or "intensiveness"—for God enjoys Actuality whole and entire.

However, not all theistic thinkers accept this account of God's relations with time. The contemporary American religious philosopher Nicholas Wolterstorff writes: "All Christian theologians agree that God is without beginning and without end."[27] (It may be noted in passing that this in fact is the common belief of orthodox Jews, Christians, and Muslims—as well as adherents of certain other religious traditions.) But they disagree, says Wolterstorff, over how God's being without beginning or end is to be construed. The dominant traditional view has been the one indicated in the preceding pages: God as eternal. Wolterstorff however argues—on both religious and philosophical grounds—for an alternative view: God as *everlasting*. Now, in everyday speech, and in popular religious language and imagery, the notions of "eternal" and "everlasting" are used more or less synonymously; certainly people often do not mark a significant distinction between

27. Nicholas Wolterstorff, "God is Everlasting," in *God and the Good*, ed. C. Orlebeke and L. Smedes (Grand Rapids, Mich.: Eerdmans, 1975); reprinted in Patterson et al., *Philosophy of Religion*, 125.

them. Nevertheless, the difference between these two notions is crucial in philosophical reflection on God.

Consider, says Wolterstorff, the relations between God and his people as represented in the Hebrew Bible, and ultimately in the saving works of Jesus Christ. "God is spoken of as calling Abraham to leave Chaldea and later instructing Moses to return to Egypt. So does not the event of God's instructing Moses *succeed* that of God's calling Abraham?" Again, "God is spoken of as leading his people through the Red Sea and later sending his Son into the world. So does not his doing the latter *succeed* his doing the former?"[28]

Clearly, Wolterstorff believes that the orthodox Jew or Christian must take these representations literally—indeed, as we have put it, univocally. But if this is so, he argues, God, like the world, must have a timeline (or, as Wolterstorff calls it, a "time-strand")—one that runs parallel to ours, while overlapping it infinitely. That is to say, God is "without beginning and without end" in the precise sense of being everlasting. For the sake of comparison with our earlier diagram, we might illustrate Wolterstorff's view as in figure 5.

When one compares this diagram with the one representing God as eternal, it becomes apparent that there are fundamental differences between the two. Whereas God as eternal is represented by a point, God as everlasting is represented by a line stretching infinitely back into the past. And each moment of our timeline is isomorphic with a moment of God's timeline, as God also develops and progresses. Moreover, just as our future is represented by a broken line, so also is God's. That is, the future is in no way present to God: for God, as for ourselves, it is "yet to be." And, if one supposes that some physical reality preceded our cosmos, it too would have been related to God in a temporal way; hence the broken vertical line to the left of the point representing the Big Bang.

Those who think as Wolterstorff does sometimes ask that their readers consider the religious practice of praying for things to happen (often referred to as "petitionary prayer"). What sense can it make to

---

28. Wolterstorff, "God is Everlasting," 127.

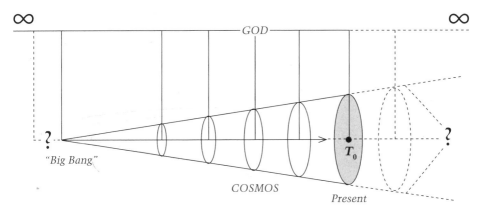

Figure 5. Relations between Cosmos and God Conceived as Everlasting

pray about future events if our future, as God eternally knows it, is "set"? Certainly, we cannot hope to "change God's mind"—for God's mind, on the model of eternality, is changeless! Thus, these thinkers say, the only sense the practice can make for those who hold God to be eternal involves the hope that we ourselves will come to feel better, or to change, for having prayed. And while such results may be psychologically important, they hardly account for the widespread occurrence of the traditional practice. Rather, those undertaking petitionary prayer hope that God will, as the Psalmist says, "come to their aid." In short, for Wolterstorff an orthodox acceptance of Judeo-Christian teachings and practice requires that we reject the perennial model of God and the universe, and substitute a model expressing God as temporal but everlasting.

Wolterstorff clearly offers a significant critique of the traditional view of God. But before undertaking a response to his challenges, let us offer in turn some critical reflections on his own view of God as everlasting. Here we shall draw on some suggestions of the Frenchman Emonet, who, although apparently not familiar with the work of Wolterstorff, offered pertinent comments on similar views. He writes, for example: "Certain philosophers, in order to analyze relations between the world and God, posit a God who changes. . . . We reject this view of God . . . God is beyond becoming and multiplicity: the First Intellect, Pure Act, the per se Subsistent Being."[29]

Emonet's apparent targets here are thinkers in the European tradition of the nineteenth-century German philosopher G. W. F. Hegel. But his statements also would apply to the movement called "process thought," developed by the Anglo-American philosopher Alfred North Whitehead and his followers such as Charles Hartshorne and, more recently, John B. Cobb. This movement, it should be noted, has been influential on a number of American theologians. Indeed, it clearly is the case that Wolterstorff's account of God as temporal but everlasting is undertaken (in Emonet's words) "in order to analyze relations between the world and God." Now admittedly, such an account makes it easier to "picture" the relations in question; but easy pictures are not necessarily correct ones. Indeed, they can be the enemy of correct thought. The reader will see, for example, that a temporal God could not be the One concluded to in Aquinas's Five Ways. Indeed, it should be asked what independent, rational, or philosophical grounds would support belief in such a God at all. The present writer frankly sees none.

Consider also the following. If certain practices or ideas of prayer seem to lack philosophical warrant on the perennial account, might this not be even more the case on Wolterstorff's account? Is his God truly immanent? Is his God immanent in the special way that requires transcendence? It would seem that the answer is No, since this God must approach the future (as we do) as that which has not yet happened. Wolterstorff's God may wish what is best for the world, and he may seek to influence the world in whatever ways are available to him;

---

29. Emonet, *God Seen in the Mirror of the World*, 103. It should be emphasized that to say that God does not "change," or that God is beyond "becoming," is not to say that God does not "act." It is simply to say that in God there is no instance of the Aristotelian category of "passion" or "passivity." (Recall the discussion of this and other categories of "accident" in section 1.2.) Indeed, God's being beyond change and becoming does not prevent God—Who is supremely Personal—from being, in an appropriate, analogical sense, "receptive." For a discussion of this point, one that calls for further exploration, see W. Norris Clarke, S.J., "A New Look at the Immutability of God," in his *Explorations in Metaphysics*, 183–210.

but, since he is temporal, he cannot know (much of) the world's future, and he cannot be truly responsible for the outcome of events. Indeed, the only point to petitionary prayer on this account would seem to be to share one's sentiments with a "higher personal power"—who, one hopes, will be sympathetic and perhaps able to do something of a practical nature to help.

Thus, contrary to what might at first be supposed, and contrary to Wolterstorff's own suggestions, there in fact is a very high conceptual price to pay in conceiving God as everlasting, rather than as eternal.

We might ask: Which conceptual price is higher—that involved in thinking of God as eternal, or in thinking of God as everlasting? And, in either case, is the price worth the "goods" received—i.e., the quality of the resulting ways of conceiving the world's relations with God? The present author's sympathies no doubt can be anticipated. From the side of the perennial tradition, one might respond to Wolterstorff's critique in the words of Aquinas himself: "(N)othing . . . prevents our saying that God's action existed from all eternity, whereas its effect was not present from eternity, but existed at that time when, from all eternity, He ordained it." (*Summa Contra Gentiles*, book II, chap. 35.) That is to say, the events recorded in the Bible—the call of Abraham, the instructing of Moses, the parting of the Red Sea, the coming of the Christ—all are objects of God's eternal will; but, as temporal, they naturally occur or take effect (and are willed by God to occur or take effect) within the temporal order. And so it is with all events, to the present day and into the future.

Regarding prayers of petition, it certainly is true that certain understandings of such prayer—e.g., that we might thereby "change God's mind"—turn out to be superstitious and without intellectual warrant. But consider the following: Might it not be the case that God eternally wills that certain events occur precisely as a response to prayer—e.g., for the sake of the edification of the faithful and the further building up of God's "kingdom"? Moreover, it is recognized by many religious people that God eternally fashions a good outcome for them, even though they are unable to articulate beforehand precisely in what such an outcome would consist. (Here we might compare a thoughtful mother who, before leaving for work, places a nourishing snack on the kitchen table for her son to eat when he comes home from school—even though he has not thought to ask her to do so.)[30] In light of all this—plus a recollection of God's intimate presence to the world throughout the course of time (or, to use a religious expression, God's "faithfulness from age to age")—we might well ask: Why should persons of faith *not* pray for important events in their lives, or in the lives of their families, or indeed of the whole human community?

Before leaving the present topic, let us consider the specific belief, common to orthodox faithful, in Creation as temporal origination. How is one to represent this? More particularly, how is one to represent the idea of God existing "before" creation? In contrast to the view of Wolterstorff (where the diagram shows God's timeline extending infinitely prior to the Big Bang), on an understanding of God developed in line with the "great tradition" this idea makes no literal sense. Indeed, it involves a conceptual mistake to speak of God's existing "before" Creation. As with all expressions indicating temporal and spatial relationships, the words "before" and "after" as used in relation to God must be taken metaphorically. Time literally begins with the Big Bang (or, if there was a precursor physical reality or realities, with the beginning of it or them). As earlier noted, God's "priority" is an ontological one, not a temporal one.

Upon reviewing these points, the present author would suggest that the conceptual price for holding God to be eternal is rather modest—indeed, that this conception of God clarifies what is essential in religious thought and practice, and at the same time helps us to avoid falling into superstitious beliefs—e.g., that God may come to have "second thoughts," or be "moved" to action by our words. However, as with many other questions in this book, further reflection on the matter must be left to the interested student.

---

30. This example I have adapted from one by Eleonore Stump and Norman Kretzmann. See their "Eternity," in *Readings in the Philosophy of Religion: An Analytic Approach*, ed. Baruch A Brody (Upper Saddle Creek, N.J.: Prentice-Hall, 1992), 404.

God as Intellect and Will—and as
Beings' Ultimate End

Let us return to the idea of Creation, and try to spell out what can be said of the operation of God's Intellect and Will. A study of such faculties as they operate in human persons occupied our attention in the preceding part of the book; here let us note some additional points about these powers, as they function in our own case.

First of all, it seems clear that human knowledge must come "after" the things that are known, in both an ontological and a temporal sense. That is to say, no actual reality can be known by us if it does not itself exist, and our coming to know individual things or their essences involves a temporal process. Moreover, as noted regarding the "critical realism" introduced in part 1, whether things actually are as we know them to be (or think we know them to be) is not a matter of our own choosing or making, but rather a matter of the "conformity" or "fit"—what Scholastic philosophers have called the "adequation" (in Latin, *adequatio*)—of our minds with the realities in question. Thus, for example, as these lines are being written the seasons are changing from summer to fall. Such change is occurring quite independently of anyone's being aware of the fact. And the truth of the proposition that the seasons are changing depends not on any human choice or action, but on the actual conditions within natural reality itself.

Regarding human willing, the matter is different in one important respect. The objects of human choice and action—states of affairs that it in some way would be good to bring about—exist intentionally, i.e., as qualities or modifications of the minds of the persons making the choices, or performing the actions, before they exist in reality. Nevertheless, the goodness of these states as types of reality that might be brought about, and thus their power to "attract" the will by way of what we identified as final causality, is a feature that already characterizes them in their state of intentional being. Thus "practical truth," or the result of right reasoning about things to be done, depends on a prior objective goodness—a goodness that reflects intrinsic suitability or desirability or appropriateness, rather than being determined in its very status as good by either human reason or human will. To extend our earlier example, the change of seasons may remind the homeowner that new insulation is needed for winter. The good of a well-insulated dwelling attracts the homeowner's will and disposes him or her to take action. This good is a characteristic of the house as such (or, strictly, the house insofar as it is composed of certain materials and is located, say, in the upper Midwest)—whether it exists only in intentional or also in physical being.

If we now reflect on our earlier philosophical results, we can see that the very reverse of the above points about knowledge and will must be true in the case of Gód. That is, God's knowing, and God's willing as conditioned by God's knowing, "precede" things, ontologically speaking. (They do not, of course, precede things temporally, since all temporal relations characterize events within finite or physical being.) Therefore, that things are as they are, and that things have the objective value they have, is a result of God's making them so. And God's "making" (or Act of Creation) is bound up with God's knowledge and will. As St. Thomas puts the matter in the *Summa Contra Gentiles*, "God's act of understanding and willing is, necessarily, His act of making. . . . [A]n effect follows from the intellect and will according to the determination of the intellect and the command of the will." (*Summa Contra Gentiles*, book II, chap. 35.) Moreover, although God is not a temporal being, God's making of temporal things in accord with intellect and will extends even to the segments of the "timeline" they occupy: "Just as the intellect determines every other condition of the thing made, so does it prescribe the time of its making. . . . as a physician determines that a dose of medicine is to be drunk at such and such a particular time, so that, if his act of will were sufficient to produce the effect, the effect [including its temporal dimension] would follow from his decision." (Ibid.)

Earlier we mentioned the idea of God's Conservation of the universe. We now can see—at least from the standpoint of philosophical analysis—that this amounts to the same thing as God's Creation. That is, Conservation consists precisely in the ultimate ontological dependence of the universe upon God, at each point in its continuing existence, however long that existence has stretched back into the past or will stretch forward into the future. And so it is with Creation—the first moment of the existence of each thing that arises from nothingness, and the first moment of the universe as a whole (supposing, with Christian revelation, that the universe had a first moment).

To summarize the foregoing paragraphs: It is because of God's knowing and willing that things exist—and that they exist when they exist, and as the types of beings they are, and with the objective meaning or value that is attributable to them.

It must be remembered, of course, that all of the above is expressed in terms of our mode of thinking. Since God is Absolute Being, Whose Existence is entirely One and Simple, there can be in God no real distinctions—in particular, among "aspects" of God's Creative Act (i.e., knowing, willing, and making), and between the act of Creating and the act of Conserving the universe. We perhaps cannot avoid the appearance of making such distinctions, if we are humanly to articulate an account of God at all. But we should keep firmly in mind that in this case all language implying division or limitation is to be interpreted metaphorically.

Let us now turn to a different question, although one related to the above discussion: Is God in any way "constrained" or "limited" in the act of Creation? Philosophers and religious thinkers throughout history have pondered puzzles such as the following: "Can God create a square circle?" Or even: "Can God create a stone too heavy for God to lift?" Regarding the latter, it may seem that this represents a genuine dilemma for the theist. If one says that God *cannot* do this, one seems to be limiting God's creative ability—i.e., saying that God cannot create a certain stone. But if one says that God *can* create this stone, one again seems to be saying there is something God cannot do—i.e., lift the stone in question.[31]

The solution to such puzzles comes with the realization that certain verbal formulas do not correspond to genuinely possible acts—

---

31. For a discussion of these puzzles, see George I. Mavrodes, "Some Puzzles Concerning God's Omnipotence," in Brody, ed., *Readings in the Philosophy of Religion,* 410–12.

that the very ideas they express involve self-contradictions. But, it may be asked, does not this "solution" itself put a constraint on God's activity? On reflection we should be able to see that it does not. For, while the theist must hold that God acts consistently with what is logically and metaphysically possible, the reason for this is that such consistency is bound up with God's own creative act. God freely creates, as we might put it, with a view to reflecting God's own perfect Essence—itself the ultimate ground of all necessity and possibility, both logical and metaphysical. From the standpoint of God, therefore, there is no actual constraint.

We occasionally have spoken (as is commonly done) of "God's relations with the world." But it should be pointed out that such relations, strictly speaking, are relations of the mind or "beings of reason" only; that is, they are not, on God's side, real relations at all. In particular, God does not really change when finite persons or things change in relation to God—e.g., when they come to know and love God (or even when they come to exist!). As a matter of fact, the same is true of relations of reason within the natural world itself: objects themselves do not change, or become augmented in their real qualities, when individuals come to be aware of them. Moreover, as Pure Actuality, God is, as earlier noted, infinite and intrinsically without change. All real changes occur among things within finite reality.

Let us now inquire a little further into what can be said of the mode of God's activity. Here—as should be no surprise—we again find ourselves following primarily the "negative way." At one place in his discussion of God's activity, Emonet quotes with approval another French writer saying: "Between God as the cause of the world and the beginning of the world there is absolutely nothing"[32]—i.e., there is no medium, no space, etc. In a similar vein, the Englishman Herbert McCabe writes that God operates "within" things, not "on" them, as if from outside; that is, God is not an "external force."[33]

This point is worth pondering, for it has implications regarding the

---

32. Emonet, *God Seen in the Mirror of the World*, 5.
33. McCabe, *God Matters*, 13.

interpretation and the ultimate applicability of our expanded cone diagram. Indeed, it seems that there are here revealed certain limitations
of our diagram—and no doubt of any diagram. For at the very least it
should be admitted that the idea of there being "absolutely nothing"
between God and the beginning of the world—or between God and the
continued existence of the world—is somewhat obscured in our diagram, even though we have pointed out that the diagonal lines should
be interpreted as representing an extra dimension, as if they "folded
out" from the printed page. Now we come to see that these lines cannot be regarded as representing any kind of distance or extension—in
which case it might be asked whether there could be an adequate representation of the world and God that involves the use of lines. Since
lines, of their very nature, seem to signify extension, they themselves
function in the present context only metaphorically. Another way of
expressing the matter would be to say that our type of diagram does a
better job of representing God's transcendence than it does of representing God's immanence. To represent the latter, we would have to
"flatten" the lines altogether—and thus, of course, obscure God's transcendence! (Such, we now should be able to see, are necessary vicissitudes in any attempt to picture God.)

Next, let us consider the implications of the classical understanding of God for the question of human freedom. It has seemed to some
thinkers that if God's knowledge is eternal, there can be no genuine
freedom of action—because God "already knows" what we will do.
Such a conclusion has been reached especially (but not only) by philosophers and theologians who have been influenced by the earlier mentioned process thought.[34] However, on reflection, we can discover a
logical mistake in this line of reasoning—at least if we are speaking
of freedom and of God as these are understood in the perennial tradition. For the idea of "freedom" in question, most simply and precise-

---

34. For a process thinker who argues in this way, see David R. Griffin's essays in John B.
Cobb and Clark H. Pinnock, eds., *Searching for an Adequate God* (Grand Rapids, Mich.: Eerdmans, 2000). For a more classically oriented thinker who propounds the problem, see Anthony Kenny, "Divine Foreknowledge and Human Freedom," in *Aquinas*, ed. Anthony Kenny
(Garden City, N.Y.: Doubleday Anchor, 1969), 255–70.

ly, is one of real causality by way of an authentic exercise of the will. To the extent that choices and acts are free, they are not subject to any natural necessity, whether of a physical or a psychological sort. (The formula "an act that is free but naturally necessitated" thus would be comparable to the earlier "a square circle"—that is, these words express a logical impossibility.)

Such logical points aside, a doubt nevertheless may remain: If God is the Creator of the cosmos, and thus the first Cause of all actuality (including the actuality of human choice and action), and if God knows all events past, present, and future (including our human choices and acts), are these choices and acts not "necessitated" in some sense? Here, once again, we find ourselves in the realm of paradox and mystery. However, there is no contradiction involved in maintaining the reality of human freedom, if we conceive (as we have) God's knowledge and causality as eternal. For it can be said that God eternally creates certain beings—in particular, human persons—to live in freedom (to the extent that we actually achieve this in our lives); and it further can be said that God, as Aquinas would put it, eternally "ordains" that certain events come about as the result of free choices and acts. Another way to express this coherence would be to say that God's knowledge involves being eternally aware of, and God's causality involves eternally "supporting" (in an ontological sense, not necessarily a moral sense) what human persons, in time, freely choose.

Yves Simon expressed the matter as follows: "The modality by which the free act is free is no less certainly caused by God than any other aspect of any act or thing." But this very fact, so far from being an "obstacle" to freedom, involves, for the school of St. Thomas, "a glorious assertion of [God's] excellence in the creation and maintenance of freedom."[35]

Similarly, the fact that God knows our future choices does not mean that, in themselves, these choices in any sense are necessitated. For while it is true in our own case that actual knowledge extends only

35. Simon, *Freedom and Community*, 66. (It should be noted that St. Thomas and his school here again follow the lead of Boethius in *The Consolation of Philosophy*.)

to those events that either already have occurred, are now occurring, or are "set" to occur (because causes adequate to bringing them about are already in motion), in the case of God, Who is eternal, knowledge extends to all events—including those that will occur in the future. Thus, although, in one important sense, events about which *we* have actual knowledge cannot (any longer) not occur, events about which *God* has actual knowledge either may or may not be of this sort. And if the events in question either consist in, or result from, free choices that human persons will make in the future, they clearly (in themselves, at this point in time) *can* not occur—i.e., they are not necessitated.

In addition to creating and conserving reality, God acts as reality's Ultimate End or Final Cause. To approach an understanding of this matter, let us recall that, on the perennial account, value and good are objectively given. Let us also recall that the term "good" functions analogously; that is, it designates an ordered set of perfections related by proportionality and, sometimes, by attribution. Now, for the tradition of Aristotle, all striving is related to some end or final cause (in Greek, *telos*), which is a good for the being, or more specifically for the act, in question. And this is the case whether the striving is, as with plants, unconscious (recall the tropisms discussed at the beginning of part 2), or, as with us, conscious (in particular, our formulations of goals and our choices of means to pursue them).

But what might be regarded as the objective end, or good, of all created being? What stands first in the ordered hierarchy of final causes? And what would be the mode of operation of this final and ultimate end, especially in relation to the free choices and acts of human persons?

Thomas Aquinas takes up such questions in his *Summa Contra Gentiles*, book III, part 1. Ordinarily, when we speak of the "ends" or "goals" of actions we mean what the agents immediately have in mind. These often are called the actions' "proximate" ends, by contrast with more ultimate ends to which the former are ordered. (Thus, when one has symptoms of an illness, one may decide to go to the doctor to have them checked; in doing so one at the same time is pursuing the further goal of restoring one's health.) Now, is there some end or good related in this way to all that we do? This we characterized in section 2.3 as the "comprehensive good"—that which would be good without qualification. Aristotle called this good *eudaimonia*; his word is usually translated into English as "happiness." (In French, as we have noted, the word used is *bonheur*—which might here be translated as "goodness itself.") But what, in fact, would constitute the comprehensive good or goodness itself? What, in fact, would be a good without any lack or qualification? In our philosophical treatment of the human person, we found ourselves in the midst of mystery on this point. We indeed were able to specify what, and why, certain things serve as proximate ends (health, family, education, etc.) and in this way point to or contribute to the achievement of our final end. But at that stage of our inquiry a positive characterization of the ultimate good eluded us.

At this point, however—having come to understand God as constituting Goodness in the highest (indeed infinite) degree—we can see that, objectively, God also must be the Final End of all being and striving. But how, it may be asked, is God's unique final causality exercised? Aquinas discusses this matter in some detail (*Summa Contra Gentiles*, book III, part 1, chaps. 18–21). Let us note some of his key points.

First of all, God cannot be like a restoration of health—first existing in our minds and then, it is hoped, coming to exist in reality. For God is the absolutely First Reality. Thus God must be things' End in the sense that they seek, in their respective ways and measures, to "attain" to God.

Elaborating this point, we may say that to attain to God is to be "like God" in whatever ways particular beings are able. Thus, for example, all beings naturally seek to maintain their own existence; and in this, consciously or unconsciously, they seek to be like God, Who is Subsisting Being Itself. Moreover, all beings seek their respective goods (to be a full-grown oak, to be a virtuous and happy person, etc.);

and, insofar as they achieve their goods, they "participate," as we have put it, in goodness. But God just is Goodness, enjoyed all at once, entirely, and without lack; thus all beings seek, in their respective measures, to be like God in this way as well. Of course, given their limitations and conditions of potentiality, finite beings cannot, on their own, fully become like God; but they are, in these ways, ordered to God and God is thus their Ultimate End.

Besides participating in existence and goodness, things seek to be like God by exercising their proper activity and causality. Insofar as a being acts in accord with its nature, it imitates God in the highest way possible for that creature. In our human case, to exercise our proper activity and causality is to act freely in pursuit of authentic good. Aquinas accordingly quotes an earlier authority (whose precise identity is unknown but who took the name Dionysius, after the follower of Paul in the New Testament): "Of all things, it is more divine to become a co-worker with God." (*Summa Contra Gentiles*, book III, part 1, chap. 21.)

Of course, even if God is understood to be the Ultimate End of all striving (including our free, human striving), the actual choices we humans make—as we saw Emonet and Simon stress earlier—all too often go against this end, because they go against the genuine good. This leads to a consideration of how we are to understand the presence of evil in the world—including, but not limited to, the evil that we ourselves bring about—in relation to what is called God's "Providence." This will be our topic in the next section.

SUMMARY

• In spite of the presence of mystery and paradox, the transcendence of God can be seen to require, and to be required by, the very immanence of God.

• The perennial tradition maintains the classical understanding of God as eternal, by contrast with certain recent attempts to conceive God as an everlasting but literally temporal being.

• God's knowledge and will are to be understood as immediately causal; in addition to being subjects of Creation, things of this world (including human beings) are moved by God as Ultimate End.

3.4 PROVIDENCE AND EVIL

Meaning of God's Providence

According to its everyday meaning, as applied to human persons, to be provident is to be responsible for (and, along with this, to "provide" for) a range of future happenings—as well as their effects on ourselves and other persons, on the natural environment, etc. To be provident is to order events—or at any rate to try to order events—so that the things for which we are responsible achieve their proper or intended outcome. Thus, for example, in our society and most others parents are expected to provide for the needs of their children, especially when the children are young. And most parents in fact do their best along this line. However, given the natural limitations (physical, psychological, economic, etc.) that affect all human knowledge and activity, it can happen that, in spite of parents' best efforts, children fail to grow up to be healthy, happy, well-educated, and productive adults. More generally, given the role of what we call "chance" in human affairs—to say nothing of our mysterious but undeniable tendency to choose evil—we must recognize that, even in matters over which human persons exercise providence via intellect and will, complete success (i.e., complete achievement of what would be a good and proper outcome) is not to be expected.

Let us now consider in what way, and with what differences (recalling that all positive and literal language about God must be analogical), the notion of *providence* can be applied to God.

From the preceding discussions we recall that God's Intellect and Will are creative—that is, they bring things into existence; moreover, they extend to all that is or can be. The early Medieval writer Boethius, mentioned above, expressed the matter as follows: "Providence is the Divine Intelligence itself as it exists in the supreme principle of all things and disposes all things." Again, he remarked that Providence is "the evolution of things temporal as conceived and brought to unity in the Divine Intelligence."[36] Being "brought to unity" here means that, in one important sense, from God's standpoint there are no truly "chance events." As suggested just above, from the standpoint of our knowledge—in light of everyday experience, the philosophy of nature, and the sciences—many events indeed are attributed to "chance." That is, we recognize that they are due to the accidental crossing of lines of causality. For this reason many things happen quite irrespective of—and even contrary to—the natural tendencies and purposes of particular agents, including ourselves: an acorn is stepped upon by a hunter, our sincere effort to console a grieving friend is rebuffed, etc. Moreover, in such cases—unless the relevant causes are already in act, and are known by us to be in act—the outcomes are quite unpredictable. But in speaking of God we must mark a great difference. For God can and does turn to God's own ultimate purposes what—from the perspective of nature—are accidental or chance events. Indeed, Aquinas says that "the order of divine providence demands that there should be coincidence and chance in things." (*Summa Contra Gentiles*, book III, part 1, chap. 74.) Nevertheless, in the "all-at-once," single, comprehensive act by which God beholds and orders all things, nothing escapes God's Intellect and Will. Strictly speaking, therefore—from the standpoint of eternity—no events are simply due to "chance." All events are ordered by God so as to produce the end for which the universe is created.

However, this rejection, from an ultimate point of view, of mere chance events does not mean that all earthly matters are subject to ne-

---

36. Regarding the term "evolution" in this quotation, we should note that Boethius knew nothing of modern scientific theories of the evolution of species. Here he is simply speaking of the gradual unfolding through time of God's eternal plan. Still, it is an interesting project for contemporary philosophers of God to develop an account of evolution in the modern scientific sense as it relates to God's Knowledge and Will. For suggestions along this line, see Emonet, *Dearest Freshness*, chaps. 14–17; and W. Norris Clarke, S.J., *The One and the Many*, chap. 15.

cessity or "fate." Only those things that are ordained by their respective natures to act and interact so as to produce determinate outcomes can be regarded as necessitated in this way. And some things—in particular, the results of human free choice—are not determined by nature (or even the intersection of two or more natures). When persons act freely, they choose among alternative outcomes they believe they are capable of bringing about. Thus the effects of their actions cannot be said to be "fated" or necessitated. Nonetheless, all things—whether resulting from natural necessity or free choice—are ordained in keeping with God's comprehensive Knowledge and Freedom. Whereas our human providence is effective in some matters and to a certain degree, God's Providence is effective in all matters and to the highest possible degree—that is, it cannot fail.

Moreover, let us note that it is only in an analogical sense that God can be held "responsible" for the outcome of the universe: God, Who freely creates natures (the source of moral obligation), must be ontologically prior to morality; therefore God is under no type of obligation in acting. Again, we can see that there are no restrictions upon God's Freedom, except what is required by metaphysical consistency—which itself, as noted earlier, is determined by God's creative act. Clearly, therefore, while there is a similarity in saying "Parents are responsible for their young children" and "God is responsible for the cosmos," there also is an unfathomable difference.

Where we have spoken just above of God's Providence as "effective," traditional accounts also use the term "efficacious." Thus Aquinas says that God's Providence is efficacious in that the things of this world minister to God's final purpose, which cannot be frustrated. (*Summa Contra Gentiles*, book III, part 1, chap. 94.) Other characteristics of God's Providence that can be affirmed as a result of philosophical reasoning include the following: it is universal, immediate, and without violence or external compulsion. Let us consider each of these in turn.

Providence is said to be "universal" in that it extends to all things; it is said to be "immediate" in that the very being of things is given by God and, while ordinarily divine Providence operates through natural and "secondary" causes (recall the discussion of the latter notion in section 1.2), it is itself the Source of the powers that operate accordingly. (See *Summa Theologiae*, I, q. 22, arts. 2 and 3.) Finally, Providence is said to be "without violence" or external compulsion (proceeding, as the Medievals put it, *suaviter*, from whose root comes our English "persuasion") in that it ordinarily effects its purpose by making use of natural tendencies, rather than by going against them. (See ibid., I, q. 103, art. 8.)

Finally, let us note that, strictly speaking—recalling that in God essence and existence are identical—God's Providence just is God, insofar as God eternally orders all events within the universe so that the end for which it was created should be realized. Thus it is with good reason that religious people sometimes say, "This matter must be left to Providence"—meaning that it must be left to God.

The "Problem of Evil"

The God of historical theistic belief—whether in the form contributed to by the perennial philosophy or other traditions of thought—is said to be all-knowing, all-good, and all-powerful. What has come to be called the "problem of evil" is seen as a challenge to this belief. The challenge has been expressed in various ways, but none more famous than that of the eighteenth-century Scottish philosopher and skeptic David Hume: "Is he [God] willing to prevent evil, but not able? Then is he impotent. Is he able, but not willing? Then is he malevolent. Is he both able and willing? Whence then is evil?"[37]

Notice that the problem of evil is a genuine and serious problem only for those who hold that God is provident as characterized above. It is not at all clear, for example, that one who accepts Wolterstorff's model of God—for Whom the future, since it does not yet exist, is not knowable or controllable in any way that is essentially different from our own—is challenged by a recognition of evil in the same manner, or

37. David Hume, *Dialogues Concerning Natural Religion*, in Peterson et al., eds., *Philosophy of Religion*, 240.

to the same degree, as one who holds the traditional model; for on the latter the unrealized future nonetheless is present to God in a single, comprehensive act, an eternal "now."

Therefore, we shall focus on the problem of evil as it arises for the perennial tradition, and we shall consider the resources of this tradition for responding to it. Let us pose the following question: Can we accommodate both a belief in an all-knowing, all-good, and all-powerful God and also the recognition of evil within a single, coherent framework of thought? Over the centuries there have been a variety of efforts to show how the traditional concept of God in fact is compatible with recognition of evil in the world. An effort of this sort is sometimes called a *theodicy*, from the Greek words for "God" *(theos)* and for "judgment" or "right" *(dike)*. Within the perennial tradition, responses to the challenge of reconciling belief in God and the recognition of evil typically have involved two steps.

The first step involves rebutting the suggestion that God creates—or directly causes or brings about—any evil. As the point is expressed by Herbert McCabe, "God brings about everything that is good, [but] does not directly bring about anything that is evil."[38] This position, at least among Christian writers, stems from the early Church Father St. Augustine. Aquinas and his school follow Augustine's lead and render the position precise. To use the technical Thomist language, evil is real, but it is a *"privation."* That is, evil is an absence of a quality or perfection—e.g., blindness in the eye of a living animal, or vice in the soul of a human person—rather than a type of reality having its own subsistence. Moreover, "absence" here does not mean mere negation; rather, it refers to a lack of a quality or perfection that is normal (i.e., that follows an intrinsic norm, based on the thing's essence) for the type of being in question. In light of this, we see that God—Who creates everything falling under the heading "what is"—cannot be said to have created evil. For "what is" in this primary sense applies only to positive, subsistent realities, that is, within the physical cosmos, substances and their various features.

38. McCabe, *God Matters*, 27.

Evil therefore is in no way a direct result of God's creative act. This holds, incidentally, regarding both what are termed "natural evils" (the results of situations that involve beings acting according to their natures, and thus producing diseases, floods, animal predations, etc.), and what are termed "moral evils" (the results of bad personal choices and acts). However, in the former case, there might be said to be a kind of "indirect" causality by God, since the natures of things themselves depend on God's eternal knowledge and will; thus it must be acknowledged that God so orders things that certain natural evils occur as concomitants of goods—i.e., as concomitants of things fulfilling their own natures (for example, a lion's stalking its prey).

Where we have spoken of "natural" and "moral" evils, Scholastic thinkers often have used the terms "evil suffered" and "evil done." To "suffer" evil is to undergo evil (whether the agent belongs to the category of inanimate being, plant, animal, or human person). But "doing" evil is possible only for intellectual or personal beings, insofar as they can deliberately act against what they recognize (or should recognize) to be authentic good.

At this point we may find ourselves wanting to ask: How is moral evil, or evil done, itself possible? And isn't such evil also brought about by God, at least "indirectly"? Here reflection reveals that the answer is No. For unlike natural evil, or evil suffered, moral evil is wholly the result of the use—or rather the misuse—of the power of free will. Let us consider why this is the case.

When a rational but finite being falls away from the good, it is not as though he or she acts completely independently of God; for, as ontologically First Cause, God's Actuality is implicit in all that occurs. (As we expressed it above, God ontologically "supports" all that is and is done.) But in the case of moral evil, the evil—precisely as such—is not attributable to God, but only to the human agent.

In this connection, Jacques Maritain distinguishes two ontological "moments" or stages in the free choice of evil. The first is the mere initiative of the will to act apart from consideration of the dictates of reason and the good (e.g., general moral norms that are discernable).

This, in itself, is simply an absence or negation, not yet a privation of a due good. Its possibility, indeed, is implied in the very idea of the will being "free." In the second moment or stage one proceeds to an act of concrete choice, one that goes against dictates of reason and the true good. Here we have a genuine privation, and thus an instance of evil—in this case, an evil done.[39] Moreover, this evil done or moral evil produces a further wound—that is, an evil suffered—within the agent himself or herself. For, if one chooses against reason and the good, one makes oneself less human (and thus less good) than one can and should be. Yet throughout this second moment the evil done and its further consequences are not attributable, even indirectly, to God.

Why Does God Allow Evil?

Yet, as McCabe says regarding evil, "I shall grant that [God] could have prevented it."[40] Thus, in effect, God must be said to "allow" evils. Many thoughtful people have asked, "Why?" or "Why so many and such terrible evils?" This is the second and more difficult aspect of the problem.

To approach this question, let us first remark that, as McCabe points out, God cannot be said to be "guilty by neglect"—as if God were shirking a "responsibility" to prevent evil.[41] For, as already noted, God's mode of acting is ontologically prior to all obligation or responsibility, and thus cannot meaningfully be said to operate under any such moral constraints.

Moreover, in the case of both natural and moral evil, God can (and according to religious believers, sometimes does) intervene to prevent the evil in question. Or, to express the point more precisely, God may eternally ordain that some expected evil is avoided—e.g., in response to prayer, or in order that someone come to embrace a life of virtue. Nevertheless, it must be acknowledged that many expected—and unexpected—evils do befall the world, including ourselves. As suggested

39. Jacques Maritain, *St. Thomas Aquinas and the Problem of Evil* (Milwaukee, Wis.: Marquette University Press, 1942), 27–31.

40. McCabe, *God Matters*, 27.

41. Ibid., 37.

above, we may well want to ask why God allows such evils to occur.

In some cases, and in some respects, we ourselves are able to appreciate God's wisdom and goodness in allowing evil. We can see, as already suggested, that certain evils are inevitable consequences of God's creating a universe of contingent natural beings, as well as a universe in which some beings (e.g., members of predator species) achieve their goods at the expense of others. We also can come to see that beings endowed with free choice (in particular, ourselves) cannot be coerced into making good choices, or prevented from making bad choices, without subverting their very freedom—which, without doubt, itself is a great good or (non-moral) value. Moreover, is it not the case that, at least sometimes, we even can come to appreciate how a particular evil—whether natural or moral—contributes to overall good, or is compensated for by some other good?

This brings to mind a suggestion of the Patristic writer St. Irenaeus, which was reformulated by the British theologian and philosopher John Hick in the middle of the twentieth century. According to this suggestion, God presents us with a world designed, so to speak, for "soul-making."[42] That is, the good pointed to in this type of theodicy is the great good of personal spiritual development—a good we might well be unlikely to pursue if our experience of the world were without trials and tribulations. And, in fact, many people affirm that such trials and tribulations have been the occasion for the "making" or improvement of their souls.

However, in the end there remain, for nearly everyone, areas of unresolved concern, indeed of terrible mystery, in the experience of evil. Here we encounter the problem of evil at its very depth.

In approaching this problem, let us first ask: Is it entailed by God's Providence that God should provide a good outcome for each individual thing, as well as for the universe as a whole? The answer, it seems clear, is No. (Remember, again, that while it is metaphysically impossible for God to directly produce evil, God acts eternally and thus with-

---

42. See John Hick, "An Irenaen Theodicy," in *Encountering Evil*, ed. Stephen T. Davis (Westminster, Ky.: John Knox Press, 1981).

out moral constraints—for the latter are, both ontologically and logically, posterior to creation.) But is the human person perhaps a special case? For, as a being with a spiritual nature, a person can be considered a "universe" in himself or herself by way of subjectivity, as well as by way of knowledge and will. Here the answer the present writer would suggest is that God's Providence requires a *fitting* or *appropriate* outcome for each individual person. It is only in this precise sense of "fitting" or "appropriate"—including what is appropriate in light of personal choices made—that God must provide a "good result" for all persons. But what actually should count as a fitting result is surely a matter of deep mystery. We are, it would seem, simply in no position to judge the appropriateness of human persons' ultimate states, in part because of our lack of genuine knowledge about such states.

To return to the question of natural evil, one may be tempted to say that God should not have created a world in which some things, according to their very natures, must suffer in order that others by their natures may be fulfilled. Now, while the inclination to say this is understandable, we should consider, in detail, how very different any alternative world would be. Would such a world be demonstrably better than the one we actually inhabit? Moreover, as in the case of questions about the ultimate states of human persons, it seems to the present writer that any making of judgments about what kind of world God should or should not create takes us significantly beyond the scope of our limited rational powers.

However, it does seem that the perennial tradition must maintain something like the following: that the all-good, all-powerful, and all-knowing God would not allow any evils that, as seen from the ultimate perspective, do not contribute to or get compensated for in creation's overall end or good. This, in fact, is said in nearly the same words by Aquinas: "Divine providence does not imply the complete removal of evil from reality, but rather the ordering to good of the evil which arises." (*Compendium Theologiae*, part I, chap. 142.)

It is a very real question whether, or to what extent, this belief about Providence can be sustained in a purely philosophical manner—

i.e., in terms of common human experience and modes of reasoning. Or, more accurately, while the belief in question indeed seems to be a "corollary" of our philosophical concept of God, it also may seem to conflict with aspects of our lived experience. Here one might note the critical analysis by the American philosopher William L. Rowe, an acute and fair-minded thinker who in fact has defended "cosmological" arguments for the existence of God—i.e., arguments like Aquinas's first three. Regarding the problem of evil, however, Rowe demurs from the perennial position; indeed, he finds the evil in the world to be a stumbling block to personal religious belief. In an essay titled "The Problem of Evil and Some Varieties of Atheism," Rowe argues that it would be "fatal" to a belief in God if one were to acknowledge "instances of intense suffering [human or animal] which an omnipotent, omniscient being could have prevented without thereby losing some greater good or permitting some evil equally bad or worse." He then asks the reader to consider the case of a fawn trapped in a forest fire; the fawn is "horribly burned, and lies in terrible agony for several days before death relieves its suffering." Surely, he suggests, there are many such instances of animal and human suffering that must be regarded as truly "pointless"—that is, as neither required for some greater good, nor necessary to prevent some evil that is equally bad or worse.[43]

Is this indeed the case? To Rowe, it obviously is; and thus for him and for many others it turns out to be personally impossible to hold theistic beliefs. For still others, however, the above conclusion is not entailed—or at any rate it cannot be known to be entailed. (Doubtless, from a purely natural point of view, any person of good will and sensitivity will be very troubled by incidents such as the one described.) The concept of God's Providence does include God's directing all things so that the proper end of the universe is realized; but this end, and the ways it might be realized, are, to say the least, not fully intelligible to finite knowers like ourselves. Thus, on reflection, we see that a person need not adopt Rowe's skeptical conclusion.

43. William Rowe, "The Problem of Evil and Some Varieties of Atheism," in Brody, ed., *Readings in the Philosophy of Religion*, 307–9.

The blade in question of course cuts both ways. On one hand, the skeptic or atheist may argue that we ought to be able to see more clearly than is possible the intentions of a loving Providence; on the other hand, the reflective believer will point out that there is no compelling reason to suppose this—especially regarding a God Whose mind is said (in the Hebrew Scriptures) to be "unsearchable," and Who has declared (in those same Scriptures), "My ways are not your ways."

The above point suggests that the full articulation and defense of the perennial tradition's concept of God may require the resources of religious faith. And, without doubt, a firm belief in Providence is held primarily—if not only—by those who embrace a religious revelation that includes reference to such a God. As we have seen in earlier sections, philosophical reason does make important contributions to the overall tradition of Christian wisdom; but it should hardly be expected single-handedly to maintain this tradition by means of its natural, and thus limited, resources.

In light of all this, it seems appropriate that we extend our inquiry, and consider—to the extent possible within the boundaries of common human experience and reason—the idea of a "revelation" from God, as well as the nature of religious faith.

SUMMARY

• The notion of "Providence" expresses God's creative knowledge and will insofar as these can be approached by the human mind—largely by analogy with the providence exercised by parents and civic officials.

• The long-standing "problem of evil" suggests that it is conceptually impossible to recognize the evil present in the world and at the same time to think in terms of an all-good, all-knowing, and all-powerful God.

• Perennial responses to the problem of evil typically involve two parts: first, pointing out that God cannot in any way be considered the direct cause of evil; and second, arguing that, while God allows serious evil, it is brought by God to ultimate good.

3.5 "GOD'S CALL" AND THE RESPONSE OF FAITH

Is It Reasonable to Anticipate a Revelation?

Let us recall one of our results from part 2: philosophical reflection on the human person reveals both the dignity and the mystery of our being. At this point it might be added that philosophical reasoning about the existence and nature of God only adds to the sense of mystery about our being. As we have seen in the preceding pages, God comes to be characterized as Source and Exemplar of all that is, including all personal being. Thus, in some real way, we ourselves must be "like God." What then, we might ask, are we as human persons that we can be compared—even analogously—to God? Moreover, in contemplating such a comparison, we might recognize within ourselves a desire to communicate with this ultimate, Personal Source of our being. But how would such communication be possible?

Philosophy itself cannot answer this question. But it can raise and perhaps answer a related question—the one indicated in the title of this subsection. However, to be properly appreciated, this question must first be more fully articulated. In light of the foregoing discussions, we in effect are asking: Is it reasonable to anticipate a revelation from a Being that has been demonstrated (or, at any rate, that it is rationally possible to believe has been demonstrated): to exist; to be such that were it not for this Being we ourselves utterly would fail to exist; and to be the Ultimate End of all natural and human striving? Moreover, we have come to understand God as possessing in a "supereminent" way all positive personal qualities such as knowledge and love. And, since we ourselves, as persons, are essentially social and communicative beings, in this respect too we must image the Creator. Further, let us recall the disturbing and mysterious discovery within ourselves of a desire to exercise freedom in ways that ignore considerations of reason and authentic good, and the anguish experienced by many because of the problem of evil, as discussed in the immediately preceding section. In light of all this, is it not reasonable to expect that God—as the Being we have concluded God to be—would wish to communicate with us and clarify our existential condition for us, so that we may understand and respond in an appropriate way?

There is, of course, no basis for saying that communication from such a Being is either logically or ontologically necessitated. (Indeed, as we have seen, no act of God is necessitated.) But, given our experience of positive, personal qualities in our own limited or "impoverished" state, and given the impenetrability of the ultimate meaning of our being if we rely on our purely natural powers, it does—at least to this writer—seem reasonable to anticipate a communication from Absolute Being, that is, to anticipate a *revelation.*

The questions of what form such a revelation might take, and by what criteria we should assess proposed revelations, are ones that seem at least very difficult to pursue philosophically. In the end, we are perhaps limited to insisting that one's ultimate framework of thought—and what one affirms as the ultimate truth—cannot contain internal contradictions or incoherencies. This is not to say that one's framework cannot contain elements of mystery. Indeed, in the course of this book we have seen many such elements even in the regions of thought traversed by unaided human reason.

The view just sketched is contrary to that of the famous German philosopher Immanuel Kant, who wrote around the turn of the nineteenth century, and who held that religious beliefs should remain "within the limits of reason alone."[44] But, we would ask, in light of the points recalled above (especially the mysteries we have encountered in the world and in ourselves): Is it not actually more "reasonable" for us to be prepared to respond to a message that can be understood to come from beyond those limits?

---

44. See Kant's book incorporating this phrase in its very title: *Religion within the Limits of Reason Alone,* trans. Theodore M. Greene and Hoyt H. Hudson (San Francisco: HarperCollins, 1958).

"God's Call," Faith, and Reflection

According to Christian tradition, *faith,* as a religious act, involves a total personal response to what one hears as, or understands to be, a call from God. Let us consider how we are to make sense of this notion.

What is it to hear "God's call"? Can we identify and express the essential aspects of this experience? Answers to these questions would constitute a kind of phenomenology of religious faith.

It seems possible to say at least the following: To hear God's call is to apprehend a summons to a life of faith, and to realize that this summons requires of oneself the deepest and most definitive personal response—whether it be one of acceptance or rejection. In relation to Christianity, such an apprehension seems to require the joint presence of factors such as these: a) being aware, in terms of some adequate expression, of the Gospel message of God's saving acts in Jesus; b) seeing, or at least supposing, that the central teachings of Christianity can be accommodated within a viable framework of thought; c) finding concrete and personal significance in the promises and admonitions of the Gospels; and d) sensing the availability—to oneself, and to the whole world—of unlimited power and self-giving love, such as is said to characterize, and to be offered by, the God of biblical religion.[45]

How should we describe the response called "faith"? It is a response of acceptance, in light of the above types of experience, of what now is apprehended precisely as a call from God. In terms of our analyses of the human person in part 2, such a response will involve both cognitive and affective dimensions. Moreover, to be genuinely human, faith must involve rational affectivity—i.e., it must involve a person's will, not merely his or her feelings or emotions. Indeed, faith may be said to be primarily an act of will that moves a person to a firm ac-

45. Some years ago, the present author undertook a phenomenological description of Christian religious experience that set out more fully the points summarized here. See "Understanding and Agreement in Religion," *The Modern Schoolman* (May 1978): 333–55. The self-giving love mentioned at d) corresponds to Greek *agape,* which surpasses both *eros* and *philia,* mentioned in section 2.3.

ceptance of things (in particular, the promises of Christ) that cannot, of their very nature, be directly known by us to be true; and also to a firm commitment to live one's life accordingly. (From the standpoint of Christian theology, it would be added that these movements of the will depend on the gracious activity of God.)

The account outlined above compares favorably, we believe, with what John Paul II wrote about the nature of faith in *Fides et ratio*, sec. 33: "From all that I have said to this point it emerges that men and women are on a journey of discovery . . . [and that] Christian faith comes to meet them, offering the concrete possibility of reaching the goal which they seek. Moving beyond the stage of simple believing, Christian faith immerses human beings in the order of grace, which enables them to share in the mystery of Christ."

Our account also is in line with a statement by Cardinal Joseph Ratzinger, later Pope Benedict XVI, as recounted in the volume *Pilgrim Fellowship of Faith*. Making use of a formula of Aquinas, who in turn drew upon St. Augustine, Cardinal Ratzinger calls faith "thinking with assent." He notes, however, that unlike the assent that can be associated with scientific investigation, where a state of "certainty 'determines' our thinking," in the case of religious faith, "assent comes about . . . not through the degree of evidence bringing the process of thought to its conclusion, but by an act of will, in connection with which the thought process remains open and still under way." Indeed, as Aquinas pointed out long ago, faith is compatible with some degree of contrary spiritual "motions"—e.g., questioning, doubt, and interior struggle. In this special type of "thinking with assent," all of "[a person's] spiritual powers . . . are at work together."[46]

This reference to our "spiritual powers" will recall certain discussions from part 2. There we suggested that the basis of human dignity is to be located in our ability to pursue the knowledge of ultimate truth, and, once we have found it, to form our lives accordingly. We also suggested that, from the point of view of natural reason, this

---

46. Joseph Cardinal Ratzinger, *Pilgrim Fellowship of Faith*, trans. Henry Taylor (San Francisco: Ignatius Press, 2005), 21–24.

pursuit of truth about the human person ends in mystery. We now may add that—from a specifically Christian theological perspective—if anyone is to come to recognize ultimate truth there is required, in addition to genuine openness on his or her part, the supernatural power of God's action within.

This account of faith can be seen to have important implications for questions of *religious freedom*. There could be no more important goal for a human person than to recognize and embrace the truth about oneself. However, ultimate personal truth (unlike the truth of a scientific theory, or even a philosophical principle) cannot be recognized and embraced apart from an act of the will. Religious faith therefore involves the engagement of the individual's deepest and most intimate resources—things that cannot fall within the scope of any human authority to command. Here we find the philosophical basis for a fundamental and universal human right—one threatened, in our own day, by religious extremists on one hand and by militant secularists on the other: the right to freedom of choice in matters of religion.

Although truths of faith can be "confirmed" only through a movement of the will, Aquinas also spoke of "preambles of faith" *(praeambula fidei)*, truths which, although they can—and usually are—accepted on faith, also are subject to specifically philosophical reasoning. (Such reasoning can be said "to run along"—Latin *ambulare*—before actual faith.) Included in this category of preambles would be the very existence of God, as concluded to in the Five Ways, as well as the immaterial nature of the human soul, as discussed near the end of part 2. A recent philosopher of the perennial tradition, Pierre-Marie Emonet, expressed the role of such rational activity as follows: "Philosophers entertain certain purely metaphysical analyses capable of conditioning the natural intelligence to receive truths coming from above reason [i.e., the truths of revelation, which can be accepted only in faith]."[47]

47. Emonet, *God Seen in the Mirror of the World*, 37. See also Ralph McInerny, *Praeambula Fidei: Thomism and the God of the Philosophers* (Washington, D.C.: The Catholic University of America Press, 2006), esp. 26–32.

Concerning truths of revelation properly speaking—e.g., for Christians, the Incarnation of God in Jesus Christ; or, for Muslims, Mohammed's status as the "Seal of the Prophets"—it bears repeating that no results of human reason can lead to their confirmation (or, of course, their disconfirmation—except for a case in which a putative revelation is shown to be incoherent). Rather, these truths can be accepted only on the basis of one's more fundamental acceptance of God as having revealed them.

Reflections that take place specifically within the life of faith, and that make use of the "data" of revelation, give rise to formal systems of theology (e.g., Christology or Trinitarian theology). Since these systems of thought relate to supernatural mysteries, no single system can give a final or exhaustive account. Mysteries of faith are always open to further exploration and articulation. However, for the Catholic tradition, at least as understood by John Paul II, another "preamble of faith" becomes relevant here. If genuine theology is to be possible, we must suppose that propositions that are authentic expressions of the content of faith stand as objective and universal. This is not to deny the essential role of the will in religious faith. But it is to affirm that the content in question includes a cognitive dimension, and that this dimension in principle can be communicated to all persons of normal intellect and affectivity. Thus the Christian philosopher must seek, among other things, to overcome what can be termed the *"symbolicism"* of Paul Tillich and similar thinkers. That is, he or she must seek to authenticate the human capacity to come, in John Paul's words, "to a knowledge which can reach objective truth" (*Fides et ratio*, sec. 82)—even if, as in the case of the teachings of Christian faith, it is truth that can be expressed only in incomplete and analogous ways.

Regarding symbolicism, let us note that while symbols indeed are vital to the life of faith, a question inevitably arises as to how we can recognize a particular symbol, or set of them, to be adequate or appropriate. In this context, "adequacy" cannot mean what it does in the context of propositions directly proposing cognitive truth—i.e., correctly expressing some empirical or essential aspect of the reality in question. Rather, religious symbols seem at once to involve something less and something more. Something less, in that—precisely as symbols— the terms in question do not try to express reality by means of genuine concepts; something more, in that no concepts alone could have the depth of personal significance associated with symbolic uses of language. Still, the question of adequacy or appropriateness remains.

Tillich, as we have indicated, did not believe that there could be any literal or designative language about God; this view is one that the perennial philosopher obviously must reject. However, if one takes certain elements of Tillich's (and other authors') accounts of religious symbolism, and combines them with the sorts of analyses developed in the present book, it would seem that there might be envisioned a genuine "synthesis"—one involving the seemingly necessary designative, albeit analogical language ("God is," "God is One," "God is Good," etc.), and at the same time symbolic expressions ("God is our fortress," "The Lord is my shepherd," "Behold the Lamb of God," etc.). Moreover, it is quite understandable that philosophers would emphasize the need for, and possibilities of, designation and objective truth, whereas specifically religious thinkers would emphasize the richness of symbolic meaning and the importance of modes of expression that "reach beyond" the literal.[48]

Responses to Remaining Challenges

Let us now turn to the third set of challenges articulated in the Introduction. These, it will be recalled, included relativism, postmodernism, and nihilism. In the context of religion, relativism often finds expression in what its proponents call *religious pluralism*. A primary figure in this movement is John Hick, who holds that "the great world faiths embody different conceptions of, and correspondingly different

48. For an example of a religious teaching that contains both aspects, consider that of "eternal life." From the cognitive standpoint, this phrase applies properly (albeit by the "negative way" and the way of analogy) to God, and only improperly to us. For, as we have seen, our being is essentially temporal. However, we can use the notion of "eternity" to symbolically express the anticipation of whatever our state will be when there is "a new heaven and a new earth."

responses to, the Real or the Ultimate from within the major variant cultural ways of being human." Moreover, while the various religious traditions have different conceptions of the ultimate state humans hope to achieve ("salvation," "liberation," "enlightenment," "nirvana," etc.), at the most fundamental level they all involve, according to Hick, "the transformation of human existence from self-centeredness to Reality-centeredness"; and, "so far as . . . observation can tell," followers of the world's diverse religious paths succeed "to much the same extent."[49] Thus, for the pluralist or relativist, the respective religious traditions have an essentially equal standing, in relation to both the correctness of their teachings and the effectiveness of their practical programs of transformation.

Now, in an age in which religious liberty and tolerance are rightly prized, it can be appreciated that religious pluralism (as well as other forms of relativism) have become popular positions, even though they challenge traditional understandings of truth, including that of the perennial philosophy. However, several problems with pluralism should be considered. First, it is widely recognized that, for the religious person, this position runs the danger of incoherence: if God in no way can be directly attained, and if the various religious traditions merely reflect culturally conditioned visions, why should we adopt one particular religion rather than another, or rather than no religion at all? Moreover, we have discerned reasons for anticipating a (genuine) revelation from God, one that would provide definitive answers to the mysteries of human life as we have come to be aware of them. Such a revelation scarcely could take the form of indefinitely many incompatible and culturally conditioned accounts. This is not to say that there cannot be important truths expressed in the various religious traditions. Nor, from the theological point of view, does it mean that only formal adherents of divinely revealed religion can achieve salvation. (In this regard, the Catholic Church and certain other Christian bodies have de-

---

49. John Hick, "A Philosophy of Religious Pluralism," in *Classical and Contemporary Readings in the Philosophy of Religion*, ed. John Hick, 3rd ed. (Englewood Cliffs, N.J.: Prentice-Hall, 1990), 425.

veloped understandings of "universal salvation"—i.e., the possibility that those who have not heard the Gospel nevertheless can be caught up in the saving work of God in Christ.)[50] However, Hick's relativistic pluralism seems to be incompatible with authentic Christianity, as well as with most other religions—and, as we have just argued, there also are philosophical reasons for questioning it.

Next let us ask how a postmodernist philosopher might react to our philosophical exploration about God. As noted in the Introduction, postmodernists such as Jacques Derrida regard all language as embedded in particular viewpoints, or, as Derrida also called them, "myths." For this French thinker the whole history of philosophy is to be regarded as a succession of controlling ideas, ones that developed out of a search for some absolute and central reality—for example, Plato's "Forms," Aristotle's "substance," or the Medievals' "God." In all cases, according to Derrida, the central idea served "not only to orient, balance and organize the structure . . . but above all to make sure that the organizing principle would limit what we might call the play of the structure."[51] With no "play" (i.e., no variation or uncertainty) allowed by the particular culture, the principle in question achieved mythical status and went unquestioned as long as the relevant forms of thought held sway.

By way of response to this position, we would note our effort to provide a common experiential basis for reasoning to and speaking of God. (The same, incidentally, could be said regarding the notion of substance, as discussed in part 1.) The idea of God, as we have pre-

50. For Catholic accounts that express deep respect for other religious traditions without adopting a radical or relativistic pluralism, see J. A. DiNoia, O.P., *The Diversity of Religions: A Christian Perspective* (Washington, D.C.: The Catholic University of America Press, 1992); and Joseph Cardinal Ratzinger, *Truth and Tolerance: Christian Belief and World Religions*, trans. Henry Taylor (San Francisco: Ignatius Press, 2004).

51. Jacques Derrida, "Structure, Sign, and Play in the Discourse of the Human Sciences," in *Writing and Difference*, trans. Alan Bass (Chicago: University of Chicago Press, 1978), 278. It is interesting to note the influence of Derrida and other postmodernists even on Catholic philosophers in France. In particular, see the work *God without Being*, by Jean-Luc Marion, trans. Thomas A. Carlson (Chicago: University of Chicago Press, 1991). For Marion (at least in the book here mentioned), the metaphysical notion of "being"—although not the God of religious faith—is a "myth" in Derrida's sense; or, as Marion himself puts it, this notion is a "conceptual idol."

sented it, is not an a priori construction brought in to limit thought (as indeed is often the case with genuine myths); rather, this idea is the result of attentive philosophical reflection—and, the author hopes, it holds potential for further fruitful reflection.

Let us consider as well how a nihilist philosopher might react to the above pages. Friedrich Nietzsche, taken by many to be a prototype of this movement, proclaimed over a hundred years ago that "God is dead," indeed that "we have killed him."[52] By this he meant that anyone who fully embraces the present age no longer has need for a concept of God. In light of this, Nietzsche no doubt would be surprised— perhaps even amused—to read the serious, positive accounts of God (and of the world's relations with God) articulated in this part of our book. But what might the nihilist actually say by way of criticism? Perhaps the following: In spite of its "official" emphasis on philosophical reason, this book and its author in fact are simply (perhaps even slavishly) following the beliefs of religious predecessors—beliefs that are outmoded and in fact demeaning to authentic human life. Moreover the book's display of rational flourishes (e.g., the logical analyses in section 3.1) simply mask this underlying mentality. Faced with such charges (versions of which also are expressed by certain contemporary authors),[53] the perennial philosopher can only respond by asking that the fair and objective reader consider the philosophical argumentation that has been presented. Do the rational elements introduced amount to mere "flourishes"—or do they contribute in a substantive way to the understanding of ultimate matters, in particular, ones re-

---

52. Friedrich Nietzsche, *The Gay Science*, trans. Walter Kaufmann (New York: Vintage Books, 1974), § 343.

53. A recent tract is *The End of Faith*, by Sam Harris (New York: W. W. Norton, 2005). Writing in the wake of 9/11—but questioning other historical expressions of "faith" as well—Harris subtitles his book *Religion, Terror, and the Future of Reason*. See also Richard Dawkins, *The God Delusion* (Boston and New York: Houghton Mifflin, 2006). A section of the book called "Thomas Aquinas' 'Proofs'" (pp. 77–79) begins with these remarks: "The five 'proofs' asserted by Thomas Aquinas in the thirteenth century don't prove anything, and are easily—though I hate to say so, given his eminence—exposed as vacuous. The first three . . . rely upon the idea of a regress and invoke God to terminate it. They make the entirely unwarranted assumption that God himself is immune to the regress." In light of our discussion in section 3.1, one may wonder whether Professor Dawkins has had occasion to reflect on the nature and philosophical significance of contingent being.

lated to our being and its source? And, if the latter is judged to be the case, the tables might well be turned; that is, one might ask: What is the true psychological basis of nihilism, including its notion of what is demeaning to authentic human life?

At this point, we also should consider the remaining challenges to perennial thought (beyond Tillich's "symbolicism" discussed above) that arise among religious believers themselves. To begin with fideism, let us consider a famous passage from the writings of the Danish thinker Søren Kierkegaard. He regularly stressed what he took to be the essentially "subjective" character of Christian faith—i.e., its relation to the personal subject, by contrast with the "objective" character of science and speculative philosophy. Kierkegaard writes, "Without risk there is no faith. . . . If I am capable of grasping God objectively, I do not believe, but precisely because I cannot do this I must believe. If I am to preserve myself in faith I must constantly be intent upon holding fast the objective uncertainty, so as to remain out upon the deep, over seventy thousand fathoms of water, still preserving my faith."[54] Here, it may be noted, there is one important element with which the perennial philosopher will sympathize. Matters of faith, properly speaking, are matters of risk and personal commitment, requiring for their acceptance acts of will as well as intellect. (And they can involve, as Aquinas was well aware, "objective uncertainty.") But Kierkegaard is saying something more: namely, that a philosophical (i.e., metaphysical) approach to God is religiously suspect; and it seems to this writer that our sections 3.1–3.3 have shown that this is not the case. Rather, a (properly modest) philosophical approach to God can be quite compatible with, and supportive of, orthodox religious faith.

It is interesting to speculate about how a fideist would react to nihilism. The fideist might agree with the nihilist that there is no positive basis in common human experience or reason to affirm the reality of God. However, unlike the nihilist—who, as John Paul put it, is prone either to "a destructive will to power" or to "a life without

---

54. Søren Kierkegaard, *Concluding Unscientific Postscript*, trans. David F. Swenson and David Lowrie (Princeton, N.J.: Princeton University Press, 1941), 182.

hope"—the fideist chooses to affirm the meaningfulness of human life precisely by way of his or her religious faith. In light of our discussions, the student may wish to consider the possibilities of combining elements of these two rather different responses to nihilism—i.e., that of the perennial, metaphysical philosopher, and that of the religious existentialist.

As we noted in the Introduction, fideism is sometimes associated with fundamentalism, the view that all ultimate questions about being, the human person, and God are already available in the Bible, and thus that philosophy is at best unnecessary and at worst a threat to religious belief. By way of response to this view, we may point to the role that philosophical elements have played in the very formulation of biblical religion. Consider, for example, the idea of Christ as God's "Word" (in Greek, *Logos*), expressed at the beginning of John's Gospel: "In the beginning was the Word, and the Word was with God, and the Word was God. All things came to be through him and without him nothing came to be." (Jn 1:1–3.) This passage reflects, among other things, the Hellenistic philosophical currents that characterized late antiquity, in which the term *Logos* expressed ideas of divine "utterance" or "emanation." The author of the Gospel, aware of this context, is claiming (contrary to other views on offer at the time) that Christ himself is the very *Logos* of God. A passage such as this would be virtually unthinkable outside the milieu of the Greco-Latin world.[55] Similar remarks would be appropriate regarding discussions of "soul" and "spirit" in the letters of St. Paul. (Recall the passage from the Letter to the Hebrews noted in section 2.1.) Thus, whether they are regarded as welcome or unwelcome, philosophical influences on Christian thought seem to be inescapable. The only real questions are which sorts of philosophy will be influential, and what kinds of influence will they have? In light of this, fundamentalism seems quite ill-considered—unless one is prepared to "immortalize" the frameworks

---

55. For a discussion of influences on the composition of John's Gospel, and specifically on the identification of Christ as the *Logos* of God, see Bruce Vawter, C.M., "The Gospel According to John," in *The Jerome Biblical Commentary*, ed. Raymond E. Brown, S.S., et al. (Englewood Cliffs, N.J.: Prentice-Hall, 1968), 416–17.

of thought of one particular historical period (a move that perennial philosophers—under the tutelage of Jacques Maritain's statement about the need for constant intellectual renewal—clearly would not support).

In fact, perennial philosophers stress the need for both substantive and critical uses of reason in the articulation of religious faith. John Paul II himself, commenting on what he called "biblicism" (i.e., fundamentalism), remarked that one cannot "make the reading and exegesis of Sacred Scripture the sole criterion of truth"; and he added that "without philosophy's contribution, it would in fact be impossible to discuss theological issues such as, for example, the use of language to speak about God . . . [or] . . . God's creative activity in the world." (*Fides et ratio*, secs. 55 and 66.) The reader will recognize in the late pope's remarks the theological relevance of sections 3.2 and 3.3 of this book. Indeed, the author hopes that a number of our philosophical results can assist in the ongoing renewal of Christian theology.

SUMMARY

- In light of the foregoing sections (which establish the rationality of belief in a Personal, Creator God, but also the deep mysteries of our being, including the tendency toward evil), it can be argued that one might appropriately anticipate a revelation.

- Religious faith involves a total personal response to what is accepted as a communication from God; the "great tradition" emphasizes the role of philosophy in developing a cognitively significant articulation of the mysteries of faith.

- Contrary to extreme postmodernists and nihilists, perennial philosophers seek rationally to articulate the meaningfulness of being and its Source; contrary to fideists and fundamentalists, they point to a need for, as well as the possibility of, uses of reason in religious matters.

QUESTIONS FOR REFLECTION (PART 3)

1. Explain the nature of deductive argument, and the role it plays in attempts to demonstrate the existence of God. How, in the case of Aquinas's Five Ways, are the arguments supposedly rooted in facts of experience, and in philosophical—by contrast with empiriological—reflection on such facts? Take one of the Five Ways, as presented in section 3.1, and discuss whether it appears to be sound.

2. Explain, using our "cone" diagram, the difference between temporal and essentially ordered (or "subordinated") series of causality; and discuss how these two types of series figure in Aquinas's first two Ways. The Third Way is thought by many perennial philosophers to be the most fundamental of Aquinas's arguments. Discuss why this might be thought to be the case, and whether it seems to you to be the case.

3. How does the Fourth Way relate to the metaphysical principle concerning participation elaborated in part 1? Why is Aquinas's example of heat an obstacle, rather than an aid, in presenting this argument today? Despite this flaw, discuss whether the argument, suitably expressed, seems to be sound.

4. Explain, with examples, what is meant by the "negative way" in speaking about God. Why does Maimonides think that, if we are concerned with literal meaning, only the "negative way" can be used without falling into idolatry? How does Aquinas's theory of analogous language provide a way that some philosophers believe goes beyond Maimonides? Discuss to what extent it really does so.

5. Why, in light of our accounts in part 1, can there be no univocal language relating the world and God? Why would an appeal to equivocity also be futile? Explain, with examples, the difference between the way of metaphor or symbolism, and the way of analogy, and discuss to what extent each seems able to contribute to an account of language about God.

6. Explain, using our diagrams, the difference between conceiving God as eternal and as everlasting. How does Wolterstorff argue that the God of biblical religion must be conceived as everlasting? How does a follower of Boethius and Aquinas respond to Wolterstorff, and how cogent do you take this response to be?

7. What philosophical account do Augustine and Aquinas give of the

reality of evil? How does this account enable them to respond to an initial problem about evil in relation to God? Does calling evil a "privation" of good adequately recognize the true nature and reality of evil? Discuss.

8. Explain, with examples, the difference between natural and moral evils. Why must the traditional theistic philosopher hold that God would not allow any evils that, in the final analysis, do not either contribute to overall good or get compensated for by good? Discuss to what extent this claim can be philosophically justified, and to what extent its acceptance seems to require religious faith.

9. Explain the author's argument that if a person has a rational belief in God (as developed, for example, within perennial philosophy), it is reasonable to anticipate a revelation. Would it be possible to show, philosophically or otherwise, that a supposed revelation constitutes a "genuine" (or an "objective") call from God? Should the answer to this question either contribute to or detract from the firmness of an individual's religious faith? Discuss.

10. Take our suggestion about how a nihilist thinker might react to the perennial philosophy of God and consider how this reaction might be further elaborated. How would a religious fideist respond to nihilism; and how would his or her response be different from one given by a thinker in the perennial tradition? Which response strikes you as more satisfactory, and why? Do you see ways of combining elements of the two? Explain.

EPILOGUE

Review of Our Philosophical Results

Under the general title *Understanding Our Being,* this book has sought to introduce students to speculative philosophy as undertaken in the perennial tradition. Let us review the principal results that have been articulated.

In part 1, after clarifying the very idea of pursuing the being of things, we began with an investigation of natural being. Results here included the "hylemorphic" structure of physical reality, according to which each thing *is* as an individual substance through the organization of primary matter by a natural, substantial form. We noted that each such form in turn is associated with specific powers and acts. It also emerged that a comprehensive scheme of explanation of natural being must include reference to a variety of types of causality (traditionally called "formal," "material," "efficient" or "agent," and "final"). We then moved to a metaphysical study of being, partly as a result of realizing that the term "being" is not intrinsically limited in its application to physical beings, and partly as a result of finding indications that the realm of natural being is not adequately self-explanatory. As the most general and most fundamental study of being, metaphysics articulates concepts (e.g., "existence," "goodness," "unity," etc.) that apply across all categories, as well as principles (e.g., those of Identity and Sufficient Reason) that underlie all particular disciplines. Within speculative philosophy itself, metaphysical concepts and principles find application in the subject matters that make up the book's succeeding parts.

We proceeded in part 2 to articulate a philosophy of our specific personal being. To be a human person is, first of all, to be a type of living being. The perennial tradition adopts the language of Aristotle and Aquinas to speak of the substantial form of a living being as "soul" (Greek *psuche,* Latin *anima*). As long as a natural substance is alive, its particular type of soul informs matter so as to compose a being with its respective life-powers. At death the living being simply is no more; it is replaced by other, non-living natural substances. We investigated two general modes of activity that characterize personal life: knowledge and affectivity. Certain aspects of each are shared with other animal species; but others—intellectual knowledge (involving universal concepts, judgments, and reasoning), and rational affectivity or will (involving deliberation and free choice)—seem to be distinctive of ourselves as human beings. Moreover, the particular forms of sociality that characterize personhood elevate this aspect of our lives as well, when compared with similar modes of behavior in other species. In the end, these points led to the conclusion that aspects of human reality are immaterial in nature, and thus that human soul, the source of these aspects, is immaterial as well.

In part 3 of the book, we explored human reasoning to God, as well as what can be said of God taken as the Source and End of being. Regarding theistic reasoning, we developed a contemporary presentation of Aquinas's Five Ways and provided materials to help the student assess whether such modes of argument should be considered sound. Regarding statements about God, a primacy of place, both historically and conceptually, was accorded the "negative way"—i.e., the development of well-grounded statements of what God is not. Perennial philosophers also seek an account of positive statements about God using the theory of analogous language. (Of course, much language about God arises from within religious communities, where the full resources of metaphor and symbol also come into play.) Philosophically, the primary designation for God is "the One Who Is"—i.e., Absolute, Eternal, and Personal Being. After discussing the view of certain recent religious writers who seek to conceive God as literally "everlasting" (and thus as fully temporal), rather than as "eternal," we undertook a philosophical discussion of God's Providence. This led to a consideration of the age-old problem of evil, which, according to those who pose the problem, shows the conceptual impossibility of recognizing the evil in the world and at the same time accepting the idea of an all-good, all-knowing, and all-powerful God. Although we challenged this claim of conceptual impossibility, we acknowledged the unlikelihood of a fully adequate response to the problem of evil in common human terms, i.e., without appealing to specifically religious themes. We concluded by considering the reasonableness, in light of the perennial philosophy, of anticipating a revelation from God, and by exploring the nature of religious faith and the role of philosophical reason in articulating the content of faith.

As we indicated in the Preface to the book, proponents of the perennial tradition, although mindful of the Christian context in which their work has flourished, believe that basic results such as the ones recounted above can be rendered compelling to persons of all ages and cultures. In practice, this raises important and sometimes difficult issues concerning intercultural dialogue.

Prospects for Intercultural and Interreligious Dialogue

Given the ever-increasing communication among peoples of the earth, as well as the tensions and even violence that sometimes accompany deep differences in perspective, it is widely accepted that all peoples must be open to intercultural and interreligious dialogue. In the Introduction we noted John Paul II's explicit hope that philosophy, as developed within the perennial tradition, might make a substantive contribution to such dialogue.

However, in pursuing such a hope we must realize that there are widely differing ideas about the nature, purpose, and conditions for the success of this enterprise. For some persons it seems that dialogue is simply a pretext for trying to convert the other to one's own point of view. For others it seems that dialogue requires each party to give up its own claim to truth—or even to give up the supposition that there is any ultimate truth to be attained. As we shall see, neither of these attitudes is compatible with intercultural and interreligious dialogue as understood by John Paul II and perennial thinkers.

In *Fides et ratio*, sec. 72, John Paul II set out three "requirements" for authentic dialogue, as this might be participated in by Christian philosophers and theologians. He regarded these requirements as both reasonable in themselves and acceptable in principle to properly motivated dialogue partners from other traditions. The three points are as follows: first, recognition of the universality or commonality of the human spirit, in particular in its search for truth; second, agreement that no religious tradition should remain "closed," or seek to affirm itself by simply rejecting others; and third, acknowledgment that Christian partners to dialogue cannot abandon what they have gained through initial "inculturation" in the world of Greek and Latin thought. Of course, themes arising in other cultural contexts indeed might help clarify those of the Christian tradition—and in fact this tradition should try to assimilate them, as long as they are not intrinsically incompatible with its original cultural inheritance. Thus, writing with particular reference to the metaphysical and religious speculations of India, the late pope declared, "It is the duty of Christians now to draw from this rich heritage the elements compatible with their faith, in order to enrich Christian thought" (ibid.). By the same token, it may be hoped that dialogue partners from other religious and philosophical traditions will find their ways of "understanding our being" enriched as well.

Let us now suggest some specific points for interreligious dialogue of the sort called for by *Fides et ratio*. Beginning with the ancient and many-layered religion of Hinduism, we might note first of all that it adheres to a fundamental and long-standing conceptual duality. The term "Atman" for Hindu thinkers represents human reality, while the term "Brahman" represents divine or eternal reality. However, the relation between the two is controverted. Some Hindu texts and scholars regard Atman and Brahman as strictly separated, whereas others regard them as in principle united. Consider the following passage from the work called *Upanishads*, in which a seeker of Truth discovers, at the moment of death, his identity with Brahman: "I see the light, which is your fairest form. I myself am He! My breath to the air, to the immortal! My body ends in ashes."[1] Study and reflection

---

1. *Isa Upanishad* 15–18, as quoted in Robert E. Van Voorst, *Anthology of World Scriptures* (Belmont, Calif.: Wadsworth, 1994), 36.

on such texts, and a comparison of them with one's own, might, for the Christian, shed light on the idea of the human person as "image" or "likeness" of God. Moreover, it seems reasonable to assume that Hindu readers of, say, the book of Genesis may find light shed in their direction as well. A further important point would be the following: although, on the surface, Hinduism is characterized by reference to many gods (Vishnu, Shiva, Krishna, etc.), it may be wondered whether these are best understood as symbols of the one true God, rather than as expressions of polytheism. As another *Upanishad* has it: "Beyond [the high mountain] is the High Brahman, the vast, hidden in the bodies of all creatures. He alone envelops everything, as the Lord."[2] A pursuit of this passage might give rise to other fruitful explorations involving Hindu and Western religious traditions.

The thought of ancient China also reveals overlaps with Christian themes that might be explored in a philosophical way. Consider this verse about the "Tao," i.e., the "Way" of the cosmos, to which the wise person will order his or her life:

> The Tao that can be walked is not the enduring
>   and unchanging Tao.
> The name that can be named is not the enduring
>   and unchanging name.
> Conceived of as having no name, it is the
>   Originator of heaven and earth;
> Conceived of as having a name, it is the Mother
>   of all things.
> Always without desire we must be found
> If its deep mystery we would sound. . . .[3]

Readers of the present book will see that these lines offer material for comparison (as well as contrast) with the perennial tradition's accounts of God and the order of the universe, including the "deep mystery" of Providence.

---

2. *Shvetashvatara Upanishad* 3.1–13, as quoted in Van Voorst, *Anthology of World Scriptures*, 34.

3. *Tao Te Ching*, 1, as quoted in ibid., 173.

Buddhism originated in India with Siddhartha Gautama (the first to experience "buddhahood" or "enlightenment"), but it took root primarily in East Asia. It also represents a dialogue partner. There are several strands of Buddhism—notably Theravada, located primarily in Sri Lanka and Southeast Asia; Mahayana, in East Asia; and Vajrayana, in Tibet. Most Buddhists do not affirm a God, and in fact place little importance on ideas of transcendent reality; moreover, most Buddhists deny the reality of the human self as an actual metaphysical subject. Nonetheless, with their themes of "Dharma" (the saving reality or path taught by the Buddha) and "Sangha" (the Buddhist community), these religious peoples express a profound understanding of human life, in particular its social aspects. It seems to the present writer that the perennial philosophical themes articulated in sections 2.4 and 2.5 might well elicit interest (although in some cases rejection) among adherents of Buddhism. And, even though there are significant incompatibilities between the two traditions, Christian thinkers might profit from such an encounter as well.[4]

Regarding the religion of Islam, it will be recalled from section 3.2 that an account of language, such as Aquinas's, that distinguishes analogy from metaphor, may be helpful in seeing what is meant by each of the Hadith's "Ninety-nine Most Beautiful Names of God." Regarding another important matter, it has long been a point of difficulty for Muslims that Christians, with the teaching on the Trinity, seem to worship three Gods—something unthinkable within Islam's own very insistent monotheism. The perennial philosopher Jacques Maritain noted a number of years ago the importance, in this context, of carefully distinguishing within the teaching about God the notions of "being," "substance," and "person"—precisely so as to remove the tendency toward "tri-theism," which Islam rightly rejects.[5]

---

4. For concrete suggestions, see James S. Dalton, "Human Dignity, Human Rights, and Ecology: Christian, Buddhist, and Native American Perspectives," in *Made in God's Image: The Catholic Vision of Human Dignity*, ed. Regis Duffy, O.F.M., and Angelus Gambatese, O.F.M. (Mahwah, N.J.: Paulist Press, 1999), esp. 35–42.

5. See Maritain, *A Preface to Metaphysics*, 95–97. For the *Hadith* passage on the names of God, see Van Voorst, *Anthology of World Scriptures*, 335–36. For a more general discus-

Regarding Native American religions, as well as other indigenous sources, we might note the common belief in a spirit-world, including, often, the "Great Spirit." Although the animism of indigenous religions is not to be found in Aristotelian philosophy, it is significant, the present writer believes, that the notion of "form" and (by extension) the notions of "essence" and "actuality" are. For these latter notions serve a purpose similar to that of what we may regard as mythical elements in indigenous religions. Specifically, they indicate that all realities share, in proportionate ways, characteristics named in common—not "spirits," strictly speaking, but that analogous set (i.e., the "forms" of things) of which "soul" and "spirit" are the highest members. As is well known, Native American cultures display great reverence for all things of the world, including the human person. The perennial tradition's emphasis on human "dignity" arises in a similar way—out of respect for what is required of and thus owed to the human spirit. By the same token, it might be suggested that perennial philosophers (and the Christian tradition generally) can learn from their indigenous counterparts that such reverence is to be extended to all things according to their respective forms.[6]

Now we must turn to a more theoretical issue: Whatever progress in mutual understanding may be achieved through dialogue, how are we to think about the very fact—apparently quite durable—of religious and philosophical diversity?

As already noted in section 3.5, the perennial philosopher will argue against religious "pluralism" as understood by John Hick, on the grounds that it seems essentially relativistic. Hick's view, in fact, is precisely what John Paul II had in mind when he wrote critically about "undifferentiated" pluralism. This relativistic type of pluralism, incidentally, has had an impact within Catholic theology. The interested

---

sion, see the comparative treatment of Islamic, Jewish, and Christian thought about God in the Middle Ages by David B. Burrell, C.S.C., *Knowing the Unknowable God: Ibn-Sina, Maimonides, Aquinas* (Notre Dame, Ind.: University of Notre Dame Press, 1986).

6. For suggestions along this line, see Dalton, "Human Dignity, Human Rights, and Ecology," esp. 42–49. See as well various essays in Anne Waters, ed., *American Indian Thought* (Malden, Mass.: Blackwell, 2004).

reader may consider the well-intentioned but controversial writings of Jacques Dupuis, S.J., and Roger Haight, S.J. These works in fact have been subject to a *monitum* (warning) by the Vatican's Congregation for the Doctrine of the Faith, indicating that they contain passages that appear inconsistent with Catholic teaching—largely on the basis of tendencies toward relativism and also, in the case of Haight, toward historicism.[7]

In light of our earlier reflections, we are in a position to see that relativistic forms of pluralism are wrong-headed. First of all, they are unsatisfactory from the standpoint of authentic religious faith and commitment, at least as traditionally understood. Moreover, they in no way are required by a correct philosophical analysis; for the notion of ultimate truth surely can be accommodated even if, as a matter of fact, the articulation of such truth is something that can only be approximated by the human mind.

Religious "pluralism," as here discussed, is often contrasted with two alternative views, called "exclusivism" and "inclusivism," respectively.[8] *Exclusivism* is the extreme opposite of relativistic pluralism: it maintains that there is one, and only one, path to salvation, and that only those who hear about and embrace this path are able to come to human fulfillment. Exclusivism is often maintained by persons we earlier called "fundamentalists," whether they are members of the Christian or some other (e.g., Islamic) tradition. It may be noted that, at least on the face of things, this view characterized certain teachings of the Catholic Church before the period of the Second Vatican Council (1962–65). In earlier eras a phrase sometimes used was *"extra Ecclesiam nulla salus"* ("outside the Church there is no salvation"). Now, however, Catholic thinkers typically embrace some form of inclusivism—in some cases reinterpreting the above phrase

---

7. It should be added, however, at least in the case of Dupuis, that his more recent writings appear to be more irenic. They might be thought to represent a very strong form of the position we shall come to identify as "inclusivism." See, in particular, Jacques Dupuis, S.J., *Christianity and the Religions: From Confrontation to Dialogue* (Maryknoll, N.Y.: Orbis Books, 2002).

8. See John Hick, "A Philosophy of Religious Pluralism," 418–32.

so as to be compatible with this position. *Inclusivism* can be characterized as holding that saving truth is intended for all humankind, and in some way is participated in by (or at any rate is available to) all humankind—even if large numbers of people are not explicitly cognizant of it. One well-known form of inclusivism was developed around the time of Vatican II by the German theologian Karl Rahner, S.J. According to Rahner, all persons who sincerely seek the truth, and all persons who sincerely hold the truth as they have grasped it, can be recognized as "anonymous Christians."[9] Moreover, John Paul II also developed positions of an inclusivist sort. For example, in his first encyclical letter, *Redemptor hominis* (The Redeemer of Man), the late pope wrote: "(M)an—every man without any exception whatever—has been redeemed by Christ; and with man—with each man without any exception whatever—Christ is in a way united, even when man is unaware of it."[10]

Two other recent theologians who are sensitive to religious diversity, but who do not fall into pluralism or relativism, are J. A. DiNoia, O.P., and Cardinal Josef Ratzinger (later Pope Benedict XVI).[11] Thus, for example, in his *The Diversity of Religions: A Christian Perspective*, DiNoia writes that, from the Christian standpoint, "the existent with which all human beings are unconditionally engaged in all religious communities is the Triune God."[12] Thinkers such as these, it may be suggested, support a proper form of "multiculturalism"—i.e., a recognition and respectful acceptance of the reality of other traditions—but at the same time a firm maintenance of the notion of truth, as well as a continuing commitment to the teachings and practices of one's own faith.

---

9. Karl Rahner, S.J., "Anonymous Christians," in *Theological Investigations*, 21 vols. (London: Darton, Longman and Todd, 1961–88), vol. 6, 390–98.

10. John Paul II, *Redemptor hominis* (The Redeemer of Man), Vatican translation (Boston: Pauline Books and Media, 1979), sec. 14. (It perhaps should be added that "man" here translates the generic Latin *homo*, which applies equally to men and women.)

11. J. A. DiNoia, O.P., *The Diversity of Religions: A Christian Perspective* (Washington, D.C.: The Catholic University of America Press, 1992); and Cardinal Joseph Ratzinger, *Truth and Tolerance: Christian Belief and World Religions* (San Francisco: Ignatius Press, 2004).

12. DiNoia, *The Diversity of Religions*, 136.

The present writer would add that the resources of perennial philosophy, as developed and extended in section 3.5, provide further support for a well-considered inclusivism. It will be recalled that we have developed arguments in common human terms for the reality of Absolute, Personal Being. Whatever the strength of these arguments, they lend support to the anticipation of a "revelation" from God—and thus to the possibility of finding ultimate truth. However, such truth would be at least very difficult to substantiate apart from religious faith itself; and, given the vast differences among the cultures of the world, it should be no surprise that different versions of ultimate truth have emerged over the long course of human history.

Further, we have suggested that faith consists precisely in a deep personal response to what one takes to be a "call from God" (or some similar experience in connection with other religious traditions); thus one who accepts our philosophical results can only respect authentic responses of this sort by other people, even if they are very different from one's own—and even if, as DiNoia suggests, one is inclined to believe that the real "existent" responded to is the Triune God of Christianity.

Perennial Philosophy and the
Common Human Future

Whatever the future may hold for the peoples of the earth, one thing is increasingly clear: our future, positive or negative, will be a common one. If, as is to be hoped, it is positive, this will mean that a variety of cultural factors have played their appropriate roles: e.g., the arts, the natural sciences and technology, religious traditions, economic strength, and even, when used judiciously, military power.

In recent decades, perhaps especially in Western nations, the sciences and technology, along with economic and military power, have been counted on to assure success on the world stage. However, it now is quite obvious that military power alone cannot assure a good outcome, for our own country or for the world as a whole. Moreover, the globalization of the economy (as suggested in section 2.4) threatens to break down cultural moorings and proper personalist values, even as it opens up opportunities for material development. Even the sciences and technology—without proper cultural guidance—can be used against genuine human good.

In light of all this, another cultural element—that of philosophical reflection—now surely must recover its strength. As we saw John Paul II remark in the Introduction to this book, "philosophical thought is often the only ground for understanding and dialogue" for people of diverse traditions; and it might provide a basis for "clear and honest collaboration between Christians . . . and all those who . . . have at heart the renewal of humanity." (*Fides et ratio*, sec. 104.)

Let us recall another point expressed in the Introduction. Philosophy is found in various "conditions" or "states," including that of common sense or common intuition as developed in and shaped by a particular culture. For John Paul II, as we have seen, common sense should serve as a "reference point" for different schools of thought. In a somewhat similar vein, we noted in part 3 Yves Simon's idea that common sense musings can express important philosophical content, although not in a "technically elaborated" manner (recall the story of the "old sailor" who at sea thinks of God). Philosophers, we may say, are called to elicit and judiciously articulate such points of common sense, and to consider in light of these efforts the possibilities of dialogue that might thereby be opened.

Of course, technically elaborated philosophical concepts themselves are always developed in one or another cultural context (e.g., Ancient Greece, Medieval Europe, early twenty-first-century America, etc.). But persons—including the present writer and reader—who think within any particular context should be open to themes and concepts arising in other contexts, insofar as the latter can be blended with and can, as appropriate, reshape or add to one's own.

As an important current example of this let us recall the idea of a "global community," as discussed in section 2.4. Some of the most serious obstacles to the actual development of such a community stem from theoretical disagreements among peoples and nations as to the proper relations between religion and society, and in particular between religion and the state.

Recalling our earlier treatment, we may say that any viable society must be rooted in a commitment to truths about the human person, as well as truths about how best to organize our interpersonal life in community. In light of this, certain forms of state—those that recognize the human tendency toward self-government—are to be preferred to those that do not. (The latter often are called "totalitarian" regimes.) Now, self-government—indeed, to be fully a "self" at all—requires, in addition to psychological maturity, the possession of and genuine ability to exercise a range of civic freedoms, including religious freedom. This in turn requires a society—and especially a form of state—that is tolerant of various religions (as well as of citizens who adopt no religion), and that recognizes the religious rights of all.

So much seems clear to the perennial philosophy today. However, it must be said that in order to come to this understanding, the perennial philosophy (and the Christian tradition with which it is associated) has had to undergo a sometimes painful process of development. For although the writings of St. Thomas Aquinas and others contain resources that can be used to develop the above positions,[13] a variety of historical and cultural factors prevented earlier authors from fully recognizing and exploiting such resources. Indeed, it was liberal Enlightenment thinkers, with their stress on individual freedoms and equality, as well as on the promise of democratic institutions, who provided the theoretical impetus for recognizing religious liberty and tolerance. (For its part, the Catholic Church came fully to recognize and proclaim these matters at the Second Vatican Council. See the Council document titled *Dignitatis humanae*, the Declaration on Religious Liberty.)[14]

---

13. See Yves R. Simon, "Thomism and Democracy," in *Science, Philosophy, and Religion*, vol. 2, ed. Louis Finkelstein and Lyman Bryson (New York: The Conference on Science, Philosophy, and Religion in Their Relations to the Democratic Way of Life, 1942), 258–72.

14. Printed in Austin Flannery, O.P., gen. ed., *Vatican Council II Constitutions, Decrees, Declarations* (Northport, N.Y.: Costello, 1996), 551–68. For a discussion of this development by an American scholar (perhaps a bit overly patriotic in tone) see John T. Noonan Jr., *The Lustre of Our Country: The American Experience of Religious Freedom* (Berkeley: University of California Press, 1998).

Now, however, the situation is really quite different. As was suggested in section 2.4, the great "liberal" political philosophies of the past have, ironically and sadly, devolved into patterns of thought that ignore (or even explicitly reject) the idea of truth about the human person, and thus truth about the ways humans should relate to one another in their various communities—including the international community. To the present author this indicates that—for the present and the foreseeable future—the best hope for philosophical support of authentic democratic institutions lies in the resources of the perennial tradition.[15]

As we have seen, in the new century now under way a principal issue will be that of a "world community"—how it is to be conceived, and by what means the human family can move toward an instantiation of it. Many present tensions, as well as conditions of outright warfare, stem at least in part from the lack of a functioning community at the international level. And it seems difficult—in fact, foolish—to ignore the fact that a prominent reason for this lack is the presence of various "exclusivisms" in people's understandings of the world. One must hope, therefore, that other prominent religious and cultural movements (in particular, Islam and, it now also appears, Hinduism) will be able to develop from the best of their intellectual resources comparable—or at least compatible—notions of human dignity, of political and religious freedom, and of the need to pursue both the truth about the human person and the global common good.[16]

Interactions now occurring, or suggested above, between perenni-

---

15. For a prediction along this line dating from the middle of the twentieth century, see John Courtney Murray, S.J., *We Hold These Truths: Catholic Reflections on the American Proposition* (Kansas City, Mo.: Sheed and Ward, 1960). See also Yves R. Simon, *Philosophy of Democratic Government* (Notre Dame, Ind.: University of Notre Dame Press, 1993); and Christopher Wolfe, *Natural Law Liberalism* (New York: Cambridge University Press, 2006).

16. Two episodes occurring in 2006 exemplify the present difficulty. First, a young Afghan man who announced that he had converted from Islam to Christianity was in danger of being convicted and executed, until the government determined that there were questions about his "sanity" and he was allowed to emigrate to Italy. Second, in a number of regions of India, state governments developed laws against religious proselytizing, if such efforts involved "force or allurement." Charges of this sort regularly have been made against Christians in India, both Catholic and Protestant. These groups believe that the new laws specially and arbitrarily target them, while favoring traditional Hindu religion.

al philosophical ideas and those of other religious and cultural traditions may well contribute to salutary effects along these lines. The author hopes that readers of this book will be moved to—and at this point also will be equipped to—take part in the ongoing dialogue.

SUMMARY

• As reflected in the Summary sections of our book's main parts, the philosophy of critical realism here developed has led to positive understandings of being (transcendental as well as physical), the human person (a creature that is both bodily and spiritual), and God (being's ultimate Source and End).

• John Paul II proposed three requirements for authentic interreligious dialogue: a) recognition of the universality of the human spirit, in particular its search for truth; b) agreement that no religious tradition should remain "closed," or affirm itself by simply rejecting others; and c) acceptance of the fact that Christian partners to dialogue cannot abandon what they have gained via original inculturation in Greek and Latin thought.

• The perennial philosophy, and the Christian tradition in which it has flourished, have substantive points of overlap—as well as points of difference—with themes developed in other contexts: e.g., Hinduism, ancient Chinese thought, Buddhism, Islam, and Native American religions.

• The development of a philosophically sound and religiously respectful "inclusivism" (by contrast with both "exclusivism" and "pluralism") can benefit from the application of a number of considerations rooted in perennial thought.

• If humankind's future is to be a positive one, philosophy—i.e., rational reflection rooted in common human experience—must play its appropriate role, along with other, sometimes very powerful, cultural forces.

QUESTIONS FOR REFLECTION

1. Of the philosophical positions articulated in this book, which strike you as most novel or most surprising? Which strike you as most in need of further development and/or rational support? Explain.

2. Take the requirements proposed by John Paul II for authentic inter-religious dialogue and consider whether any of them would be difficult for potential dialogue partners to agree to. To the extent that they would, discuss how well a supporter of the late pope's proposal might respond to the parties' concern.

3. Which of this Epilogue's suggestions about prospects for dialogue with adherents of other cultural and religious traditions seem most significant or most promising to you? Why?

4. How different, in actual fact, do the positions identified as religious "inclusivism" and "pluralism" (or, alternatively, religious "inclusivism" and "exclusivism") seem to you? Explain.

5. Supposing the people of the earth face a "common future," what role might philosophy play in helping to bring about a future that is positive, by comparison and contrast with one or two of the following: the arts, the natural sciences, religious traditions, economic forces, and military strength?

GLOSSARY

Terms listed in this Glossary have been introduced in *italics* in appropriate sections of the book.

abstraction: process by which the intellect forms universal concepts—which, in principle, represent common, essential features of things.

accidents: as identified by the perennial tradition, the nine categories of being (quality, quantity, relation, etc.) that depend upon substance.

act or *actuality:* in the primary philosophical sense, concrete reality; sometimes divided into "first act" (i.e., existence) and "second act" (activity or other real feature of an existing thing).

action: type of act that involves the maintaining of a perfection, or the bringing about of a change, either in the agent itself or in another or others.

affective keys: notion adapted from existentialist philosophers and psychologists, designating a person's most general affective responses to the world (e.g., hope or despair).

affectivity: dimension of living beings according to which they are attracted to or repelled by features of reality and act accordingly.

agent cause: see *efficient cause.*

agent (or *active*) *intellect:* intellect in the act of forming concepts or universals. (Contrast *possible intellect.*)

agnosticism: position holding that we cannot know or properly believe anything about God—including whether God exists.

analogous: use of language according to which a common term has meanings that are related to one another, rather than being completely the same or completely different—often divided into analogy of "attribution" and analogy of "proportionality"; features of reality that form the basis of analogous uses of language.

analytic philosophy: a prominent twentieth-century school of philosophy, and especially methodology, according to which philosophical progress depends primarily on clarification of matters of language.

appetite: (1) as a most general term, a synonym for affectivity; (2) as used more particularly, a natural seeking, whether sensory (as in a drive or instinct) or intellectual (as in the human mind's appetite for truth).

argument: instance of explicit reasoning, whether deductive or inductive.

atheism: position holding that God does not exist.

beauty: transcendental property of being according to which, when a thing is perceived or understood, it awakens delight.

being: (1) that which is—e.g., in the natural world, substances with their features or accidents; (2) the transcendental perfection by which each thing is; (3) the act of existing; (4) in the phrase "being as being," the formal subject matter of metaphysics.

biblicism: view holding that all knowledge about being, persons, and God is available in the Bible, without recourse to natural reason.

cardinal virtues: virtues that are the "hinges" (Latin *cardines*) of the whole moral life; traditionally listed as prudence, justice, fortitude or courage, and temperance.

category: most basic type of being; identified by followers of Aristotle and Aquinas as substance plus nine types of accidents (quantity, quality, relation, etc.).

causality: real relation of dependency between or among beings.

central (also *common*) *sense:* internal sense power whereby discrete data from the external senses are composed into whole sensory objects (a tree, a man, etc.).

change: any type of coming to be (or becoming) of formed matter; "the actualization of what exists in potency insofar as it remains in potency" (Aristotle).

choice: ultimate movement of the will, focused on a concrete act.

Christian philosophy: approach to philosophy which, while respecting the discipline's proper autonomy, receives inspiration from the practitioner's Christian faith.

civil society: large-scale community of persons organized for the purpose of securing common goods such as public defense, public order, and the fulfillment (to the extent possible) of the basic human needs of all citizens.

cognition: see *knowledge* or *cognition.*

common good: good of community life such that it is both a good of each member and at the same time a good of all (e.g., in a family, the good of mutual love and concern).

common sense: (1) see *central sense;* (2) set of beliefs, opinions, views, etc.— often unarticulated—that can be attributed to the human understanding in its untutored or pre-theoretical state.

community: social group that is bound together by a set of common goods, and that has some system of authority for the pursuit of those goods.

complementarity or *mutuality:* relation whereby two types of being (e.g., male and female) have a specific natural orientation toward joint action, or toward contributing to each other's fulfillment.

comprehensive good: the good as such; or the good understood as that which would be fulfilling in all respects.

concept: product of abstraction, which exists as a quality of the intellect, and by which, ideally, the nature of some object comes to be known.

concupiscible: in traditional Scholastic psychology, character of sensory appetites concerned with desire and aversion. (Contrast *irascible.*)

conscience: power of practical intellect reasoning about things to be done or avoided; it involves the reflective application of moral principles as grasped by the agent.

contingency: in speculative philosophy, property of a being such that it can not-be.

cosmological: (1) pertaining to the world (Greek *kosmos*) as a whole; (2) in the phrase "Cosmological Argument," a type of reasoning to the reality of God (e.g., that found in Aquinas's first three Ways), which begins with facts about physical reality as such.

Creation: relation according to which all of finite reality depends for its being on God. (Although Western religious traditions speak in terms of a "first moment" of Creation, the idea of absolute temporal origin is not included in the purely philosophical meaning.)

deductive: type of argument according to which, certain statements being proposed as true, a further statement is said to follow by logical necessity, and thus itself to be true.

definition: characterization of a type of being; divided by perennial philosophers into "real" (where it is believed that an essence is correctly represented), and "nominal" or "verbal" (where the meaning of a term is given, one that is adequate for certain practical but not for strict theoretical purposes).

degree: in the theory of abstraction, a term designating the extent of a concept's removal from matter, by contrast with other concepts of the same general order. (Within the study of nature, for example, philosophical concepts have a higher degree of abstraction than those of the empirical sciences.)

deism: belief that a God began the cosmos—but is not active in, or concerned about, its current state.

deliberation: activity of practical or moral reasoning, the conclusion of which is presented for choice as a concrete act to be undertaken.

demonstration: in perennial logic and philosophy, a sound deductive argument that is known to be sound. (Demonstrations can be either *"propter quid"* or *"quia."* The former establish both the truth of the conclusion and the ontological reason for its truth; the latter establish the truth of the conclusion only.)

designative: see *literal.*

dialectical: type of reasoning, especially about fundamental issues, in which the unacceptable consequences of holding a particular view are pointed out.

dianoetic: Maritain's term for knowledge by way of a thing's nature or essence. (Contrast *perinoetic.*)

docta ignorantia: Latin phrase for "learned ignorance"; as used in speculative philosophy, especially regarding the essence of God, knowing that one does not know, and knowing why one does not know.

drive (or *instinct*): animal appetite rooted in sensory affectivity—e.g., toward the seeking of food.

dualism: view holding that there are two fundamental types of reality (e.g., matter and spirit).

efficient cause (also *agent cause*): of the four types of causes articulated by Aristotle and his followers, that which brings about a change in or the very existence of a being.

eminence or *supereminence:* feature of perfections predicated of God, due to the fact that God, as First Cause, must share (or simply be) all transcendental and pure perfections in a way that utterly goes beyond the ways they are shared in by the dependent realities of our experience.

emotions: movements of animal affectivity (e.g., fear and joy or sorrow); higher human emotions are particularly influenced by intellectual powers and acts.

empirical: characteristic of modern natural science insofar as its statements and theories ultimately are grounded in sensory experience (from Greek *emperein,* "to experience").

empiricism: modern philosophy of knowledge, developed by David Hume and others, according to which all genuine knowing is strictly rooted in sensation (or, in the case of logic and mathematics, in the recognition of relations among ideas).

empiriological: Maritain's term designating approaches to knowledge (especially in the modern natural sciences) that seek accounts of physical reality that are resolvable into sensory experience, rather than into more general principles and causes of being. (Contrast *ontological.*)

end: in speculative philosophy, that toward which a nature or power or act is ordered.

entitative (being): existence as shared by a thing itself (e.g., as a substance or accident).

epiphenomena: in certain recent accounts of the mind, realities which often are supposed to be "mental," but which in fact depend for their existence upon, and ultimately are reducible to, physical realities (e.g., "thoughts" and "decisions" as ultimately consisting of brain activity).

epistemology: theory of human knowledge.

equivocal: use of terms according to which the same word has two or more distinct and unrelated meanings (e.g., in English, "bat" as used of the nocturnal winged animal and the hitter's instrument in baseball).

essence: what a thing is; a thing's nature or type, in principle specifiable by way of a set of necessary, defining features—by contrast with the thing's very existence.

estimative sense: in traditional Scholastic psychology, feature of animal awareness (shared by humans) whereby a being assesses the practical value or disvalue of a thing apart from any formal reasoning.

eternal: mode of duration and existence whereby a being (God) has complete possession of its reality in an "all at once" manner, without undergoing successive states.

everlasting: according to certain modern understandings, property of a reality (in particular, God) whereby it is without beginning or end, but nonetheless undergoes successive temporal states.

evil: opposite of *good;* for perennial philosophy, always an absence of some due or appropriate good.

evil, problem of: problem faced by classical theists in reconciling their characterization of God as all-good, all-knowing, and all-powerful with the experience of evil in the world.

exclusivism: belief that only one religion or ultimate view is correct, and all others are simply false.

existence: the actual being of a thing; the act whereby a thing exists.

existentialism: type of philosophy arising in the twentieth century (although with precursors such as Søren Kierkegaard), according to which the thinker's focus is on existence and concrete experience, rather than on supposed essences; some existentialists (e.g., Gabriel Marcel) have been Christian, others (e.g., Jean-Paul Sartre) atheist.

experience: a matter of direct awareness (perception, emotion, etc.), especially as interpreted by the mind.

fact: a reality that is judged to be such by experience, or the equivalent of experience (e.g., a very well-grounded theory).

faith: total personal response to what is accepted as a call from God; sometimes the term connotes in particular an intellectual adherence to truths taken to be revealed.

family: fundamental form of human life in community—in its most basic expression, male and female parents and their children; in other cases, social arrangements properly so designated by analogy or extension.

fideism: philosophy of religion according to which faith (Latin *fides*) is the complete and adequate basis for beliefs and practices, with no positive role assigned to reason or intellect.

final cause: in the system of four causes or explanatory factors developed by Aristotle and his followers, that which attracts an object as an end of activity.

form: (1) that which organizes matter so as to be an individual of a specific type (in the case of a "pure form," the organization is without matter); (2) in an Aristotelian, realist theory of knowledge, a sensible or intelligible *species* (Latin) by which an animal or a human person comes to be aware of a reality.

formal cause: in the Aristotelian system of four causes or factors in the explanation of physical reality, that which operates by organizing matter; form in its role as cause.

freedom or *free will:* the type of causality uniquely available to persons, according to which acts that result from deliberation and choice are not determined by material forces.

freedom, right to: in political society, the right of individuals and groups to choose their modes of belief and action, especially regarding ultimate matters. (Perennial theories of freedom recognize certain constraints on such liberty in light of the society's common good.)

fundamentalism: position held by some Christians, as well as adherents of other religions, according to which all basic truth about being, the human person, and God is contained in revealed Scriptures, which usually are interpreted literally.

good or *goodness:* (1) transcendental property according to which each real being, in some appropriate respect, is desirable; (2) the general object of affectivity.

historicism (sometimes *progressivism*): view that human knowledge, in all its dimensions, is progressive, or that ideas developed later in human history are always or even necessarily better than ones developed earlier.

hylemorphism: in Aristotelian natural philosophy, the account of physical reality as composed of matter and form.

idealism: in speculative philosophy, a position holding that all reality is mental, or mind-dependent.

imagination: internal sense by which data from the external senses are composed apart from concern for the result's correspondence or non-correspondence with physical reality.

immanence: (1) mode of existence involving immediate presence, especially said of God's presence to all of creation—contrast *transcendence;* (2) property of an act whereby the effect remains in the agent, as the case of an animal's breathing—contrast *transitive act.*

immaterial: not composed of matter.

immortal: not able to die; once alive, always alive.

inclusivism: belief that while one and only one religion or ultimate view is completely and objectively correct, good-faith adherents of others can reach a state of human fulfillment through or because of it.

inductive: type of reasoning that goes from particulars to generalizations based upon them.

insight: as understood in perennial philosophy, the mind's grasp of a point related to essence.

instinct: see *drive.*

intellect (sometimes "intelligence"): power of soul, and of individuals possessing it, that is expressed in understanding, judgment, and reasoning. ("Intelligence" in this sense is to be distinguished from measurable aptitude or performance, the term's primary referent in empirical psychology.) Intellect can be theoretical or practical (e.g., moral).

intelligibility: the transcendental property (also called "truth") according to which all beings, just insofar as they are, can be apprehended and understood by some mind.

intelligible form or *species:* that by which a form of reality comes to be known in its essential features by the human intellect.

intentional (being): existence as a feature of some mind (e.g., as an object of thought or decision-making).

intuition of being: Maritain's term for the reflective act by which we understand that all real being shares in existence in an analogical manner.

irascible: in traditional Scholastic psychology, character of sensory appetites that respond to perceived threats to goods, or perceived likelihoods of evils. (Contrast *concupiscible.*)

judgment: act by which the mind, making use of concepts, expresses how things are or are not; sometimes called the "second act" of intellect.

justice: (1) the cardinal virtue according to which one seeks a proper distribution of goods, rewards, punishments, etc. for all persons; (2) the condition of a society insofar as it reflects a proper distribution of goods, rewards, punishments, etc.

knowledge or *cognition:* sensory or intellectual awareness of things.

liberalism: type of political philosophy promoting the maximization of individual freedoms; often but not necessarily rooted in the speculative view that questions about matters of ultimate significance are not subject to cognition, but only to choice.

literal: as referring to a use of language, one according to which the intention is to express features of reality by means of genuine concepts; in this text, sometimes also called "designative."

love: (1) synonym for "affectivity" in the most general sense; (2) as said of human persons, a relationship whereby either (a) one desires in a primarily sensory and emotional way to be with, or even "possess," another (Greek *eros*), or (b) one wills the genuine good of the other just as another person or self (Greek *philia*); (3) in the specific context of Christianity, orientation of self-giving that mirrors and participates in God's love for the world (Greek *agape*).

manifestation or *phenomenon:* an object of sensation or perception as such.

material cause: that out of which a thing is made or comes to be; one of the four types of cause, or factors in real being, identified by Aristotelian tradition.

materialism: in speculative philosophy, the view that all of being is comprised of matter.

matter: for perennial philosophers, any subject of form; said especially of that ultimate substrate ("primary" or "first matter") which is sheer potentiality for physical form.

memory: internal sense whereby objects originally presented by way of the external senses are again brought to awareness. (Analogously, "memory" also can be applied to the retrieval of an intellectual awareness.)

metaphorical: use of language according to which meaning is carried from one type of context to another without implying corresponding relations in reality.

metaphysics: most general form of speculative inquiry; the study of being as such.

mixed perfection: real feature of being that can be present only in a thing that is material (e.g., color or weight).

monism: position holding that all of being is of a single, fundamental type.

monotheism: belief in one God.

mystery: an object of concern, or a truth, that can be entered into by personal beings, although not one that can be made the object of intellectual understanding.

natural act: an act that is conducive to the fulfillment of a physical being according to that being's form and end.

natural being: being that is composed of primary matter and substantial form, or is an accident or feature of such a being.

natural philosophy: study of natural being just as natural—i.e., as composed of matter and form, as subject to relations of physical causality, etc.

natural science: in contemporary usages, study of natural being that focuses on empirical or observable aspects of its subjects (sometimes as mathematically ordered or related).

nature: (1) as commonly understood, the order of physical reality; (2) in perennial philosophy, the specifying principle—consisting of generic form plus the kind of matter associated with it—according to which a physical being is the type of being it is, with associated powers and acts.

necessary: (1) in the case of a statement, one that cannot fail to be true; (2) in the case of a being, one that cannot not-be.

negative way: approach to developing statements about God in terms of what God is not.

nihilism: philosophical view holding that reality has no intrinsic meaning or value.

non-cognitivism: philosophical view holding that reality, or a particular aspect of reality, cannot be known or literally expressed. (The theory of religious language referred to in this book as "symbolicism," as developed, e.g., by Paul Tillich, would be an instance of non-cognitivism.)

objective: feature of reality, or an aspect of a reality, as it is in itself—by contrast with a feature (sometimes called "subjective") that depends on the individual experiencing or conceiving it.

oneness: transcendental property of being (also called "unity") according to which each thing, insofar as it is, is a type of whole.

ontological: (1) having to do with being, or the properties of being; (2) Maritain's designation for approaches to knowledge that seek to articulate an understanding of the world by way of general principles and causes—being, potency, act, end, etc. (contrast *empiriological*).

order: (1) in the perennial philosophy's theory of abstraction, one of three general types of concepts (physical, mathematical, metaphysical), taken in terms of their objects; (2) a general type or realm of being (e.g., the mathematical, by contrast with the physical order; or the natural, by contrast with a supernatural order); (3) relationship according to which one type of reality provides an element of teleology for another (e.g., the human will as ordered to the comprehensive good).

panentheism: belief that God exists in and through the cosmos.

pantheism: belief that the whole cosmos is identifiable with God.

participation: (1) in metaphysics, the real feature of things according to which certain qualities (the transcendental and pure perfections) are shared in respective manners and degrees; (2) in philosophy of the human person, that relation according to which, as social beings, our fulfillment involves appropriate engagement with others in community.

passion: (1) (also called "passivity") category signifying being acted upon; (2) feeling, especially one strongly felt—e.g., anger.

per se nota: characteristic of a proposition "knowable through itself"; that is, if one understands the essences referred to by the individual terms of the proposition, one understands that it must be true. The per se knowability of such a proposition can be considered either "in itself" (Latin *in se*), or "to us," i.e., to given individuals (Latin *quoad nos*).

perception: sensory knowledge, as formed by animal or human minds.

perennial philosophy: a realist form of philosophy, both speculative and practical, originally developed by Aristotle, transformed in the Christian Middle Ages, and subject to successive renewals to the present day.

perfections: positive features of real beings; distinguished into mixed, transcendental, and pure.

perinoetic: Maritain's term for knowledge of the physical, not by way of things' natures or essences, but by way of facts about it that are available to sensory experience. (Contrast *dianoetic.*)

person: as understood in perennial philosophy, a basic existent (supposit) whose nature is rational or intellectual.

personalism: twentieth-century philosophy emphasizing the unique features of human, personal life: self-reflection, relationships, self-giving, conscious participation in common goods of family and society, etc.

phenomenalism: philosophy of knowledge and especially of reality according to which all that is can be grasped in sensation.

phenomenology: philosophical methodology that seeks to understand essences by "bracketing" all prior conceptual apparatus, and by focusing on reality precisely as experienced.

philosophy: love of or search for wisdom, i.e., a most general understanding of how things are ("speculative philosophy"), or of how we humans should act ("practical philosophy").

philosophy of nature: see *natural philosophy.*

physicalism: philosophical theory according to which all that is, is physical. (Typically, physicalistic theories have been reductive, holding that, in principle, references to the non-physical can be eliminated in favor of reference to only the physical; but recently there have been proposed "non-reductive" forms of physicalism, which hold that all reality is physical but that references to the non-physical, e.g., the psychical, are not—or are not fully— eliminable in terms of references to the physical.)

polytheism: belief in many gods.

positive science: another name for empirical science (plus, sometimes, mathematics).

positivism: philosophical position holding that all knowledge (or all knowledge worth pursuing) is restricted to the positive sciences. (The variant called "logical positivism" has held even more radically that statements that are not subject to procedures of empirical verification are not cognitively meaningful.)

possible intellect: the human intellect as receptive of the intelligible forms of things. (Contrast *agent intellect.*)

postmodernism: view holding that "modern" philosophical ideas (especially the rationalism characteristic of Descartes and others) are to be rejected as unfruitful relics of the past. (Many postmodernists also embrace non-cognitivism and relativism.)

potency or *potentiality:* state of "can be"; that which is actualized in coming to be.

practical philosophy: see *philosophy.*

premises: in deductive reasoning, statements that are set down and from which a conclusion is derived.

principle: (1) starting point of the being of a thing (e.g., matter and form as principles of natural being); (2) most basic statement within a discipline, including a branch of philosophy (e.g., in metaphysics, the Principle of Identity, Principle of Sufficient Reason, or Principle of Finality); (3) in moral and other affective matters, general statement from which a process of deliberation can begin.

privation: (1) in relation to change, condition or state of not having a particular quality; (2) condition or state in which a quality that by nature is due or appropriate is not present.

process thought: twentieth- and now twenty-first-century philosophical movement holding that traditional Aristotelian categories (especially substance) are to be replaced by ones suggested (according to proponents) by the modern natural sciences (e.g., "event" and "process").

progressivism: see *historicism.*

providence: as understood in perennial discussions of God, that awareness by which all things are present to God, and by which all of reality is ordered to, and ultimately is brought to, a final good. (When used as a name for God, the word traditionally is written with a capital "P.")

pure perfection: feature of real being that can be present only in beings that are not in themselves material (e.g., intellectual understanding or moral virtue).

quality: one of the nine categories of accident; a thing's color, characteristic sound, etc.

quantity: another of the nine categories of accident; a physical reality insofar as it is measurable, countable, etc.

rationalism: philosophical theory (characteristic of, e.g., Plato and Descartes) according to which, in principle, all features of reality are open to human reason, often on the model of mathematical deduction.

realism: philosophical theory according to which the human mind can, and ordinarily does, gain some knowledge of reality as it is (rather than, e.g., simply as it is experienced).

reality: being that is actual.

reasoning: act by which the mind moves from one or more truths to another or others; sometimes called the "third act" of intellect. In the case of practical intellect, reasoning is called "deliberation."

reductionism: theory according to which all elements of one order (e.g., psychical phenomena) can be reduced to those of another (e.g., physical phenomena).

relation: one of the nine categories of accident identified by perennial philosophy; relations involve two or more elements.

relativism: in philosophy, position holding that fundamental perspectives (metaphysical, religious, ethical, etc.) are inevitably relative to societies, cultures, or individuals, and that there cannot, even in principle, be rational grounds for favoring one such perspective over another.

religious freedom: within a proper civil society, the right of individuals to beliefs and practices regarding transcendent matters that accord with considered personal choices.

religious pluralism: in recent philosophy of religion, relativism in relation to religious perspectives. Often religious pluralists hold that all the world's religions are "equally good" in the sense that—their mutually contradictory views notwithstanding—each provides a way to reach ultimate human fulfillment.

revelation: teachings, or the source of teachings, accepted in faith as having been given by God, either directly or through inspired authors.

science: (1) traditionally, any knowledge established on the basis of other knowledge, and ultimately on the basis of first principles intuitively known; (2) as typically understood today, knowledge of the form pursued in the specifically empirical disciplines, often with the addition of mathematics.

scientism: philosophical view concerning knowledge according to which all genuine knowledge follows the pattern and the methods of science in sense (2).

secularism: cultural movement originating in the Modern period, and continuing to be influential in Western societies today, according to which the only matters that are real, or the only matters that humans should be concerned about, are temporal or earthly ones. (Secularism is to be contrasted with "secularity," which supposes only the relative autonomy of human affairs, even if—as the U.S. Founders, for example, believed—the temporal order depends on one that is higher.)

sensation: an animal's or a human person's mode of awareness of physical reality by way of sensory organs and powers (touch, sight, hearing, taste, smell); also an individual instance of such awareness.

sensible form or *species:* that by which features of sensible reality (color, sound, etc.) come to be in animal or human awareness.

soul: formal principle by which primary matter is organized so that the being is able to exercise powers of life (nutrition and growth, sensation and local movement, understanding and choice, etc.).

soundness: feature of deductive arguments such that, in those that have it, the premises are true and the conclusion genuinely follows from the premises; the conclusion of a sound deductive argument is true by logical necessity.

space: feature of physical being according to which its parts can be understood and measured in relation to one another in terms of place.

speculative philosophy: see *philosophy.*

spiritual: having to do with life and existence that is not, or is not totally, bound by matter.

state: (1) a condition; (2) a civil society, precisely as organized for the purpose of providing for, or safeguarding, common goods that cannot be guaranteed by smaller forms of community such as the family.

subject: (1) in metaphysics, equivalent to supposit; (2) in logic, that about which something is said (the latter is called the "predicate"); (3) in the philosophy of the human person, a conscious self.

subjectivity: (1) in metaphysics, equivalent to subsistence; (2) in the philosophy of the human person, that feature of selves that enables them to develop as individual selves and take responsibility for their choices and beliefs.

subsidiarity: (1) a synonym for "participation" in its second sense; (2) in the "Principle of Subsidiarity," the state of affairs in which social decisions (e.g., regarding traffic laws or city tax rates) are made locally, by the smallest capable unit, with broader forms of community (e.g., the state or nation) providing assistance (Latin *subsiduum*) as necessary.

subsistence: metaphysical property according to which a being is capable of independent existence.

substance: for the perennial tradition, the first category of being; that which exists and is understood in itself, rather than as a feature of another.

sufficient reason: cause or explanatory factor that is adequate to account for the effect. (The "Principle of Sufficient Reason" holds that for every reality—even God's existence—there is a "reason," even if not a "cause" in the strict sense used in natural philosophy.)

supposit (Latin *suppositum*): something that exists in a primary way; in rational or intellectual beings, equivalent to person.

symbol: expression of reality not by way of a literal concept, but by way of an image or metaphor.

symbolicism: see *non-cognitivism.*

teleological: (1) in speculative philosophy, pertaining to a thing (a nature, power, act, etc.) in relation to its proper end; (2) in the phrase "Teleological Argument," a type of reasoning to the reality of God (e.g., Aquinas's Fifth Way) that begins with the end-directedness encountered in nature.

theism: belief in God as traditionally understood in Western religions, especially insofar as this belief is articulated philosophically.

theodicy: philosophical and/or theological effort to render consistent one's theistic beliefs with a recognition of the evil in the world.

theology: study of God; by contrast with philosophy, a study of God, and of the world's relations with God, not primarily by way of rational reflection on common human experience (although this too may be involved), but by way of statements that are accepted in faith as matters of revelation.

time: characteristic of natural being according to which change is numbered as to before and after.

transcendence: mode of existence beyond the limits of the natural world. (Contrast *immanence* (1).)

transcendental perfection: property of real being (e.g., intelligibility, goodness, or oneness) that is present across all the categories and levels of being.

transitive act: type of act in which the effect takes place in a being other than the agent. (Contrast *immanence* (2).)

truth: (1) the adequation of mind to reality, or an instance of such adequation; (2) the transcendental property also called "intelligibility."

ultimate end: that toward which all real being is ordered; understood by perennial philosophers and theologians to be God.

understanding: act whereby the mind develops concepts and thus represents to itself universal features and essences of things; sometimes called the "first act" of intellect. In addition to speculative there can be practical understanding, e.g., the grasp of basic moral principles.

unity: see *oneness.*

universal: a form, and the intelligible features of a form, that can be found in many individuals.

univocal: use of language according to which, in each instance of a term's literal employment, it has the same meaning.

validity: property of certain deductive arguments according to which, if the premises are true, the conclusion also must be true.

virtue (moral): state of a person, and in particular of personal soul, according to which the will becomes effectively ordered toward choosing a particular type of good, and/or avoiding a particular type of evil.

will: power of affectivity in personal beings by which they are ordered toward and can achieve goods by way of understanding and reasoning.

wisdom: for philosophy, most general understanding of how things are (speculative wisdom), or of how we human beings should act (practical or moral wisdom).

wonder: awe at the being and nature of things; the deepest source of all human inquiry.

BIBLIOGRAPHY

The entries here listed all contribute to the perennial tradition as understood and explained in the Introduction. The sets of references for each of the book's three main parts begin with texts from Aristotle and St. Thomas Aquinas. These are followed by recent expositions, discussions, and extensions of perennial philosophy, as well as expressions of other contemporary perspectives that might be incorporated into the ongoing tradition.

The standard English editions of Aquinas's two major works are: *Summa Contra Gentiles*, translated, with introductions and notes, by Anton C. Pegis, James F. Anderson, Vernon J. Bourke, and Charles J. O'Neil, 4 vols., Doubleday, 1955–57; reprinted by University of Notre Dame Press (Notre Dame, Ind., 1975); and *Summa Theologiae (Summa Theologica)*, 5 vols., translated by the Fathers of the English Dominican Province, Benzinger Brothers, 1947; reprinted by Christian Classics (Westminster, Md., 1981). A modern English translation, with notes and glossaries, is to be found in the sixty-volume Latin/English Blackfriars edition of *Summa Theologiae*, Thomas Gilby, O.P., general editor (London: McGraw-Hill, 1964–73). Translations of Aquinas's commentaries on Aristotle's *Nicomachean Ethics, Physics, De Anima* (On the Soul), and *Metaphysics* have been reprinted, with forewords by Ralph McInerny, in the Aristotelian Commentary Series, Dumb Ox Books (Notre Dame, Ind., 1993–99). Also of note is the ongoing Hackett Aquinas Project from Hackett Publishing (Indianapolis, Ind.). Each volume in this new series contains a fresh translation of the selected texts, together with a commentary. Initial volumes are Robert Pasnau, trans., *The Treatise on Human Nature: Summa Theologiae 1a 75–89* (2002); Brian Shanley, O.P., trans., *The Treatise on the Divine Nature: Summa Theologiae 1a 1–13* (2006); and Peter King, trans., *On Being and Essence* (2007).

English versions of Aquinas's *Summas* are available electronically. For the *Summa Theologiae (Summa Theologica)*, translated by the Fathers of the English Dominican Province, see www.newadvent.org/summa/; for the *Summa Contra Gentiles*, translated by Joseph Rickaby, S.J., see www.nd.edu/Departments/Maritain/etext/gc.htm. Other Internet resources for students of perennial philosophy include the website of the Jacques Maritain Center, University of Notre Dame, at http://maritain.nd.edu/jmc/; Stephen Loughlin's Home

Page—St. Thomas Aquinas at www.desales.edu/~philtheo/Aquinas/; the web-site of Thomas International, including the McInerny Center for Thomistic Studies, at www.thomasinternational.org/; Mark F. Johnson's Thomistica web-site at www.thomistica.net; Joseph M. Magee's website Thomistic Philosophy at www.aquinasonline.com/; and the website of the Society for Aristotelian Studies at www.aristotle-aquinas.org.

    See also The Radical Academy, including the Mortimer J. Adler Archive and other resources at www.radicalacademy.com; and the philosophy section of James Arraj's website, Inner Explorations, at www.innerexplorations.com.

INTRODUCTION

Ciapalo, Roman T., ed. *Postmodernism and Christian Philosophy*. Washing-ton, D.C.: American Maritain Association/The Catholic University of America Press, 1997.
Dennehy, Raymond. "The Philosophical Catbird Seat: A Defense of Marit-ain's Philosophia Perennis." In *The Future of Thomism*, edited by Deal Hudson, Notre Dame, Ind.: University of Notre Dame Press, 1992.
Gilson, Etienne. *The Christian Philosophy of St. Thomas Aquinas*. New York: Random House, 1956.
John Paul II. *Fides et ratio* (On the Relationship between Faith and Reason). Vatican translation. Boston: Pauline Books and Media, 1998.
Maritain, Jacques. *Science and Wisdom*. Translated by Bernard Wall. Lon-don: Geoffrey Bles, 1940.
———. *A Preface to Metaphysics*. London: Sheed and Ward, 1945.
Nichols, Aiden. *Discovering Aquinas*. Grand Rapids, Mich.: Eerdmans, 2002.
Owens, Joseph, C.Ss.R. *Towards a Christian Philosophy*. Washington, D.C.: The Catholic University of America Press, 1990.
Pieper, Josef. *Guide to Thomas Aquinas*. Translated by Richard and Clara Winston. San Francisco: Ignatius Press, 1991.
Ramos, Alice, and Marie I. George, eds. *Faith, Scholarship, and Culture in the 21st Century*. Washington, D.C.: American Maritain Association/ The Catholic University of America Press, 2002.
Smith, Timothy L., ed. *Faith and Reason*. South Bend, Ind.: St. Augustine's Press, 2001.
Wippel, John F. "The Possibility of a Christian Philosophy: A Thomistic Perspective." *Faith and Philosophy* 1 (1984): 272–90.
Wojtyła, Karol (John Paul II). *Person and Community*. Selected essays, trans-lated by Theresa Sandok, O.S.M. New York: Peter Lang, 1993.

PART I

Aristotle and St. Thomas Aquinas. Among the many writings of these semi-nal authors, the following are especially relevant to the topics of part 1:

a) Aristotle. *Categories, Physics,* and *Metaphysics.* All are available in English in a variety of print editions.

b) Aquinas. *Commentary on Aristotle's Physics, Commentary on Aristotle's Metaphysics, De Ente et Essentia, De Potentia, Summa Contra Gentiles,* and *Summa Theologiae.* All are available in English, at least in part, some in a variety of editions.

Aertsen, Jan A. *Medieval Philosophy and the Transcendentals: The Case of Thomas Aquinas.* Leiden and Boston: Brill Academic Publishers, 2004.

Anscombe, Elizabeth, and Peter Geach. *Three Philosophers.* Ithaca, N.Y.: Cornell University Press, 1961.

Blanchette, Oliva. *Philosophy of Being: A Reconstructive Essay in Metaphysics.* Washington, D.C.: The Catholic University of America Press, 2003.

Bobik, Joseph. *Aquinas on Being and Essence: A Translation and Interpretation.* Notre Dame, Ind.: University of Notre Dame Press, 1965.

Cahalan, John C. *Causal Realism.* Lanham, Md.: University Press of America, 1985.

Clarke, W. Norris, S.J. *Explorations in Metaphysics.* Notre Dame, Ind.: University of Notre Dame Press, 1994.

———. *The One and the Many.* Notre Dame, Ind.: University of Notre Dame Press, 2001.

Connell, Richard J. *From Observables to Unobservables in Science and Philosophy.* Lanham, Md.: University Press of America, 2000.

Conway, Pierre. *Faith Views the Universe: A Thomistic Perspective.* Edited by Mary Michael Spangler. Lanham, Md.: University Press of America, 1997.

Copelston, F. C. *Aquinas.* London: Penguin Books, 1981.

Davies, Brian. *Aquinas.* London and New York: Continuum, 2002.

Dennehy, Raymond. "Maritain's Theory of Subsistence: The Basis of His Existentialism." *The Thomist* 39 (1975): 542–74.

———. "Maritain's Realistic Defense of the Importance of the Philosophy of Nature to Metaphysics." In *Thomistic Papers VI,* edited by John F. X. Knasas. Houston, Tex.: The Center for Thomistic Studies, 1994.

Dewan, Lawrence, O.P. *Form and Being.* Washington, D.C.: The Catholic University of America Press, 2006.

Doig, James C. *Aquinas on Metaphysics.* The Hague: Martinus Nijhoff, 1972.

Emonet, Pierre-Marie, O.P. *The Dearest Freshness Deep Down Things.* Translated by Robert R. Barr. New York: Crossroad, 1999.

Geach, Peter. *God and the Soul.* New York: Schocken Books, 1969. Reprint, South Bend, Ind.: St. Augustine's Press, 2001.

Gilson, Etienne. *From Aristotle to Darwin and Back Again.* Translated by John Lyon. Notre Dame, Ind.: University of Notre Dame Press, 1984.

Haldane, John. "A Thomist Metaphysics." In *The Blackwell Guide to Metaphysics*, edited by R. Gale. Oxford: Basil Blackwell, 2001.

——, ed. *Mind, Metaphysics and Value in the Thomistic and Analytic Traditions*. Notre Dame, Ind.: University of Notre Dame Press, 2002.

Henle, R. J. *Theory of Knowledge*. Chicago: Loyola University Press, 1983.

John Paul II. *Fides et ratio* (On the Relationship between Faith and Reason). Vatican translation. Boston: Pauline Books and Media, 1998.

Kane, William H., O.P. "Review of Jacques Maritain, *The Philosophy of Nature*." *The Thomist* 16 (1953): 127–31.

Klubertanz, George P., S.J. *Introduction to the Philosophy of Being*. 2nd ed. reprinted. Eugene, Ore.: WIPF and Stock, 2005.

Knasas, John F. X. *Being and Some Twentieth-Century Thomists*. New York: Fordham University Press, 2003.

Krapiec, Mieczyslaw Albert, O.P. *Metaphysics: An Outline of the History of Being*. Translated by Theresa Sandok. New York: Peter Lang, 1991.

Kretzmann, Norman. *The Metaphysics of Theism*. Oxford: Clarendon Press, 1997.

Maritain, Jacques. *A Preface to Metaphysics*. London: Sheed and Ward, 1945.

——. *Existence and the Existent*. Translated by Lewis Galantiere and Gerald B. Phelan. New York: Pantheon, 1948.

——. *The Philosophy of Nature*. Translated by Imelda C. Byrne. New York: Philosophical Library, 1951.

——. *The Degrees of Knowledge*. Translated under the supervision of Gerald B. Phelan, presented by Ralph McInerney. Notre Dame, Ind.: University of Notre Dame Press, 1995.

McGlynn, James V., S.J., and Sr. Paul Mary Farley, R.S.M. *A Metaphysics of Being and God*. Englewood Cliffs, N.J.: Prentice-Hall, 1966.

McInerny, Ralph. *St. Thomas Aquinas*. Notre Dame, Ind.: University of Notre Dame Press, 1982.

——. *Aquinas and Analogy*. Washington, D.C.: The Catholic University of America Press, 1998.

——. *Aquinas*. Cambridge: Polity Press, 2004.

Owens, Joseph, C.Ss.R. *An Elementary Christian Metaphysics*. Houston, Tex.: Center for Thomistic Studies, 1985.

Pugh, Matthew S. "Maritain and Postmodern Science." In *Postmodernism and Christian Philosophy*, edited by Roman T. Ciapalo. Washington, D.C.: American Maritain Association/The Catholic University of America Press, 1997.

——. "Maritain, the Intuition of Being, and the Proper Starting Point for Thomistic Metaphysics." *The Thomist* 61 (1997): 405–24.

Reith, Herman, C.S.C. *The Metaphysics of St. Thomas Aquinas*. Milwaukee, Wis.: Bruce Publishing, 1958.

Renard, Henri, S.J. *Wisdom in Depth.* Milwaukee, Wis.: Bruce Publishing, 1966.

Simon, Yves R. *An Introduction to Metaphysics of Knowledge.* Translated by Vukan Kuic and Richard J. Thompson. New York: Fordham University Press, 1990.

———. *Foresight and Knowledge.* Edited by Ralph Nelson and Anthony O. Simon. New York: Fordham University Press, 1996.

———. *Philosopher at Work.* Edited by Anthony O. Simon. Lanham, Md.: Rowman and Littlefield, 1999.

———. *The Great Dialogue of Nature and Space.* Edited by Gerald J. Dalcourt. South Bend, Ind.: St. Augustine's Press, 2001.

Stump, Eleonore. *Aquinas.* London and New York: Routledge, 2003.

Wallace, William A., O.P. *The Modeling of Nature: Philosophy of Science and Philosophy of Nature in Synthesis.* Washington, D.C.: The Catholic University of America Press, 1996.

———. "Is Nature Available to the Mathematical Physicist?" In *Science, Philosophy, and Theology,* edited by John O'Callaghan. South Bend, Ind.: St. Augustine's Press, 2006.

Wippel, John F. *Metaphysical Themes in Thomas Aquinas.* Washington, D.C.: The Catholic University of America Press, 1984.

———. *The Metaphysical Thought of Thomas Aquinas.* Washington, D.C.: The Catholic University of America Press, 2000.

———. *Metaphysical Themes in Thomas Aquinas.* Vol. 2. Washington, D.C.: The Catholic University of America Press, 2007.

PART 2

Aristotle and St. Thomas Aquinas. The following are especially relevant to the topics of part 2:

a) Aristotle. *Nicomachean Ethics, On the Soul,* and *Politics.* All are available in English in a variety of editions.

b) Aquinas. *Commentary on Aristotle's De Anima, Commentary on Aristotle's Nicomachean Ethics, Disputed Question on the Soul, Summa Contra Gentiles, Summa Theologiae.* All are available in English, at least in part, some in a variety of editions.

Adler, Mortimer J. *The Difference of Man and the Difference It Makes.* Introduction by Deal W. Hudson. New York: Fordham University Press, 1993.

Braine, David. *The Human Person, Animal & Spirit.* Notre Dame, Ind.: University of Notre Dame Press, 1992.

Clarke, W. Norris, S.J. *Person and Being.* Milwaukee: Marquette University Press, 1993.

———. *Explorations in Metaphysics.* Notre Dame, Ind.: University of Notre Dame Press, 1994.

———. *The One and the Many.* Notre Dame, Ind.: University of Notre Dame Press, 2001.

Copelston, F. C. *Aquinas.* London: Penguin Books, 1981.

Crosby, John. *The Selfhood of the Human Person.* Washington, D.C.: The Catholic University of America Press, 1996.

———. *Personalist Papers.* Washington, D.C.: The Catholic University of America Press, 2004.

Davies, Brian, ed. *Aquinas's Summa Theologiae: Critical Essays.* Lanham, Md.: Rowman and Littlefield, 2006.

Dennehy, Raymond. *Reason and Dignity.* Washington, D.C.: University Press of America, 1981.

Douglass, R. Bruce, and David Hollenbach, eds. *Catholicism and Liberalism.* Cambridge: Cambridge University Press, 1994.

Emonet, Pierre-Marie, O.P. *The Greatest Marvel of Nature.* Translated by Robert R. Barr. New York: Crossroad, 2000.

Finnis, John. *Aquinas: Moral, Political, and Legal Theory.* Oxford: Oxford University Press, 1998.

Fuller, Timothy, and John P. Hittinger, eds. *Reassessing the Liberal State: Reading Maritain's Man and the State.* Washington, D.C.: American Maritain Association/The Catholic University of America Press, 2001.

Furton, Edward J. *What Is Man, O Lord? The Human Person in a Biotech Age.* Boston: The National Catholic Bioethics Center, 2002.

Geach, Peter. *Mental Acts.* London: Routledge and Kegan Paul, 1967. Reprint, South Bend, Ind.: St. Augustine's Press, 2001.

———. *God and the Soul.* New York: Schocken Books, 1969. Reprint, South Bend, Ind.: St. Augustine's Press, 2001.

George, Marie. "Thomas Aquinas Meets Nim Chimpsky: On the Debate About Human Nature and the Nature of Other Animals," *The Aquinas Review* 10 (2003): 1–50.

Haldane, John, ed. *Mind, Metaphysics, and Value.* Notre Dame, Ind.: University of Notre Dame Press, 2002.

Hancock, Curtis L., and Anthony O. Simon, eds. *Freedom, Virtue, and the Common Good.* Notre Dame, Ind.: American Maritain Association/ University of Notre Dame Press, 1995.

Held, David. *Democracy and the Global Order: From the Modern State to Cosmopolitan Governance.* Stanford, Calif.: Stanford University Press, 1995.

Kenny, Anthony, ed. *Aquinas: A Collection of Critical Essays.* Notre Dame, Ind.: University of Notre Dame Press, 1976.

———. *Aquinas on Mind.* London and New York: Routledge, 1993.

Krapiec, M. A. *I-Man: An Outline of Philosophical Anthropology.* Translated by Francis J. Lescoe and Roger B. Duncan. New Britain, Conn.: Mariel Publications, 1985.

Machuga, Ric. *In Defense of the Soul.* Grand Rapids, Mich.: Brazos Press, 2002.

MacIntyre, Alasdair. *Dependent Rational Animals.* Chicago: Open Court, 1999.

Magee, Joseph M. *Unmixing the Intellect: Aristotle on Cognitive Powers and Bodily Organs.* Westport, Conn.: Greenwood Press, 2003.

Marcel, Gabriel. *Creative Fidelity.* Translated by Robert Rosthal, preface by Merold Westphal. New York: Fordham University Press, 2002.

Maritain, Jacques. *Challenges and Renewals.* Edited by Joseph W. Evans and Leo R. Ward. Notre Dame, Ind.: University of Notre Dame Press, 1966.

———. *The Person and the Common Good.* Translated by John J. Fitzgerald. Notre Dame, Ind.: University of Notre Dame Press, 1966.

———. *Integral Humanism.* Translated by Joseph Evans. New York: Charles Scribner's Sons, 1968.

———. *Man and the State.* Washington, D.C.: The Catholic University of America Press, 1998.

Maritain, Jacques, and William Sweet. *Natural Law: Reflections on Theory and Practice.* South Bend, Ind.: St. Augustine's Press, 2001.

McInerny, Ralph. *Ethica Thomistica.* Rev. ed. Washington, D.C.: The Catholic University of America Press, 1997.

Novak, Michael. *Free Persons and the Common Good.* Lanham, Md.: Madison Books, 1989.

O'Callaghan, John. *Thomist Realism and the Linguistic Turn.* Notre Dame, Ind.: University of Notre Dame Press, 2002.

Owens, Joseph, C.Ss.R. *Human Destiny: Some Problems for Catholic Philosophy.* Washington, D.C.: The Catholic University of America Press, 1985.

Pasnau, Robert. *Thomas Aquinas on Human Nature.* Cambridge and New York: Cambridge University Press, 2002.

Pieper, Josef. *Reality and the Good.* Translated by Stella Lange. Chicago: Henry Regnery, 1967.

———. *Josef Pieper: An Anthology.* San Francisco: Ignatius Press, 1989.

———. *A Brief Reader on the Virtues of the Human Heart.* Translated by Paul C. Duggan. San Francisco: Ignatius Press, 1991.

Pinckaers, Servais, O.P. *Morality: The Catholic View.* Translated by Michael Sherwin, O.P. South Bend, Ind.: St. Augustine's Press, 2001.

Reichman, James B., S.J. *Philosophy of the Human Person.* Chicago: Loyola University Press, 1985.

Reimers, Adrian J. *The Soul of the Human Person: A Contemporary Philo-

sophical Psychology. Washington, D.C.: The Catholic University of America Press, 2006.

Reith, Herman, C.S.C. *Introduction to Philosophical Psychology.* Englewood Cliffs, N.J.: Prentice-Hall, 1956.

Rourke, Thomas R., and Rosita A. Chazaretta Rourke. *A Theory of Personalism.* Lanham, Md.: Rowman and Littlefield, 2004.

Simon, Yves R. *Freedom of Choice.* Edited by Peter Wolff. New York: Fordham University Press, 1969.

———. *A General Theory of Authority.* Notre Dame, Ind.: University of Notre Press, 1980.

———. *The Definition of Moral Virtue.* Edited by Vukan Kuic. New York: Fordham University Press, 1986.

———. *An Introduction to Metaphysics of Knowledge.* Translated by Vukan Kuic and Richard J. Thompson. New York: Fordham University Press, 1990.

———. *Practical Knowledge.* Edited by Robert J. Mulvaney. New York: Fordham University Press, 1991.

———. *Philosophy of Democratic Government.* Notre Dame, Ind.: University of Notre Dame Press, 1993.

———. *Philosopher at Work.* Edited by Anthony O. Simon. Lanham, Md.: Rowman and Littlefield, 1999.

———. *Freedom and Community.* Edited by Charles P. O'Donnell, with an introduction by Eugene Kennedy. New York: Fordham University Press, 2001.

Sokolowski, Robert. "Soul and the Transcendance of the Human Person." In *What Is Man, O Lord? The Human Person in a Biotech Age,* edited by Edward J. Furton. Boston: The National Catholic Bioethics Center, 2002.

Stump, Eleonore. "Non-Cartesian Substance Dualism and Materialism without Reductionism," *Faith and Philosophy* 12, no.1 (October 1995): 505–31.

———. *Aquinas.* London and New York: Routledge, 2003.

Trapani, John G., Jr., ed. *Truth Matters: Essays in Honor of Jacques Maritain.* Washington, D.C.: American Maritain Association/The Catholic University of America Press, 2004.

Weithman, Paul J., ed. *Religion and Contemporary Liberalism.* Notre Dame, Ind.: University of Notre Dame Press, 1997.

Wojtyła, Karol (John Paul II). *The Acting Person.* Translated by Andrzej Potocki, edited by Anna-Teresa Tymieniecka. Boston: Reidel, 1979.

———. *Person and Community.* Selected essays, translated by Theresa Sandok, O.S.M. New York: Peter Lang, 1993.

Wolfe, Christopher. *Natural Law Liberalism.* New York: Cambridge University Press, 2006.

PART 3

Aristotle and St. Thomas Aquinas. The following are especially relevant to the topics of part 3:

a) Aristotle. *Metaphysics.* Available in English in a variety of print editions.

b) Aquinas. *Commentary on Aristotle's Metaphysics, Summa Contra Gentiles,* and *Summa Theologiae.* All are available in English, the latter two in a variety of editions.

Adler, Mortimer J. *How to Think about God.* New York: Collier Books, 1991.

Augustine. *Confessions.* Translated by Henry Chadwick. New York: Oxford University Press, 1992.

Bobik, Joseph. *Veritas Divina: Aquinas on Divine Truth.* South Bend, Ind.: St. Augustine's Press, 2001.

Boethius. *The Theological Tractates and The Consolation of Philosophy.* Edited by H. F. Stewart, E. K. Rand, and S. J. Tester. Cambridge, Mass.: Harvard University Press, 1973.

Braine, David. *Reality of Time and the Existence of God.* Oxford: Oxford University Press, 1988.

Burrell, David, C.S.C. *Aquinas: God and Action.* London: Routledge and Kegan Paul, 1979.

———. *Freedom and Creation in Three Traditions.* Notre Dame, Ind.: University of Notre Dame Press, 1993.

Catan, John R., ed. *Saint Thomas Aquinas and the Existence of God: The Collected Papers of Joseph Owens.* Albany: State University of New York Press, 1980.

Clarke, W. Norris, S.J. *Explorations in Metaphysics.* Notre Dame, Ind.: University of Notre Dame Press, 1994.

Copelston, F. C. *Aquinas.* London: Penguin Books, 1981.

Davies, Brian, ed. *Aquinas's Summa Theologiae: Critical Essays.* Lanham, Md.: Rowman and Littlefield, 2006.

Emonet, Pierre-Marie, O.P. *The Dearest Freshness Deep Down Things.* Translated by Robert R. Barr. New York: Crossroad, 1999.

———. *God Seen in the Mirror of the World.* Translated by Robert R. Barr. New York: Crossroad, 2000.

Geach, Peter. *God and the Soul.* New York: Schocken Books, 1969. Reprint, South Bend, Ind.: St. Augustine's Press, 2001.

Gilson, Etienne. *The Christian Philosophy of St. Thomas Aquinas.* Translated by L. K. Shook, C.S.B. New York: Random House, 1956.

Hankey, W. J. *God in Himself: Aquinas's Doctrine of God as Expounded in the Summa Theologiae.* New York: Oxford University Press, 1987.

Hughes, Christopher. *On a Complex Theory of a Simple God: An Investigation in Aquinas's Philosophical Theology.* Ithaca, N.Y.: Cornell University Press, 1989.

Jenkins, John I., C.S.C. *Knowledge and Faith in Thomas Aquinas.* Cambridge: Cambridge University Press, 1997.

Kretzmann, Norman. *The Metaphysics of Creation.* Oxford: Clarendon Press, 1999.

Levering, Matthew. *Scripture and Metaphysics: Aquinas and the Renewal of Trinitarian Theology.* Malden, Mass.: Blackwell Publishers, 2004.

Maimonides, Moses. *Guide of the Perplexed.* Translated by S. Pines. Chicago: University of Chicago Press, 1963.

Maritain, Jacques. *St. Thomas and the Problem of Evil.* Milwaukee, Wis.: Marquette University Press, 1942.

———. *Approaches to God.* New York: Harper and Brothers, 1954.

———. *Untrammeled Approaches.* Translated by Bernard Doering. Notre Dame, Ind.: University of Notre Dame Press, 1997.

McCabe, Herbert, O.P. *God Matters.* Springfield, Ill.: Templegate Publishers, 1991.

McGlynn, James V., S.J., and Sr. Paul Mary Farley, R.S.M. *A Metaphysics of Being and God.* Englewood Cliffs, N.J.: Prentice-Hall, 1966.

McInerny, Ralph. *Characters in Search of Their Author.* The Gifford Lectures, Glasgow 1999–2000. Notre Dame, Ind.: University of Notre Dame Press, 2001.

———. *Praeambula Fidei: Thomism and the God of the Philosophers.* Washington, D.C.: The Catholic University of America Press, 2006.

Owens, Joseph, C.Ss.R. *An Elementary Christian Metaphysics.* Houston. Tex.: Center for Thomistic Studies, 1985.

Ratzinger, Joseph Cardinal (Benedict XVI). *God and the World.* Translated by Henry Taylor. San Francisco: Ignatius Press, 2002.

———. *Truth and Tolerance: Christian Belief and World Religions.* Translated by Henry Taylor. San Francisco: Ignatius Press, 2004.

———. *Pilgrim Fellowship of Faith.* Translated by Henry Taylor. San Francisco: Ignatius Press, 2005.

Rocca, Gregory P. *Speaking the Incomprehensible God: Thomas Aquinas on the Interplay of Positive and Negative Theology.* Washington, D.C.: The Catholic University of America Press, 2004.

Rosen, Stanley. *Nihilism.* South Bend, Ind.: St. Augustine's Press, 2000.

Rowe, William L. "Two Criticisms of the Cosmological Argument." In *Readings in the Philosophy of Religion: An Analytic Approach,* edited by Baruch A. Brody. Upper Saddle Creek, N.J.: Prentice-Hall, 1992.

Simon, Yves R. *Freedom of Choice.* Edited by Peter Wolff. New York: Fordham University Press, 1969.

———. "On Order in Analogical Sets." In *Philosopher at Work,* edited by Anthony O. Simon. Lanham, Md.: Rowman and Littlefield, 1999.

Sokolowski, Robert. *The God of Faith and Reason.* 2nd ed. Washington, D.C.: The Catholic University of America Press, 1995.

Stump, Eleonore. *Aquinas.* London and New York: Routledge, 2003.

Stump, Eleonore, and Norman Kretzmann. "Eternity." In *Readings in the Philosophy of Religion: An Analytic Approach,* edited by Baruch A. Brody. Upper Saddle Creek, N.J.: Prentice-Hall, 1992.

EPILOGUE

Ashley, Benedict M., O.P. *The Way toward Wisdom: An Interdisciplinary and Intercultural Introduction to Metaphysics.* Notre Dame, Ind.: University of Notre Dame Press, 2006.

Burrell, David, C.S.C. *Knowing the Unknowable God: Ibn-Sina, Maimonides, Aquinas.* Notre Dame, Ind.: University of Notre Dame Press, 1986.

Dalton, James. "Human Dignity, Human Rights, and Ecology: Christian, Buddhist, and Native American Perspectives." In *Made in God's Image: The Catholic Vision of Human Dignity,* edited by Regis Duffy, O.F.M., and Angelus Gambatese, O.F.M. Mahwah, N.J.: Paulist Press, 1999.

DiNoia, J. A., O.P. *The Diversity of Religions: A Christian Perspective.* Washington, D.C.: The Catholic University of America Press, 1992.

John Paul II. *Redemptor hominis* (The Redeemer of Man). Vatican translation. Boston: Pauline Books and Media, 1979.

Maritain, Jacques. *Science and Wisdom.* Translated by Bernard Wall. London: Geoffrey Bles, 1940.

———. *A Preface to Metaphysics.* London: Sheed and Ward, 1945.

Murray, John Courtney, S.J. *We Hold These Truths: Catholic Reflections on the American Proposition.* Kansas City, Mo.: Sheed and Ward, 1960.

Noonan, John T., Jr. *The Lustre of Our Country: The American Experience of Religious Freedom.* Berkeley: University of California Press, 1998.

Ratzinger, Cardinal Joseph (Benedict XVI). *Truth and Tolerance: Christian Belief and World Religions.* Translated by Henry Taylor. San Francisco: Ignatius Press, 2004.

Schall, James V., S.J. *At the Limits of Political Philosophy.* Washington, D.C.: The Catholic University of America Press, 1996.

Simon, Yves R. *Philosophy of Democratic Government.* Notre Dame, Ind.: University of Notre Dame Press, 1993.

Woznicki, Andrew N. *Transcendent Mystery in Man: A Global Approach to Ecumenism.* Bethesda, Md.: Academica Press, 2007.

INDEX

Understanding Our Being: Introduction to Speculative Philosophy in the Perennial Tradition was designed and typeset in Trump Mediaeval by Kachergis Book Design of Pittsboro, North Carolina. It was printed on 60-pound Natures Natural and bound by Thomson-Shore of Dexter, Michigan.